# Lessons
# for
# New
# Teachers

*Vito Perrone*

Boston   Burr Ridge, IL   Dubuque, IA   Madison, WI
New York   San Francisco   St. Louis
Bangkok   Bogotá   Caracas   Lisbon   London   Madrid   Mexico City
Milan   New Delhi   Seoul   Singapore   Sydney   Taipei   Toronto

*To the Students and Their Mentors Who Worked So Closely with Me
over the Years in the Harvard Teacher Education Programs*

# McGraw-Hill Higher Education

A Division of The **McGraw-Hill** Companies

LESSONS FOR NEW TEACHERS

Copyright © 2000 by The McGraw-Hill Companies, Inc. All rights reserved. Printed in the United States of America. Except as permitted under the United States Copyright Act of 1976, no part of this publication may be reproduced or distributed in any form or by any means, or stored in a data base or retrieval system, without the prior written permission of the publisher.

This book is printed on acid-free paper.

2 3 4 5 6 7 8 9 0 DOC/DOC 0 9 8 7 6 5 4 3 2 1 0

ISBN 0–07–232446–5

Editorial director: *Jane E. Vaicunas*
Sponsoring editor: *Beth Kaufman*
Developmental editor: *Cara Harvey*
Marketing manager: *Daniel M. Loch*
Project manager: *Sheila M. Frank*
Senior production supervisor: *Sandra Hahn*
Coordinator of freelance design: *Michelle D. Whitaker*
Senior photo research coordinator: *Carrie K. Burger*
Compositor: *York Graphic Services, Inc.*
Typeface: *10/13.85 Palatino*
Printer: *R. R. Donnelley & Sons Company/Crawfordsville, IN*

Freelance cover designer: *Jamie O'Neal*
Cover image: © *Jim Cummins/FPG International*
Photo research: *LouAnn K. Wilson*

**Chapter Opening Photos:** Preface: Courtesy of Harvard University, Office of News and Public Affairs; 1: © David M. Grossman/ Monkmeyer; 2: Elizabeth Crews; 3: © Tharpe/Monkmeyer; 4: © Elizabeth Crews; 5: Courtesy of Harvard University, Office of News and Public Affairs, photo by Jon Chase; 6: © Spencer Grant/Monkmeyer; 7: Courtesy of Harvard University, Office of News and Public Affairs; 8: © Candice Cochrane; 9: © Elizabeth Crews/The Image Works; 10: © Candice Cochrane; 11: © Elizabeth Crews; 12: © George Zimbel/Monkmeyer.

The credits section for this book begins on page 191 and is considered an extension of the copyright page.

**Library of Congress Cataloging-in-Publication Data**

Perrone, Vito.
    Lessons for new teachers / Vito Perrone. — 1st ed.
        p.    cm.
    Includes bibliographical references (p.  ) and index.
    ISBN 0–07–232446–5
    1. First year teachers—United States.    2.    Teaching—United
States.    I.    Title.
    LB2844.1.N4P47        2000
    371.102—dc21                                                                99–32561
                                                                                    CIP

www.mhhe.com

# *Contents*

# *Preface*

*Lessons for New Teachers* is in many ways an extended conversation about selected aspects of teaching and learning. Its large purpose is to create a basis for
ongoing reflection on the teaching and learning exchange, what I consider central to growth in teaching. While I am addressing myself in this text primarily
to *new teachers* in the late stages of their teacher preparation programs or initial years of teaching, I assume, as well, that more experienced teachers who
wish to make connections to their earlier motivations will find the book useful. In fact, many experienced teachers with whom I work have found the reflective activities and educational formulations introduced in this text extremely beneficial.

A dilemma with this kind of book, directed as it is on reflection about teaching-
learning practice, is that it might seem at odds with much of the educational
discourse that has become so dominant and that doesn't appear to place much
value on teacher reflection, teacher decision making and curriculum making,
decentralization, personalization at the school and classroom level, and support for racial, cultural and linguistic differences. While I bring forward some
of the central elements of the current discourse—learning standards for each
subject area, grade level by grade level, tests for purposes of promotion and
graduation, competition for scarce resources, and increasing centralization—I
do so mostly in relation to my efforts to place the work of teachers in historical perspective. The issues I engage most fully matter more to teachers in their
day-to-day work with children, young people, and families than the large policy issues that currently surround schools.

It should be noted that most elements of this book follow closely the outline of my core teacher education course at Harvard, a course constructed
around the Teaching for Understanding Framework (discussed in Chapter 8)

and based heavily in my students' ongoing practice in the schools, along with their reflection on that practice. Preparation for teaching within this course is defined as an inductive process enriched by the power of collective thought. It draws in this regard on John Dewey's formulation of the need for teachers to become "students of teaching," persons steeped in their practice and able to make use of that practice as circumstances change.

The book is organized around twelve chapters and an epilogue. Chapter 1, "Reflections on Teaching: Learning to Teach and Teaching to Learn," is a personal reflection of forty years of teaching. I begin here to establish a context, to introduce myself and the teaching-learning issues that matter to me. It may seem at times too personal, but teaching at its best *is* personal; it always has important connections to our experience, to our social and intellectual commitments. The next two chapters, "The Social Conditions of Schools" and "American Education: A Historical Overview" are meant to provide a large context for our work as teachers, providing some of the social and economic conditions that surround schools, as well as a critical historical perspective. It is too easy to view schools as institutions separate from the realities of the larger society. "A Philosophical Stance" begins a sequence of chapters relating directly to teaching and learning practice and represents an acknowledgment that our work as teachers needs to begin around purposes, a set of beliefs about children, young people, and the society. In Dewey's terms, it places questions about purpose within our ongoing experience. "A Place for Passion" addresses our need to get close to the learning that has mattered the most for us, to consider the passion associated with that learning in our ongoing work as teachers. "Approaches to Teaching" is a discussion of various instructional approaches, constructive ways of thinking about the teaching-learning exchange. "Curriculum Construction" moves some of the ideas in the previous chapter toward the actual building of a curriculum to teach, starting from the premise that teachers need to be curriculum makers around carefully considered "generative" topics. "Toward a Pedagogy of Understanding" presents the Harvard-developed Teaching for Understanding Framework, putting forth a performance-oriented view of teaching and learning. "Developing and Maintaining Productive Classrooms" makes the point that moving a classroom and its instructional purposes along has more to do with thoughtful planning and the mutuality of respect than with rules and control mechanisms. "Connecting Assessment, Teaching, and Learning" offers a perspective on the importance of the teacher in the assessment process and the need for schools to be critical centers for evaluation. "Relationships with Families" acknowledges the need for a partnership and suggests some of what parents should expect from teachers and schools and some of the ways teachers can meet those expectations. "Standardized Testing:

How Did We Get Here?" places the testing that exists in and around the schools into historical perspective and brings definition to the various technical formulations associated with tests. Each of the foregoing chapters closes with a short section "for reflection," where I have posed questions for readers to consider, mostly in relation to personal experience. The text closes with an "epilogue," a reaffirmation of the need for teachers to be students of teaching. A number of appendices have been added—essentially, guides and outlines that might prove helpful to teachers in the early stages of their careers to assist in ongoing reflection.

This book is not meant to be prescriptive. It begins with the belief that those going into teaching already possess strong social and intellectual commitments, that they are desirous for ways to think about teaching and learning, schools and communities, in more constructive ways, to develop stronger dispositions toward reflection, a more powerful professionalism. This book is also premised on the understanding that teachers want the teaching-learning exchange to be more productive and the schools more engaging for children and young people.

I wish to acknowledge my debt to the many students and teachers who have worked through the issues in this text with me. I know they are more thoughtful practitioners because of our work together. And, of course, I have learned much from them. I acknowledge also Jan Still, my staff assistant, who prepared much of the manuscript and, throughout, showed considerable interest in the work; Carmel Perrone, my spouse, who read the manuscript carefully and offered many useful suggestions, especially in regard to word use; Deborah Meier, principal of the Mission Hill School in Boston, who read several sections and posed good questions, along with important encouragement; Carla Fontaine, a colleague and an experienced teacher, who provided a number of suggestions for improvement; and Vicki Jacobs, another colleague, who read parts of the text but, more important, at many points talked through elements of the course that formed the basis for the text. I wish also to thank the following scholars for their comments and direction: Arthur Newman, *University of Florida;* Annette Digby, *University of Arkansas;* Virginia McCormack, *Ohio Dominican College;* Joan Henderson-Sparks, *California State University – Fresno;* Nancy I. Gaylen, *Western State College of Colorado;* Vicki Olson, *Augsburg College;* Sharon Thomas, *Miami-Dade Community College.*

*Lessons for New Teachers* is better because of their thoughtful contributions.

Vito Perrone
*Cambridge, Massachusetts*

# About The Author

VITO PERRONE is a member of the learning and teaching faculty and director of teacher education at the Harvard Graduate School of Education. He
has been a secondary school teacher of history and social studies and continues to be deeply involved in the life of elementary and secondary schools.
Prior to coming to Harvard, he was a professor of history and dean of common learning and graduate studies at Northern Michigan University
(1962–1968) and professor of history, education, and peace studies and dean
of the New School and Center for Teaching and Learning at the University of
North Dakota (1968–1986). In addition, Dr. Perrone has served since 1972 as
coordinator of the North Dakota Study Group on Evaluation, a national organization of teachers, school administrators, community organizers, and
university scholars. He has written extensively on issues such as educational
equity, curriculum, progressivism in education, and testing and evaluation.
He is currently involved in a large-scale research and evaluation project
related to the Annenberg Rural Challenge. His most recent books are:
*Portraits of High Schools; Working Papers: Reflections on Teachers, Schools
and Communities; A Letter to Teachers: Reflections on Schooling and the Art
of Teaching; Expanding Student Assessment;* and *Teacher with a Heart:
Reflections on Leonard Covello and Community.*

# CHAPTER 1

# Reflections on Teaching

## Learning to Teach and Teaching to Learn

In . . . shared activity, the teacher is a learner and the learner is without knowing it a teacher." (Dewey [1916] 1961, p. 160)[1]

Writing before the turn of the century, John Dewey suggested the need for
teachers to be "students of teaching," persons able to establish and maintain a
reflective capacity as well as to be articulate about instructional intentions.[2]
When I first read Dewey's philosophical stance regarding reflection and in-
tentionality, it had immediate resonance, in large measure because I had long
reflected on teaching practice, understanding fully that there were many critical lessons in the teaching-learning exchange, in and out of schools. I have been
guided for many years by these lessons.

By carrying you through a *small* part of my reflective journey, which is
my intention, I hope to provide encouragement for those of you reading this
text, whether you are in a preservice program or well along in a teaching career, to work your way through aspects of your own learning about teaching. Concurrently, I am using my reflections to make a number of observations about teaching, learning, and schools that I hope will guide some of our
collective work as educators—though I can manage only the surface of this
critical territory.

As a matter of context, it is important to acknowledge that I was a teacher
long before my baccalaureate degree and teacher certification. I suspect this
was also true for many of you. In the neighborhood in which I grew up, almost all the younger children learned how to play outdoor games from me—
baseball, football, basketball, soccer, hockey, four square, volleyball, newcomb,
paddleball, tennis, badminton, dodgeball, and kick-the-can. There wasn't a
game I didn't have a working knowledge of or was unable to actively teach
with confidence. This kind of teaching continued throughout my high school
and college years, extending beyond sports and recreational games to crafts,
literature, reading and writing, community studies, and religious education.

What did I learn from all this early, preprofessional teaching? I learned,
most of all, that teaching is not telling; that readiness for learning matters; that
exemplars—actual, visible performances and products—are critical. Learning
to play baseball meant in the end actually playing baseball; becoming a reader
meant actually reading real books, real texts. This was, as it turned out, a powerful base for my ongoing work as a teacher and teacher-educator.[3]

My postbaccalaureate teaching, which I also value greatly, has brought me
into intensive exchange with young children, adolescents, and adults in early
childhood centers, elementary and secondary schools, community settings, colleges, and universities. Needless to say, I have enjoyed my teaching at every
level, unable, even when pressed, to speak of a preference.[4] That may be the
case because I have come to see my approach to teaching to be more similar

than different at all the levels. Asking a young child "Why do you think that is?" or "What if you tried it another way?" is not so different from the questions I ask adults in the university setting. Deborah Meier, former principal of Central Park East Secondary School, New York City, and currently the principal of Mission Hill School in Boston (author of *The Power of Their Ideas*, Beacon Press, 1996) notes, in this regard, that Central Park East Secondary School features a pedagogy that can be easily associated with a good kindergarten.[5] I understand that. To the degree that a good kindergarten teacher takes children's intentions seriously and understands that children need to construct meaning for themselves, practice at this kindergarten level could easily guide practice at all levels, including the university. John Dewey offered a similar perspective about kindergarten teaching and university teaching needing to be more alike.

There has always been something natural about teaching—complementary relationships with others, conversation, and most of all learning. I emphasize learning because teaching, it seems to me, is the most powerful venue for learning that exists. Those who believe, for example, that the crucial preparation period for teaching occurs during preservice have lost sight of the power of ongoing teaching, actively reflected on, as an even more potent source for learning about content, curriculum, and pedagogy.[6]

My student teaching, at age 20, occurred in West Junior High in Lansing, Michigan. At the time, it was not a favored setting, being as central-city as a Lansing public school could be.[7] The teaching I observed fostered considerably more passivity than activity on the part of students—the educational process governed mostly by textbooks, questions at the ends of the chapters, and the completion of blank spaces in various sentences and paragraphs. There was little genuine discussion and few demands for inquiry, interpretation, or speculation. All the energy and enthusiasm was in the hallways, the gym, and the concrete playgrounds that surrounded the school. At the time, I thought a great deal about the contrast between the energy of students at West Junior and those I had worked with for many years outside of school—who used their active impulses as a base for learning.

Lisa Schneier (1990), one of my current classroom teacher colleagues, wrote a remarkable essay several years ago, contrasting the energy of students in the school hallways and in classrooms at her school. Regarding the latter, she writes, "A boy sits at a table (in my room) with his head down and covered by his arms when a few minutes before he had been dancing in the halls. . . . If we see, in the classroom, students who have withdrawn their vitality, if we see them turning for that time into shadows, it must be, at least partially, that this is all that we call forth." (p. 1). I agree with Lisa that much of what students are asked to do in school settings makes few connections to their lives, to what matters for them. They are certainly not challenged "to use their minds well" or actually do something with their learning.[8] That many become shadows may even be understandable.

When I first read Lisa's account, I was immediately taken back to West Junior—and many of the other schools that have been a part of my life over the years. At the same time, based on good personal experience, observation of such schools as the Urban Academy and Central Park East in New York and the Pilot School and the Fenway in Cambridge and Boston, respectively, as well as from my review of thoughtful portraits of many schools across the country that are providing their students with a particularly powerful education, it is clear that classrooms can be places for serious inquiry, intellectual energy, and personal engagement. Not surprisingly, these classrooms are in schools that have made classroom energy and high-quality teaching and learning intentional goals that are worked at actively *day after day*. Good classroom practice takes such ongoing attention. These are also schools in which the curriculum is the product of ongoing teacher exchange in the school site, assessment is primarily school-based, and the purposes are fully visible in what people do day in and day out. These are schools that have intentionally been designed to fit the students and not schools that ask only that students fit the schools (to paraphrase John Dewey). Lillian Weber, former director of the Workshop Center, City College, New York, and an inspiring teacher, has made it clear in regard to such examples, "if good practice exists in even one place, it is possible everywhere."[9] That is an understanding we ought to keep in mind throughout our careers. Our challenge is to help those in every school—as well as in every college and university, see for themselves that their settings can be different, that there can, in fact, be "dancing in the classrooms" as well as "dancing in the halls."[10]

I also grasped more fully while at West Junior the ways that students of color, who were poor, were marginalized. Given my own history, I entered the setting aware of the segregated housing patterns and economic inequities that existed. They were too sharp to go unnoticed. I remembered as well the occasions in school when questions about race and associated issues of class were put off, when race and class-related discussions I thought were important seemed always to be brought to abrupt conclusions. But, in this new role as a classroom teacher, I was pushed to think about all of this anew. The conventional wisdom is that new teachers, based on their long experience as students, enter settings they know a great deal about, yet young teachers have long shared with me what I also learned, that sitting "behind the teacher's desk" makes what may have seemed familiar ground a different, even strange place.

Black-white racial divisions, two worlds, were particularly evident at West Junior. I thought the negative effects on teaching and learning should have been apparent. But, as I noted carefully in my journal writing at the time, "issues of race and matters of equity are *never* discussed. 'Things are as they are' is the prevailing view."

Race needed to be discussed then. It needs desperately to be discussed now. Can we really believe that the barriers that now exist, that keep us from achieving the democratic ideals, social justice, and economic progress that we hold out in our public discourse, will ever fall away without confronting more directly matters of race in the schools and society? How many more generations of silence can we endure? As it is, inquiries into matters of race in schools and in colleges and universities are awkward, guilt-ridden, sometimes hostile, but mostly absent. Where beyond schools and college classrooms are young people to learn to discuss matters of race with intelligence and sensitivity? How else but through active consideration of race will teachers and administrators in schools assume a higher level of awareness and take more seriously the effects of inequitable educational opportunity? I continue in this regard to be surprised by the denial of differential education for students of color—overplacement in special education and in lower-level courses, higher levels of suspension, lower graduation rates, and higher dropout rates. When will such problems matter enough to actually do something about them? They don't exist by chance.[11]

I was also particularly conscious at West Junior of the fact that there were no African American teachers in the building, even though the African American student population was very high. It was not really different in the schools I attended, but, in this teaching role, with what seemed a heightened awareness, the lack of African American teachers was more highly visible. As I learned through my questions then and in later studies, the composition of the teaching staff in the school was not unique in Lansing or anywhere outside the then-segregated schools in the South. What is dismaying today is that most schools in the United States *still* have an overwhelmingly Euro-American teaching staff, and we are more than four decades beyond the *Brown* decision and in a new world regarding the demography of the student population. As things stand, most students in our schools can still expect to complete their K–12 schooling and not have a single teacher of color. This, I believe, is a tragedy for all students, regardless of their racial-cultural backgrounds, denying them a critical cultural education. What are we doing to change all of this? [12]

After the student teaching semester and graduation from college, I completed a two-year military obligation with very few expectations. I have begun to think about this again, especially since one of my students who served a four-year stint in the Marines prior to entering our Harvard program observed that our Teaching for Understanding Framework (described fully in Chapter 4) matched well much of what he experienced in his military training. His comments brought me quickly back to my own observations of the military as school, something I actually thought about a good deal as I was going through it. Much of the teaching I observed through six months of intentional instructional activity was precise; the purposes were clearly delineated, known at the outset, with much of the evaluation having a performance base and an ongoing quality. One was expected to demonstrate the learning by doing something. In its own way, it clearly had many of the ingredients of what is currently held out as good teaching, as teaching for understanding.

I noted in letters to former teachers and friends how successful the military instructors were in getting everyone to a reasonably high level of proficiency in tasks that were not rooted in most people's experience—for example, reading and making successful use of contour maps of particular terrains, finding obscure places with the aid of compasses and designing, and hooking up and making use of complex communications systems. While not high-level "academic" tasks, they all demanded high levels of concentration and active experience. That it was not the telling environment of the schools was clear.

For my last year in the military, I was involved in educational and cultural programs that were far removed from the mainstream of Army life, working mostly with civilians who directed theatrical productions from *Hamlet* to *Showboat*, organized a variety of musical concerts and taught courses in visual arts and crafts. This immersion into the performance-oriented world of the arts was new for me. The instructors acted every bit like the coaches Ted Sizer and the Coalition of Essential Schools have actively promoted for the schools—persons who stand alongside their students. Their teaching was personal and highly interactive, with room for "the students" to be inventive, making the work their own. What was obvious was the naturalness of what they did. There was little of the didactiveness that dominates so much of the teaching practice in our schools and colleges.

Observing in this environment took me back to my early teaching experiences. It also reminded me of occasions in school when my learning was more powerful than usual. I noted in particular becoming my school's expert on National Socialism—the Nazi movement—in Germany, the product of five months of intensive research as a high school junior. Helping students gain *personal* control over a body of knowledge was clearly a goal of my history teacher. It ought to be every teacher's goal in all courses, at all levels. How much different the teacher-student exchange would be if such a purpose existed.

Over the past several years, as part of a research project on Teaching for

Understanding,[13] I have been asking students, mostly at the middle school, high school, and undergraduate college levels, about times when they were most engaged intellectually, when their understandings were larger than usual, when their learning had a "special" quality. Needless to say, the responses took me back once again to my junior year in high school, to my last year of military service, and to many more personal experiences in schools since, in which teaching and learning assumed more active directions. Among other things, students spoke enthusiastically about working on projects they chose, that they cared about, with *time* to pursue their work intensively, gaining in the process what they acknowledged to be a form of expertness. Teachers were described as persons who worked actively *with* them, posed questions, didn't appear to have fully determined ends in mind with regard to individual projects, seemed genuinely interested in getting them to wrestle with ideas, and even learned from them. Why isn't that the norm—the common experience—for students in our schools and in our colleges and universities?[14]

Entering a secondary classroom as a first-year professional teacher in Michigan was to be yet another powerful learning experience—another place for serious reflection on teaching and learning. I have thought a good deal about that beginning experience in relation to all the debates that have raged over the past forty years (and, as I have learned from my studies of educational history, long before) around the question—"Are new teachers prepared sufficiently to teach at high levels?" I often wonder what such a question actually means. I was clearly ready to make a beginning, and I understood that I was, in fact, beginning a journey in which I anticipated learning more and more, day by day. That I would be a much better teacher after five years or twenty years was very much with me, even as I was confident about being successful in this very first year, fully expecting to serve the students well.[15]

In light of such an outlook, how have I come to think about teacher education?[16] In the 1960s and 1970s, I had the privilege of working in an experimental college (at the University of North Dakota) that prepared teachers primarily through liberal arts courses, occasions in which prospective teachers reflected carefully on their experiences as learners (essentially autobiographical inquiry), close observation of children, intensive one-on-one teaching experiences (in many respects related to Piaget's clinical interviewing), and extensive internship experiences in "cooperating schools" in which the students had full teaching responsibilities for one academic year, along with weekly reflective seminars, classroom research, and intensive journal writing. The quality of the teaching of these students was exceptional—inquiry-oriented, active, filled with high-level learning of the various subject matters, and imaginative in regard to literacy activities and ongoing assessment, including self-evaluation, the use of community resources, and connections to parents. That experience shapes much of my continuing thought about teacher education.

Over the years, in spite of all the reform agendas, I have come to believe that the best we can do in teacher preparation programs, through a variety of courses and clinical experiences in intentionally selected schools, is to help academically able and socially committed students enter teaching with constructive dispositions and skills relating to young people, curriculum content, pedagogy, and the power of collective thought; with well-developed habits of observation and reflection; and with reasonable confidence and an understanding that they are entering a process of learning something important every day, working *toward* the largest of possibilities. Regarding the last, it is important to keep before us, in all that we do as teachers, the best classrooms and schools, the most productive exchange with students, the most interesting and engaging curriculum, and the most useful connections to parents and communities we can imagine, believing with Alfred North Whitehead (1929) that "when ideals have sunk to the level of practice, the result is stagnation" (p. 3). I also think a great deal, in this regard, about Erich Heller's (1959) related admonition: "Be careful how you define the world, it is like that." (p. 205). Keeping before us a more uplifting vision gives us something to work toward.

When students who are considering teaching ask me about what they might do prior to beginning their preparation programs that would be particularly helpful, I suggest they try for an extended period of time to be careful observers of children and young people in the natural environment, watching them in subways and buses, in the streets, and at parks and playgrounds; listening to their talk with each other and with adults; and getting a larger view of the similar and different patterns. Teaching, after all, is about *knowing* children and young people well—outside as well as inside schools. What we often learn through such observations is that children and young people are more competent, responsible, imaginative, and attentive to what is around them than the public media or our narrow observations in schools might suggest. Given the structures in many of our schools, and the heavily negative media accounts of young people, it is quite easy to see them as having few of these constructive qualities.

One of the most critical lessons I learned in my early years of teaching, and I am intentionally breaking from the teacher education discussion, was the importance of knowing the students well, coming to know what they care about, beginning always with their meanings, seeing the need to make connections with what we do in school and the world beyond school. How is it possible to teach students well without knowing them well? As I think about this, many examples come to mind, but I will share one experience in particular, from my fourth year of teaching at a very large, integrated secondary school in Lansing, Michigan.

There were two brothers in my tenth grade history course who were very quiet, doing too little with the course, often late to class. When I talked with them about getting to class late, they told me they ran traps in the morning, and sometimes it took longer than they anticipated. Since we were in the city, nothing about the traps made sense to me. As it turned out, they lived outside the city in a semiswamp area. They asked without hesitation if I would like to walk their trap line with them. How could I say no? We made arrangements for me, and my 2½-year-old son, to go to their house on a subsequent Saturday morning. Getting to the house meant driving through parts of the swamp on a perilous road that gave me many second thoughts. They lived with their parents in a very neat cottage the father and sons had built. It was the beginning of a most engaging three-year conversation.

These two young men had what I considered impressive knowledge about the flora and fauna that surrounded their home setting. They were first-class naturalists, who seemed to comprehend everything possible to know about the growth of plants and the habits of various wildlife, yet they were struggling with their biology class (and their teacher never did learn about their wilderness lives). They were also excellent landscapers and builders, and there was little they couldn't do with an automobile—whether engine or body work. Moreover, they produced wooden bowls and sculptures that were truly works of art. (Their woodworking teacher, whom I met at one of their exhibits, *did* know a great deal about their talents. He also was a model for the kind of teacher I hoped to become, the ultimate exemplar of the teacher as coach.) I found these young men's abilities and understandings inspiring, yet they were hardly making it at the school, they did not see themselves as exceptional learners, and they were given virtually no encouragement to believe they could be successful academically or should consider any post-secondary education.

What if their strengths had been the basis for their education? Many such young people are invisible to many of us in the schools. The need to know my students well, to be in a position to work from their strengths, their interests, and their intentions has stayed with me. It still animates my work as a teacher. It also shapes some of the ways I think about school structures. We clearly need to think about smaller school communities, with smaller numbers of students working with a core of teachers who plan together, who gain individual and collective insights into the students they work with in common, and who can engage the discourse of curriculum and standards with the seriousness such matters deserve, with their students continuing to be the focus of their attention. [17]

When teachers are asked to reflect on what makes their work captivating—what from their collegiate backgrounds and ongoing reflection contributes most to their successful practices—what do they say? The technical pieces—lesson plans, record books, academic majors and minors, the policy debates, which are often the core of teacher education programs—fade quickly. They don't say, "I wish I had had another course on how to use textbooks, interpret standardized tests, or be a leader." Everything takes on a more complex direction. The design for better teacher preparation, they suggest, has more to do with dispositions toward inquiry and reflection, curiosity, a particular intellectual passion, a social commitment, a set of beliefs, a love for the unexpected, a general interest in human growth and development.

The exceptional teachers I know are passionate about learning. They have deep interests in a particular aspect of learning—history, literature, science. They are so steeped in this passion that they could manage well if all the textbooks, workbooks, and curricular guides that fill the schools suddenly were to disappear. They see connecting points everywhere. It is not possible to take a walk with them without noting that they are almost always seeing around them possibilities for their students. They make particular note of books, insist on "checking out" libraries and museums, and write down addresses of people and places. Schools need to promote and support passion of this kind. Teachers need more opportunities to reflect on their learning, on how they first came to the interests they possess and how to revitalize those interests. They need to be in schools that are authentic centers of inquiry, intellectually oriented settings where they can share their learning with others, read together, and have opportunities for writing and further study. Whether we are in schools or colleges and universities, our task is to help build such learning communities.

One means of creating a fully generative learning community—intellectually and socially challenging environments in which teachers' learning and commitments to the learning of their students grow deeper by the day—is for schools to be reciprocally engaged in a collaboration with colleges and universities. Of course, that is not a new story, and such partnerships can go in many directions. The models are, in fact, large. I want to share, however, a recent experience that has generated exceptional enthusiasm, especially among teachers as a direction that is attractive to me, as it starts with the belief that teachers can be the serious scholar teachers Dewey wrote about, capable of charting their own directions and even producing a literature of their own.

In a program funded by the American Council of Learned Societies (ACLS), eight to twelve teachers per year, over a three-year period, were freed from their classrooms for 40 to 60 percent of the time to attend Harvard courses in humanities fields, to use the libraries, and to participate in a weekly collective seminar around a humanities text and its classroom potential. They were also expected to serve as resources to teaching team members in their respective schools. To have a chance to read and explore ideas was particularly generative. These teachers demonstrated an inspiring level of scholarship. During one of the later years of the project, one of the teachers completed a book on poetry, while doing research on Langston Hughes, that enriched his classroom greatly. It also enriched the work of everyone else in the seminar. Another entered, saying she wanted to learn, among other things, how to draw and paint, having been told in the third grade she "was a hopeless artist." She took to the seminar each week some of her work in progress, an outgrowth of her studies. Her work got increasingly better, and she put up an impressive exhibit of thirty pieces at the Cambridge High School Library at the end of the year. She was also able to articulate an inspirational, freshly developed view of learning. A third participant, a sixth grade teacher who left her sixth graders at 10:30 each morning, was asked by her students early in the year, "Where do you go each day?" She told them about the courses she was taking in philosophy and religion. They asked about what she was learning and what she was reading. From then on, she spent part of each day sharing with her students the ideas she was exploring, the examples the professors used, what she made of what she was reading, and the questions she had. The students' enjoyment of all this was overwhelming, causing this teacher to ask about the curriculum—whether it was challenging enough, personal enough. I can multiply these kinds of stories by the number of participants.

Why isn't such experience more commonplace? These teachers made it clear that they desire continuing professional development around ideas, real texts, the world—not more workshops on how to teach reading or writing, or learning styles, or on new teaching techniques and not more occasions to share what they think of a curriculum being devised somewhere else. [18]

Why was I a teacher of history? That is a question I have often been asked. The short answer is that I have long enjoyed historical study. I was engaged throughout my schooling by historical accounts—in particular, biographies. However, I wasn't always enamored with history courses, which seemed too expansive, always rushed, with the details more important than the human drama, the possible meanings. As a college student, I understood early on that the courses were mostly about coverage, even as the time frame grew shorter over the undergraduate years. My interests moved me in the direction of wondering about the anomalies embedded in human events, and I posed quite regularly such questions as "How did they do that?" and "How and why did that happen?" As it was, such questions didn't seem to matter much in the courses. I suspect that attending to them seriously would have seemed too time-consuming. I was often in awe—for example, as I observed the fine jewelry of the early Egyptian civilization—only to find that the course I was taking wanted me, instead, just because a few weeks had passed, to think about government in Rome, thousands of years later. It was clear to me that history was more than coverage, even as coverage was the model for most of the history courses I took.

I brought such a critical perspective to my early teaching—making inquiry my base—*understanding* history was always my overarching purpose. Getting through everything became less and less important with each year of experience. As it turned out, I had implicit support for such work. I understood this more fully in my fifth year of teaching, as a veteran history teacher of thirty years said to me one day, "I wish I could do the things you do." When I asked him what that meant, he said, "The principal would never let me develop my own curriculum, put the textbook aside, work only on multiweek projects." It hadn't occurred to me that the principal had anything to do with it, but I have come to understand that administrators can influence practice. Whether I knew it or not, I clearly had support to teach history for understanding. All teachers should have such support and the dispositions to work toward ends that matter.

I learned over time increasingly more about inquiry—about the kind of help students need to engage in inquiry, about the power of questions, about the importance of resources and the consequential nature of time. I found slow, carefully measured beginnings—times when the students and I were learning together how to read primary documents, how to pose questions, how to use reference materials, how to do interviews, how to do careful note taking, how to present ideas (all around specific content)—to be particularly helpful. The quality of later work always seemed higher for the time devoted to preparing to do good work. How many students don't do good work because they don't know what good work is or how to do it, or they don't understand that good work is *their* work and not work they do only for the teacher?

I also found that when the students gained a sense of control and confidence around a small topic (a person's life, an event), they were eager to fill out pieces of the story surrounding these areas. They read more history. I think a great deal about this now as the lists of what students are "supposed to know" expand, along with the corresponding belief that if everything isn't covered by the teacher, much will be missed. I worry that enthusiasm for the subject matter will be the largest missing piece, and in the end that will assure that the content being worried about will also be missed, certainly forgotten quickly.

I had many other good experiences early in my teaching that helped set some constructive patterns, and that helped shape as well as deepen my philosophic orientation—my moral and intellectual stance—to teaching and learning. There are two instances from my initial year that I want to share, as they have continued to influence the ways I think about assessment (and, of course, teaching and learning more broadly). The first is about one of my students in a world history course who handed in blank papers each week for the first four weeks of school, prompting me *finally* to ask him about it. His response was very straightforward, "I don't know how to read or write." As we talked, he said, "How would it be if I gave reports to the class?" Given the fact that I was still wondering about why he had not acquired any knowledge of reading and writing, or what kind of neurological problem he might have, I quickly said, "That seems like a good idea." For the rest of the year, every other week or so, he gave 15- to 20-minute reports. Those I recall most vividly were about pyramids, rockets, how birds fly, how to build a skyscraper, and how the telephone works. These presentations always included interesting drawings on the board. He got the information principally from pictures, photos, and television, although he must have gleaned some of it from personal observation in the environment. He was not always accurate with the information, but everyone listened to him respectfully and applauded at the conclusion of each presentation. He established for me a basis for ongoing conversation with him that was rooted in real content—even though it was not always related to what we were studying at the time. Learning to connect well with him greatly expanded my ability to make connections to other students. That lesson remains critical for me. Moreover, the quality of his classroom participation was much greater than had been usual for him in school, and he taught others in the class a great deal about matters of difference. At the same time, I was forced to reflect more seriously about what constitutes learning and how it is to be assessed, as well as the situational aspects of teaching and learning.

The second instance came with the first big unit examination on the ancient world—three complex essay questions. Overall, the students did not do as well as I had expected, and I established times to meet one-on-one with students who had done especially poorly. The first student I met with told me that he had not done well because I had asked the wrong questions. I then asked him to share with me what questions would have given him the opportunity to inform me about his knowledge, his understandings of the ancient world. To my surprise, he did just that. In the process, it was clear that he had taken away from the unit far more than his performance on my test had indicated. I clearly had not tapped what he had actually learned.

I did not give another test that year, or for many years after, that did not leave room for the students to write three or four questions each believed important to what we were studying, and then to answer two or three of them, always understanding that their questions were important indicators of their understanding. I also did not engage in a unit of study that did not include a number of opportunities for students to demonstrate understanding through a performance activity—an oral presentation, a dramatic interpretation, a comparative essay, a model, a drawing, or a research project. Before that year was over and for all the years that have followed, my students' work has always been built on previous work—everything is scaffolded, always constructed so that all students complete work that matters to them. Everything is about success, not failure. Students are not faced with surprises.

It was clear to me very early, and it has been reinforced since, that the important assessment questions must be about what students understand and are able to do, *not* what they don't know, although there is obviously power in not knowing as a base for generating new understandings. In recent years, the focus of much of what passes for assessment, primarily rooted in an assortment of multiple-choice tests, is on what students don't know or don't know how to do well enough according to someone who is far removed from the actual setting in which the teaching-learning exchange is occurring.

With regard to assessment, as I moved to a performance base—to get closer to what I understood to exemplify important learning—I had to rethink what constituted appropriate standards. How was I to deal with the students in my classes who entered with wide variations of skill levels and prior knowledge and experience? It seemed that I had to individualize the assessment process, but could I individualize the process without tying together instruction and assessment and finding ways to see patterns in student growth over time? Having students maintain "portfolios"—which I called "work folders" at the time—seemed natural. Self-evaluation around work over time also seemed natural. I haven't worked all of this out yet, but I have certainly grown more confident about assessment. As assessment has grown more complex, cumulative, personal, and internal, it has assumed greater meaning for the students, encouraging risk taking and leading to higher and higher quality work. The point is that instruction and ongoing assessment are intertwined, never separate.

I have learned that teaching can be approached in many ways. Over the years, I found ways to team teach; to do extensive, several-month projects; and to create new courses with students. The power of writing became apparent early, and journals were a staple. Using documents, the local community, and personal experience always made what we did more engaging. The power of cooperation and collective thought was so clear that my talk in a classroom declined consistently over the years that I was in a secondary school. That also influenced greatly how I thought about university teaching, which began in a department of history, where I taught courses in Western civilization, American history, and historiography.

The style in the university setting was lecture, but I moved away from that format rather quickly, seeing my own contribution increasingly to be the selection of interesting and challenging materials to read, the posing of questions that pointed toward anomalies or provoked more questions, providing assistance to students to help them assume the dispositions of historians, able to engage in genuine historical inquiry, and construct their own historical narratives. Given such an outlook, I also understood the need to assume a role of careful responder to students' work and ongoing synthesizer of ideas, which I still put into writing in the form of regular letters to students.

Lectures are still the dominant mode of teaching in the schools and colleges—even as reading materials and media are more accessible than ever. Lectures are, without doubt, often useful. I enjoy going to lectures to hear various people I admire share part of their lives and some of their thinking, but I wouldn't want an entire course of lectures. I would prefer to read the lectures and enter into a conversation, consider alternative views, seek other possible explanations, and speculate about possible connections to other formulations, other topics, and different experiences.

However, so much of what students experience in their education, especially at the collegiate level, is lectures, one after another. Teacher education students often discuss with me, mostly with disdain, all the lectures they receive in various education courses about the power of cooperative learning, the need to listen carefully to their students, the importance of the dialogue that Paulo Freire, a Brazilian educator who has had considerable influence on teaching and learning practices in the United States, wrote so much about, and the constructivist nature of most learning that matters. They have no problem understanding that there is a good deal of parody here.

Another lesson that I learned very early and have refined since and that still plays a critical role in my teaching is the importance of my completing the various exercises I ask students to do. By doing the exercises, I have come to understand more fully the complexities embedded in them; have learned about more of the nuances; have considered more productive questions to pose; and have found, in the process, that I could respond more constructively. I also developed a point of sympathy, to use Dewey's formulation.

Those of us who work in education schools—where most of our students are preparing to teach or are teachers seeking additional challenge, confirmation, or revitalization—need to be conscious of our teaching and all that can be learned from it. How do we meet our students—as if it is an encounter of persons wishing to learn from one another, as a dialogue in which the students' questions matter, or as a process aimed at extending learning in fresh directions? Do we ask our students to read the most challenging materials we know about? In relation to what we ask our students to read, who are the writers? Do they represent various intellectual and cultural traditions? Does their experience mirror sufficiently the diversity of our society? How does all this relate to children and young people in the schools; to the ways schools are organized; and to curriculum, pedagogy, and the social realities that surround school practice? Even though I have been at this work for forty years, my journey is still in progress. I am still learning. We should all still be learning. That is our ongoing challenge.

## FOR REFLECTION

You might begin writing an autobiography of your learning. Think about occasions when your learning in school took you to larger levels of understanding and caused you to be more intellectually engaged. What were the conditions? What made the difference?

Reflect also about occasions when you were called on to teach something to another person or help another person understand your views about something important. When the teaching was successful, when the other person came to understand what you wanted him or her to understand, what do you remember doing and saying? What made the difference?

You might also begin to think about matters of difference around race and class. When did you first understand that differences exist? How did you think about them then? How do you think about them now?

Finally, as you think about yourself as a teacher, what would you most want your students to say about you? How would you like to be described?

---

[1]This chapter is essentially my AERA (American Educational Research Association) DeGarmo lecture (April 1996), which was given during my fortieth year of teaching. As fortieth years have had special significance in our society, one of those marking occasions, it seemed the right time to share some of my learning over the years about teaching and learning in relation to my work as a teacher-educator and active participant in the life of schools. It also seems now to be an appropriate way to begin this book.

[2]Dewey ([1938] 1976), pp. 249–272. I add to the definition of "students of teaching" at many points in the text.

[3]Most of the preservice teachers with whom I have worked acknowledge quickly those occasions when the teaching and learning exchange has worked well for them. In the process, they begin to define the characteristics of good teaching.

[4]I have now formally taught in the schools for seven years and in university settings for thirty-six years. While teaching at the secondary school level, I consistently taught in the summers in children's programs. Within my work at the university level, I have on several occasions gone back to the schools to teach. I also have been in schools on a regular basis, almost weekly.

[5]Meier 1987.

[6]This suggests, I believe, our need to see preservice and inservice education as a continuum, not as distinct elements.

[7]As I learned much later from Malcolm X's autobiography, West Junior High played a prominent role in his life.

[8]T. Sizer uses the formulation of "using their minds well" in his *Principles of the Coalition of Essential Schools* (1984).

[9]L. Weber, "Presentation, North Dakota Study Group Meeting," Grand Forks, ND, 1972. See also *Looking Back and Thinking Forward: Reconsiderations of Teaching and Schooling* (1997).

[10]Most of our schools are not like Central Park East or the Urban Academy in their intentions or practice. They could be. I encourage teachers to see such settings as exemplars of what is possible, something to work toward, understanding always that in many settings it means small steps. Keeping an idea about what is possible before us, though, is critical.

[11]See the report by the National Coalition of Advocates for Students (1985) for a fuller discussion of the longstanding inequities in and around schools. In a school in Vermont, a teacher teaching what she described as "lower-level" literature classes invited strong senior students to join her as coteachers. They planned with her and helped her carry out the instructional program. In the process, the senior students shared with the teacher that they remembered many of the students in the "lower-level classes" from elementary school as students who didn't dress very well, who weren't "very attractive," and who didn't get much support from teachers or peers. The senior students weren't surprised that these students were struggling in high school and have begun to ask serious questions about tracking, about how social class inequities are played out. They gained a wideawakeness that also pushed the teacher to a larger wideawakeness. We might think more about this as it applies to our experience in schools. Possibly it will help us understand more fully the ways race and social class have impacted children and young people and their educational opportunities.

[12]Currently there is an emphasis in our schools on multiculturalism, an understanding that we need to support differences, construct a more inclusive curriculum, and seek ways of honoring the backgrounds, cultures, languages, and histories of all our students. Such efforts are important. Our task, though, is to assure that such efforts go beyond the tokenism that exists—for example, hosts of one-day celebrations that feature a particular population, photographs of prominent African Americans or Latinos posted here and there, an occasional short story written by an Asian writer.

[13]The work is described fully in Wiske (1997).

[14]I invite readers to reflect on their own experiences with learning that had a special quality.

[15]This first year was more difficult than I had ever imagined. It had a day-and-night quality, consuming virtually all my physical and intellectual energy. Not everything worked well. Some of my assignments were not clear enough, in need of much more background work—more scaffolding—than I had provided. Further, I was surprised about all I didn't know about the content I was teaching. I was not always prepared for the questions students asked me. But I learned a great deal, and students knew that I cared about them and their learning, that I was serious about the work. All of that mattered. Currently there is interest in programs in which new teachers teach a less-than-full schedule and receive ongoing mentoring from an experienced teacher. Such efforts can clearly be beneficial to new teachers. In my case, I found mentors, exemplary teachers who were willing to share their thinking with me.

[16]I offer this perspective to help readers think more about the current debates surrounding teacher education, possibly placing their preparation for teaching into perspective.

[17]Over the past decade, interest in small schools has re-emerged. Such schools make it easier for students and teachers to know one another well, for teachers to work together, and for the school day—the schedules—to become more flexible. Many of these small schools—either separate or within larger schools—have been started by classroom teachers who want to construct a more positive climate for serious teaching and learning.

[18]The ACLS work has been transformed into the "Teachers as Scholars" program, which now involves 700 teachers from Boston area schools in seminars related to the humanities, math, and science. The same level of enthusiasm for ideas prevails. Similar programs are being developed in many parts of the United States.

# CHAPTER 2

# The Social Conditions of Schools

In Chapter 3, as a way of getting closer to the fuller context of our work as educators, I have provided a historical review of American education. In this chapter, I present a social-ecological view of the schools as a means of helping us move beyond the simple, mostly negative, accounts of schools that fill the popular media and influence so profoundly public attitudes. It is my way of responding to the questions I receive about such matters as the size and scale of schools and school districts, the demographics of school-age populations, the social context that exists and the financing of schools. While clearly an overview, it has proven helpful for teachers.[1]

Overall, there are 14,900 independent school districts in the United States, serving approximately 47 million students—28 million in elementary schools and 19 million in the secondary schools.[2] In 1920, there were closer to 200,000 school districts. The consolidation movement, growing from the belief that bigger is more efficient and better, has been strong.[3]

Close to 25 percent of all public school students, approximately 11 million, are in the largest 100 school districts (a very small fraction—less than 1 percent—of the districts that exist). New York City, for example, has 1,090,000 students, Los Angeles 650,000, Chicago 480,000, Miami 250,000, Philadelphia 200,000, Houston 190,000, Detroit 180,000, Fairfax (Virginia) 170,000, Columbus (Ohio) 110,000, and Boston 60,000.

After accounting for the 100 largest school districts, however, what should be clear is that the vast majority of American schoolchildren are in relatively small districts. Cambridge, Massachusetts, has 7,500 students in K–12 and Lincoln-Sudbury (twenty minutes away) has 2,000. Lansing, Michigan has 20,000, and Okemos (twenty minutes away) has 4,000. These are fairly typical. In the rural areas of our country, though, school districts with 200–300 students are not uncommon. While high schools in Grand Forks, Fargo, Bismarck and Minot, North Dakota, have between 1,000 and 2,000 students, the average high school in North Dakota has fewer than 100 students in grades 9–12. There are at least twenty states with high school characteristics similar to those in North Dakota.

The overall size of schools has grown significantly over the past half century. Schools in the United States in 1940 had, on average, under 200 students; the average today is 650.[4] The belief is that there is greater efficiency in large schools and that large schools can offer a wider array of educational programs and services. The losses, though, have been substantial. Students are less well known in the larger schools; many fall through the cracks. Also, control efforts assume greater prominence as schools get larger. Moreover, there is little evidence that the larger schools are more productive academically or socially.[5]

Funding for the public schools is still heavily based on local taxation. In such a system, where one lives makes a significant difference. As a result, inequities abound.[6] The wealthiest districts in Massachusetts spend five times more per child than do the poorest, and the differences are visible. The inequities, though, are greater in many other states. Jonathan Kozol's *Savage Inequalities* outlines the problems of school funding in particularly graphic form, showing conclusively the terrible price paid over many decades by those most in need. Prior to the change in school finance in Michigan, which I will describe briefly in the next paragraph, Detroit spent $3,900 per child; Grosse Pointe, on Detroit's eastern border, spent $9,000; and Bloomfield Hills, to the north, spent $10,500.[7]

In 1995, the highest court in Massachusetts declared funding mechanisms for schools inequitable and unconstitutional. The supreme courts of New Jersey, Kentucky, Montana, New Hampshire, and Texas have come to the same conclusion within the past decade. And, three years ago, arguing that the inequities could never be overcome as long as the local property tax was the determining factor, the state legislature in Michigan passed a law prohibiting local taxation for schools. Increased sales taxes—dedicated to schools—have been established to make up for the local revenue lost. There is still, however, considerable confusion, and, in districts that now have had limits placed on how much they can spend, there is great anger.[8]

In the midst of this essential debate about resources, a question that is increasingly being posed by many legislators and those who believe they are already heavily taxed is "Does money really matter?" Would Boston's schools be better, they argue, if the expenditures were $7,500 per child rather than the current $6,700 per child? Could the $6,700 be better spent, producing a better education? Economists who study dollar inputs in relation to educational outputs (mostly test scores) don't agree on how much difference more money—beyond a "reasonable base"—makes.[9] I believe money matters a great deal; the visible differences are stark between high-spending and low-spending schools. Nonetheless, it also depends a great deal on how the money is spent. Considerably more money, for example, gets to classrooms in Concord-Carlisle (a suburban district) than in Boston, although both have approximately the same amount of money to spend per child. In New York City, much less gets to classrooms than is true in the state as a whole.[10] Would the educational enterprise be better if individual schools (rather than the districts) were to receive funding, deciding at that level how to expend the resources? Charter schools are supposedly testing that issue, as are a number of experimental schools within many school districts. The fact that class sizes have been substantially reduced in many of these settings, through different kinds of staffing and curricular decisions, might suggest that such directions are worth emulating.

Racially, 71 percent of the total school population is Euro-American. Among the 29 percent students of color, 16.2 percent are African American, and 9.1 percent are Hispanic. Given birthrates and the flow of immigration, however, the population of students of color is expected to increase significantly over the next decade or two. Early in the twenty-first century, students of color will be in the majority overall, although most school districts will not reflect the changes unless geographic boundaries and housing patterns undergo substantial change. The fastest growing populations in the schools are Hispanics from the Dominican Republic, El Salvador, Nicaragua, Guatemala, and Mexico and Southeast Asians from Vietnam, Cambodia, Laos, and the Philippines. Cambridge, Rindge and Latin School (in Massachusetts) has fifty-six language and cultural groups today. Twenty years ago, there may have been ten to fifteen. In many respects, Lowell, Massachusetts, is a new city demographically, changed dramatically in the past twenty years. The schools now have a significant Cambodian population. Twenty years ago, the school population was mostly Euro-American. Many communities across the United States have undergone such transformations.

For many Americans, these changing demographic patterns have brought about considerable worry. Proposition 187 in California and the increasing anti-immigrant sentiment portend more difficult times. While we have a history of not educating well enough the country's diverse populations, we must embrace this growth as our challenge and not succumb to all the hysteria that now exists. A similar hysteria existed in the years prior to the 1924 change in immigration policy, which essentially limited immigration. Immigration was reopened in 1965. There is, though, a good deal of current interest in reducing substantially the numbers of new immigrants.

Although the student demographics have changed dramatically, there has been little change in the teacher population, which remains overwhelmingly Euro-American. This must be seen as a crisis. The peak year for teachers of color—approximately 13 percent—was 1972. After several years of decline, we are again beginning to approach the 1972 level. Teachers with a strong bilingual base are also in short supply. This, too, is troubling, especially if we are serious about promoting high-quality, democratic education.[11]

Overall, urban schools have a much higher percentage of students of color than the national data might imply, and their percentages are rapidly expanding. In twenty-three of the twenty-five largest school districts, for example, African Americans, Hispanics, and Asian Americans now constitute the majority. In several districts, they are close to 90 percent of the school population. Those teaching in many of our urban communities are in schools in which more than 90 percent of the students are African American, Hispanic, or Asian American.

In contrast, America's suburban and rural settings, especially outside of the South, are virtually all white.

Gary Orfield, a faculty member in the Harvard Graduate School of Education and the national chronicler of desegregation, noted in his recent studies that racial isolation in our urban schools is greater now than was the case thirty years ago, when desegregation orders flowed from the federal courts.[12] This is discouraging, suggesting that socioeconomic conditions and housing patterns have not changed much. In this regard, Orfield cites the Detroit decision in 1972 as the turning point when the Circuit Court overruled a lower court decision regarding metropolitization for purposes of desegregation. By keeping Detroit's suburbs out of the desegregation struggle, Detroit had nowhere to go but toward greater racial isolation. Interest in redrawing school district boundaries, encouraging more crossing of boundaries, is growing as a means of reducing racial isolation, but little change has actually come about.[13] The hoped-for integration of our neighborhoods and schools is still far away. The democratic premises, so much a part of the language of our society, remain part of an unfulfilled promise.[14]

In recent years, America's cities have brought us to a reality of two cultures—a world of high-rise buildings, well-stocked shops, and gentrified neighborhoods alongside deteriorating housing and extreme levels of poverty. In 1965, when the war on poverty began, there was considerable poverty in our urban centers, but most neighborhoods had, from an economic standpoint, a greater mix of people than currently exists. Large numbers of those with economic resources have left their urban neighborhoods, leaving them much poorer than they were in earlier times. Many urban neighborhoods, especially those housing mostly people of color, have unemployment rates of 40 to 60 percent.

As physical settings, urban schools are more like the deteriorating housing than the uptown shops, and urban students are closer to poverty and discouragement than to America's promised good life. In the thirty-seven cities constituting the Council of Great City Schools, more than one-third of all public school buildings are more than 50 years old and in need of reconstruction—only 4 percent are less than ten years old. In Chicago, nearly one-fifth of all school buildings were constructed before the turn of the century. I would never argue that learning is not possible in old structures, but age is only one of the issues. An estimate of what it would take to bring New York City's schools to modestly acceptable standards is close to $6 billion, and New York is only one city.[15]

What other realities exist? About 23 percent of all children of school age in the United States reside in families living below the poverty line. The poverty rate for school-age children is greater now than it was a decade ago. We have to go back to the Great Depression for poverty levels of such magnitude.[16]

Additionally, as I implied earlier, in regard to immigration levels, life to-day is much like 1900. Close to 12 percent of the students in our schools are non-English-speaking or English as a second language students. However, these new immigrants, unlike those who, in earlier times, came mostly from Europe, face racial as well as linguistic and cultural discrimination. This is a heavy burden, one not always acknowledged sufficiently. The need for language support is particularly critical, yet we are faced with growing political pressures to limit bilingual services. We need to stand with those in need of language support as part of their transition to English. We should also support the desire of so many of our new immigrants to maintain their cultural roots. Our country can only be the richer for such support.[17]

Add to the portrait some of the realities surrounding academic achievement. There is evidence that overall literacy levels have remained stable over the past ten years—that overall knowledge of history, science, mathematics, and the arts is not at a level most Americans believe is acceptable. Moreover, the belief is that education for citizenship is in a deteriorating state. However, there are schools where such concerns don't fit. I was questioned often while I was working with teachers in the West Bank recently about reports that U.S. schools "are in a rapidly declining state when compared with schools in other industrialized countries of the world." We have the paradox of having schools equal to the best in the world, with some better than schools anywhere in the world, while also having schools that are far below what anyone in this country should accept. We can do better.

Dropout rates, while plateauing in recent years at about 22 percent nationally, remain too high. And, in our largest cities as well as in some rural areas, particularly in the South, dropout rates are closer to 40 percent. This is a societal tragedy, as it places too many limits on too many young men and women.

In virtually all these matters, the schools mirror the society. What does this reality say to us? Quite simply, we have much to do, individually and collectively. While none of us is likely to be in a position to alter very many of the global circumstances substantially, we can, in our individual classrooms and schools, contribute to constructive change. By understanding the context, we can help alter the discourse and, ultimately, the practice more broadly.

Tolerance of low-level learning activities is not acceptable—and low-level learning activities dominate in too many of our schools. Basic skills should never mean marginal skills and low-level thought. Neither should the arts, inquiry science, and world languages be seen as frills available only to the few in selective schools or in the suburbs. We need better schools in all our communities, and those better schools depend on thoughtful, committed, intellectually inspired teachers. I trust that is why we have chosen to enter teaching.

Having presented some of the reality of schools, what are some of the issues
that are up for debate?

- Can the diversity of our population be handled in integrated schools?
  Would some students be better off in racially or culturally separate schools?
  Several cities have developed black male academies—believing that some
  black males need special support if they are to succeed socially and academically. Further, women in some settings are being placed in all-female
  math and science classes.
- Should large school systems be more fully decentralized—with each school
  becoming a cost and curriculum center? Should large schools be decentralized into several more autonomous small schools?
- Should the distinctions between public and private schools be blurred, with
  choice being more central?
- Should bilingual education be eliminated, expanded, or reconstructed
  philosophically?
- What will be the impact of the new standards movement on populations
  that have long been underserved?[18]

I have only entered the surface of the questions and issues. My own view
is that we don't have, on an overall scale, the schools that we need, yet we
know how to get better schools. The will, a genuine passion for change, is not
yet with us. As a result, the promise of American education remains a distant
dream, and too many of our young people continue to languish.

## FOR REFLECTION

Reflect on the communities you have lived in. In what ways are they the same
or different from fifty years ago, twenty-five years ago, ten years ago? How do
you think about this?

Think about the demographics of the elementary and secondary schools you
have attended. What were the ethnic, racial, social-class, and cultural backgrounds
of the students and teachers? Did you think about these kinds of demographics
at the time you were a student? What do you have to say about them now?

Reflect on your high school. How did the size affect personal relationships,
class sizes, course offerings, academic intensity, and rules and discipline patterns? Also, what would cause you to say or not to say that all students received a high-quality, equitable education?

Finally, why is it so difficult to bring greater equity to schools—in their
financing, materials, and outcomes?

[1]My preservice teachers are not particularly close to most of what I present, although they know pretty well the popular accounts that describe many of the "problems" of schools. More experienced teachers are generally aware of conditions in their own schools and school districts but are less aware of conditions globally.

[2]We are currently in a period of growth in the school-age population. Secondary school enrollments, in particular, are expected to rise substantially over the next decade.

[3]Another way to think about the changes is to consider that there were approximately 1.4 million school board members in 1920, while there are only 80,000 today. From the point of view of civic participation, this cannot be viewed positively. Educationally, it has also moved decision making away from local schools, greatly enlarging bureaucratic structures. I would argue this has not been salutary.

[4]Averages, of course, mask a great deal. High schools have gotten much larger over the past fifty years. Few high schools in our urban areas, whether small or large cities, have fewer than one thousand students, and there are high schools with as many as four to five thousand students.

[5]Based on my observation of schools over many years, I would keep elementary schools under two hundred and secondary schools under four hundred. In such settings, greater simplicity of organization is possible, control issues decline, students become better known and are able to be taught more effectively, greater academic intensity is possible for all, and students and families tend to feel more comfortable. (See Cotton [1996].) Recognizing that schools often are much larger than this, we need to consider ways of creating autonomous schools within schools.

[6]Nationally, 48 percent of school funding comes from state governments, 46 percent from local property taxes and 6 percent from the federal government. There is, however, great variation among states. In many of the New England states, funding is considerably heavier at the local level, well over 60 percent.

[7]We have lived with these kinds of inequities for much of the twentieth century. Schools with the poorest children, those with the greatest educational needs, have long had inadequate resources. The rhetoric, at least since the Second World War, has been "equality of educational opportunity," but the reality has been considerable inequality of educational opportunity. Few industrialized countries have the inequities of funding that exist in the United States.

[8]As it has turned out, high-spending districts in Michigan have found ways to keep their spending high. Although the hardest-pressed school districts have seen an enlargement of resources, equality still hasn't been accomplished.

[9]When scores on standardized tests are the measure for determining the value of increased expenditures, poor and minority schools will likely always show up badly. Standardized test scores have a long history of understating the abilities, knowledge, and skills of children and young people from poor, culturally and linguistically different, and racial minority populations.

[10]Urban centers argue that they have far larger costs for transportation (related to court-ordered desegregation) and special education and bilingual education than do suburban and smaller city school districts. They also argue that their facilities are older, and the costs of maintenance are far greater. There is considerable truth to such claims. One response from critics sympathetic to these arguments is that they still appear to spend far too much on administrative, bureaucratic structures, keeping substantial amounts of money out of classrooms. For genuine equity to occur, however, most of our urban schools and large numbers of our isolated rural schools genuinely need substantial increases in resources.

[11]I would not argue that black teachers cannot effectively teach white children or that white teachers cannot effectively teach black children. I do believe, however, we need far greater balance in our teaching population. I discussed this issue more fully in the first chapter of this book.

[12]See Orfield et al. (1996).

[13]Commitments to desegregation remain intact, but the increasing levels of racial isolation have left many long-time supporters discouraged. There is increasing pressure to make something constructive out of the racial isolation, to see potential, for example, in schools that serve African Americans exclusively being excellent schools, culturally rooted and powerful.

[14]Beginning with *A Nation at Risk*, the 1983 report of the National Commission on Excellence, we have heard much about other times when the schools "were uniformly better," a belief in some idyllic period in which everyone learned to read and write effectively, studied physics and foreign

languages, and gained a strong historical and cultural background. That is clearly a distorted history in need of constant challenge. We just didn't have such a history. Moreover, given the long history of de jure and de facto exclusion, the gross inequalities of our educational system, we have no period that should be looked to as idyllic. The schools have never been on a large scale as good, as equitable, and as democratic as they needed to be.

[15]I realize that my focus here on urban communities may appear to disregard the fact that large numbers of our schools are in suburban and rural settings. I do so because such a large percentage of our most vulnerable children and young people are in urban settings. Regardless of where we reside or what our experience is, we need to be concerned about urban circumstances, and we need to care about vulnerability in suburban and rural settings as well.

[16]It is particularly discouraging to read so much about the great economic boom the United States has been experiencing over the past decade and to know that poverty rates have been unchanged. It should also be noted that, of the eighteen industrialized countries in the Luxembourg Income Study, the United States has the highest child poverty rate—50 percent higher than all the nations studied. This receives little attention in the various international achievement comparisons.

[17]I cite the racial aspect of discrimination against new immigrants inasmuch as this is a critical difference from the mostly European immigration of the latter nineteenth and early twentieth century. It needs greater recognition, and it needs to be addressed more vigorously.

[18]These are among the public policy-oriented issues that we debate in my ongoing work with preservice and inservice teachers. While I have framed them in rather objective terms, there is a large social and moral context that surrounds them. I make sure that context is present.

# CHAPTER 3

# American Education

## A Historical Overview

Historical perspective is important, a means of understanding more fully the roots of our work, helping us make connections with other educators and approaches to the teaching-learning exchange over time and place. While most of us involved in teaching have likely had various American history courses, some related to schools and educational practices, often framed around a language of reform, we seem to lose touch quickly with what we may once have learned. To help us reconnect with some of the important threads of our American educational history, I offer here a version that teachers I work with have found particularly useful.[1]

One important message to keep in mind is that the public schools, as we know them, in their more universal forms, are not particularly old institutions and that secondary schools are even more recent. Another important message is that a reform impetus has almost always been present and that, in spite of the conditions, there have been numerous individuals and groups who believed the schools could be better, capable of serving a higher percentage of the nation's school-age populations and contributing more fully to a democratic society.

While there were a variety of means of providing schooling during the colonial period[2] and the first three decades of the nineteenth century, organized mostly by families or arranged by voluntary societies, the numbers of children who attended these schools were exceedingly small, and literacy as we now understand the term was not extensive. The system of schools we now have had its most direct origins in the 1840s in the North and West (what we now call the Midwest) and in the South after the Civil War as states began to accept more fully what was long understood as their legal responsibility for making education through the elementary grades universally accessible.

Leadership for these Common Schools came from such reformers as Horace Mann in Massachusetts, Henry Barnard in Connecticut, and John D. Pierce in Michigan. All were inspired by the mass elementary school systems that had begun earlier in Europe. They saw in these German, French, and Swiss systems models for state systems in the developing United States.[3] They were also inspired, however, by their definitions of the republican character of this country, envisioning school settings in which "all of America's children could meet, democratic life [be] nurtured, strong character [be] built and economic and cultural growth [be] guaranteed." They used the language we now tend to hear only in political speeches. In their day, however, such "larger than life" talk was more common. The nation was still new, still viewed by political and civic leaders as the democratic beacon for the world. While the schools didn't become in their lifetime the enlightened settings of their rhetoric, they did take hold rather quickly, becoming incorporated into the fabric of American society.

This period of educational growth has been particularly fertile for historians. Some, Lawrence Cremin among them, acknowledge the importance of the republican vision set forth by Mann—the deep concern for building a more elevated democratic and egalitarian society alongside provisions for continuing social and economic progress. Cremin's book *The Transformation of the Schools,* as well as aspects of his monumental three-volume work on the history of American education, pick up on this progressive view of an ever better system for providing education on a more egalitarian scale.[4]

Others see the growth of the common schools as an attempt by the state to *fix* various social and economic problems, defined in the latter half of the nineteenth century as rapid immigration, urban crowding, and unemployment. In *Broken Promises,* an enormously interesting and convincing history of America's concerns about children and young people, Marvin Lazerson and Norton Grubb argue that "doing something about the kids" has, beginning in the 1840s, been the political response to fears of social and economic disintegration. They explain current reform efforts as part of that longstanding pattern—arguing that "doing something about the schools" is always seen as easier than tackling the problems of jobs or housing, urban blight or trade.[5]

Still others, such as Michael Katz, Samuel Bowles, Herbert Gintis, Clarence Karier, and Joel Spring, see in the development of schools a conscious attempt by those in positions of economic and political power to maintain a class system.[6] This position grew in popularity in the 1960s and 1970s as Marxist analyses became more fashionable, although it has waned more recently, seen as too narrow a view, not sufficiently explanatory of the regional differences that emerged. To offer yet one more perspective, Carl Kaestle, in *Pillars of the Republic,* suggests the Common School movement grew out of efforts to preserve American Protestant culture in the face of a rapidly enlarging Catholic immigrant population.

What is clear is that traces of all these motives and beliefs can be found somewhere without explaining fully how quickly the schools became such an important, hope-filled, folklore-rich institution. What seems apparent is that easy generalizations are difficult when applied to *all* the settings in which these public schools developed. The concerns about the growing immigrant populations, especially the Irish Catholics in New York and Boston, don't explain, for example, the ways schools developed in rural Michigan, Ohio, Wisconsin, and Minnesota. Moreover, while it is true that the poor were dominant in the Common Schools of Philadelphia for many years, this wasn't the case in upstate New York or in Iowa. And, while the schools in Philadelphia were segregated, those in western Massachusetts and in most areas of Michigan were not.

As it happened, the schools grew more rapidly than Mann and others envisioned, particularly in the post–Civil War period. Given the growth, keeping up with the demands for teachers was extremely difficult. One thing that made it all possible was the part-time character of the schools. They were only open for four to five months a year in most settings. Those who farmed could often teach as well as farm. The school year, however, grew longer, in the 1880s reaching six months on average and by 1900 seven to eight months. In those early years, before teaching became a full-time profession, most teachers were men. By the 1880s and 1890s, the men had begun to drop out, and teaching became increasingly a "women's profession." (Nancy Hoffman's *The Woman's "True Profession"* provides a good historical background of this shift.)

As the schools increased in number and became incorporated into state systems, they also became more systematized and formal. The graded structures of today's schools had become the norm by 1870. Covering the material encompassed within first, second, and third grade readers became a dominant theme in the schools. Memorization took up much of a child's time. As the factory became a dominant force in the American economy by the latter nineteenth century, the metaphor of the factory pervaded the language of the broader culture, including schools. Bureaucratic forms of organization took hold. Could it have been otherwise? Was there a real alternative to the formalism, the age stratification, the separate subject matters, and the enlarging school districts? Michael Katz (1992) argues that it didn't have to come out this way—that a decentralized, more democratic system, in which each school, with its own governance process and pursuing a more independent path, was certainly possible. I also believe the wrong choices were made but am not sure which right choices could easily have been made.[7]

The debates over centralization-decentralization and standardization-uniqueness have never fully subsided. Interestingly enough, the intensity of the debate has grown enormously in the past decade. The belief that decentralized settings and less standardization, for example, bring more teacher and parent commitment has gained considerable support in recent years.[8]

Chicago was decentralized in 1991. Under the decentralization law, each of the 601 schools was to be governed by a locally elected school committee responsible for selecting principals and establishing curriculum, along with a substantial dismantling of the old central bureaucracy. Currently, under new legislation, a recentralization is occurring. This could have been a good test of a large-scale decentralization. In addition, many school districts have created opportunities for teachers and parents to create new schools with looser ties to the centralized systems. These new schools are part of an effort to make large schools smaller—as in New York City or as part of state charter initiatives in which teachers, community people, businesses, and colleges and universities are being invited to organize schools *outside* the authority of local districts (but with public funding). Close to half the states now have a form of charter legislation. Further, interest is growing in moving away from age stratification and school patterns that have supported such stratification. The Coalition of Essential Schools is pioneering many of these changes at the secondary school level.

While universalism was the stated goal in the mid- to late nineteenth century, it was difficult to achieve. Fewer than 25 percent of those who began school in the nineteenth century completed elementary programs. And, in spite of the best hopes of egalitarians such as Mann, these schools, as noted earlier, especially in the East, served a disproportionate number of poor and lower-middle-class children.

Widespread public support for secondary schools did not develop until the closing decades of the nineteenth century. Unlike the elementary schools, secondary schools in the late nineteenth century were classically academic in nature and attracted few young people from working-class or newly arrived immigrant families. Not until the 1920s did the high schools begin to attract these populations in any significant numbers. By then, the high schools had become different institutions, with a broader curriculum, vocational education programs, and diverse levels of academic expectations.[9] (I will comment further on secondary schools at a later point in this chapter on page 39.)

The nineteenth-century effort to expand educational opportunities was fraught with difficulties not unlike those currently faced by a myriad of developing countries. Fiscal support was inadequate, and school facilities could not be built rapidly enough to accommodate the increasing numbers who wished to attend. Moreover, the surrounding social order was in a state of rapid transition, especially in the urban areas. Urban population, for example, increased from 9.9 million in 1870 to over 30 million by 1900. Many major U.S. cities doubled in population in this thirty-year time period, and racial, ethnic, linguistic, and religious concerns related to the massive migration and immigration in the latter nineteenth century proved vexing in public schools.[10]

In this late-nineteenth-century period of social and economic transformation, concerns raised about the directions of schools foreshadowed what was to become a burgeoning progressive reform movement in the early years of the twentieth century. The basic challenges focused on breaking the linear curriculum chain, the rote nature of teaching and learning, the formalism, and the growing centralization of schools. Brooks Adams, a prominent historian and Boston School Board member, framed the critique as well as anyone in an 1879 *Atlantic* essay. He wrote, "Knowing that you cannot teach a child everything, it is best to teach a child how to learn," and proceeded to show that most school practice had no connection to such a purpose.[11] Such a critique was elaborated on enough by a sufficient number of educators and educational critics to encourage the beginnings of an important reform movement.

Among early reformers, Francis W. Parker, referred to by John Dewey as the "Father of Progressive Education," stands out. Accepting the superintendency of Quincy, Massachusetts, in 1873, Parker made a public commitment to "bring back enthusiasm for teaching and learning." Influenced greatly by Pestalozzi's ideas, Parker quickly initiated policies to end the linear, lockstep curriculum along with the traditional graded readers and spellers. Further, Parker encouraged teacher initiative in the development of curriculum; recommended using newspapers, magazines, and field trips into the community as a base for local history and geography; and introduced manipulative devices for teaching arithmetic.

He wanted students to make learning their own, something internal and usable beyond school. Nothing, he believed, should be taught in isolation; the weekly spelling list was one of his most potent examples of wasted opportunities for learning. Student interest, he believed, was critical to learning. According to Parker, the ways in which teachers approached children and their learning, the content they stressed, the materials they used, and the relationships they forged between what was studied and the world were more important than coverage of *any* specific curriculum. In many respects, such a perspective would seem as radical today as it was in Parker's time.[12]

Given his reform agenda, controversy swirled all around him. Some of his critics in the State Department of Education thought the Quincy schools were abandoning reading, writing, and mathematics and were "experimenting with children." Parker responded, in his 1879 annual report to the school committee, with words often repeated by reformers in subsequent eras:

> I am simply trying to apply well established principles of teaching. . . . The methods springing from them are found in the development of every child. They are used everywhere except in school (quoted in Cremin, 1961, p. 130).

This is a perspective most of us understand. In fact, you might want to think about how you learned to ride a bicycle, throw a ball, shoot baskets, cook, knit, or paint—anything that mattered deeply to you. How did that learning differ from school learning? Parker thought schools should emulate that kind of learning.

As the nineteenth century drew to a close, proposals to focus on the child rather than subject matter, on active rather than passive learning, began to come from a wide range of sources outside as well as inside the organized educational establishment. We may think that the public attention to schools we now have is new. It is important to know that schools have long been the grist for the media. Educational ideas were regularly debated in the various public affairs journals.

One of the most interesting reports of this late-nineteenth-century period was written by Joseph Rice, a pediatrician, who in 1892 visited schools in thirty-six cities as a base for a series of articles for the *Forum,* a monthly journal. His report, which ran over the course of a year (Rice, 1892-1893) was scathing. It was also extremely popular, contributing to an active debate, especially in the cities on which he focused. (*A Nation at Risk* seems mild by comparison.) Rice was extremely critical of the routine of schools. Classrooms, he wrote, should be "glowing with life and warmth," rather than being "mechanical, damp and chilly." He painted a dismal picture of incompetence and classroom practices that were little more than sing-song drill, repetition, and disconnected knowledge.

Another important external source fueling a reform impetus in the early years of the twentieth century was the settlement house movement. Unlike many of the reformers in the schools, those in the settlement houses had an expansive agenda, which included improved housing, the development of child-labor laws, neighborhood recreational facilities, and provisions for medical care, including a national health insurance plan and the construction of more elementary schools. Leaders in the settlement houses, Jane Addams being the most prominent, called for a different kind of education, one that concerned itself with children's physical and social well-being along with their intellectual growth. Members of many of the settlement houses organized cooperative nurseries, conducted kindergarten programs, and provided a variety of opportunities for intergenerational learning. They tended to view education as having a relationship integral to their efforts at improving the quality of community life (Hall, 1971). While there were occasionally some connections between the settlement houses and schools, they were mostly a world apart. Schools still have difficulty aligning themselves with such external reform efforts.

It was, however, John Dewey—a product of nineteenth-century America, who maintained an active intellectual life to the middle of our current century—who, more than any other person, gave the progressive reform movement in education its intellectual leadership. Through his writings, he continues to provide inspiration to many who seek more progressive practices in schools. Given the importance of Dewey to American education, it might be worthwhile to look at some biographical information as well as some of his principal educational ideas. Most people in the schools know that Dewey has been extremely influential in American education and understand that he and his ideas have become popular again, yet actual knowledge seems limited.

Born in Burlington, Vermont, in 1859, Dewey saw the outcome of both war and industrialization. He was deeply concerned about each, and the influence of these concerns can be seen throughout Dewey's life. Unlike most educational reformers of his day and now, Dewey's circle was extensive and inclusive.

Beginning with his work at the University of Chicago and later at Columbia, he was at the center of every major social reform movement of the first half of the twentieth century, in and out of education, serving as an important intellectual spokesperson, putting forward a powerful vision of the common good. He could be found marching with labor in support of improved working conditions; he was involved with the founding of the NAACP; he had card #1 in the American Civil Liberties Union; he wrote often about matters of equity in housing, social welfare, and justice in the *New York Times*, the *New Republic*, and the *Nation*.

In contrast to most educators of his day, Dewey could not separate schooling from the surrounding social and economic conditions, seeing them as necessarily connected. (He was, in this regard, influenced greatly by his wife, Alice, and close friend Jane Addams.) He grasped early that industrialization and urbanization were changing radically conditions for growing up, for schooling, and for community life. In his view, the schools were foundering because they had lost their connection to a society undergoing rapid change, being encumbered by an outlook of America as a small town with tree-lined streets and lovely single-family homes, with an economy fueled by agriculture and sustained by common religious beliefs and cultural backgrounds. Dewey spoke of the growing anonymity, the increasing alienation from the productive side of labor, and the decline in personal and community standards—that sense of the commonwealth. He argued for an understanding that America was a culturally diverse country and that democracy was losing ground. And he wasn't reaching back to a more idyllic time, to a golden age, against which to place his contemporary world. He wanted, in Maxine Greene's (1978) terms, a wideawakeness to the world as it was and what it could become. Some of Dewey's central educational ideas might be useful to review. As a means of illuminating the meanings, I have offered a number of interpretive comments and examples:

- *Education and life are part of the same social continuity—not separate experiences.* For Dewey, the separation—education here, life there—took the natural energy out of learning, emptying it of its fullest possibilities. So much of what students study in school has meaning almost exclusively in the school—it has little connection to what is being debated in the world and to what young people are doing and observing day in and day out in the streets. What do we say when students convey to us that they learn more in their classrooms about Peru than about their local communities, or when they say that little that goes on in their schools seems useful in the world beyond school? Moreover, students hear constantly, "You'll need this when you enter college, when you're a mother or a father, when you reach middle age." Dewey wanted us to understand that an education that matters has to be

about the life children and young people are living *now*. If that was attended
to well—by answering the questions students posed and were genuinely
perplexed by—the future, he suggested, would take care of itself.

- *Education at its best is growth*—in understanding, capacity, self-discovery, in
control of events, and the ability to define the world. It is a formulation
that suggests the need to *work toward* the better, the fuller, the most potent.
In this sense, when instruction works well, it is always generative, leading
somewhere. So much of what passes for education, though, has a fixed-
end quality. We learn X, then take a test on X, and then forget X. At its best,
education is dynamic; the ideas have multiple possibilities. What is studied can be entered at many different levels, and the possibilities for extension are virtually unlimited. One way to think of growth in these terms is
to consider one of our passions. As you likely know from experience, our
passions keep us invested for many years. They have few fixed-end points.
We don't say about things we love, "I studied that and there is nothing
more to learn." We find ourselves, for example, listening to Coltrane again
and again, hearing new things year after year. And it is natural to reread
particular texts—those that matter to us—because each time we read them
it is almost like reading them for the first time.

- *Continuity of experience is basic to growth,* the thread that brings about consolidation of ideas and their meanings. Dewey argued for connections between fields of inquiry and personal experience as a means of keeping ideas
alive. We might be studying the Italian language and find ourselves examining the architecture of Siena, becoming fascinated by the archaeology
of Rome and Agrigento, or falling in love with the genius of Leonardo. In
this regard, Dewey believed our current understandings are the foundation for new understandings, the old and the new always overlapping, new
relationships always developing. Where else except in school, Dewey
asked, are people expected to stop and start every twenty to forty minutes,
to see everything as segmented. In Dewey's terms, instruction should be
developed around *large* themes, large ideas with natural connections to
other themes and ideas. Because they are large, they need extended periods of time. *Patterns* would be an example. It is clearly generative in relation to language, logic, numbers, music, art, and design. From Dewey's
perspective, teachers need to select topics with an eye toward continuity,
their capacity for connectedness. These are topics that can be reexamined,
as their possibilities are endless. Can we ever know enough about immigration, or evolution, or the solar system, or relationships?

- *Experience is the basis for all genuine education,* even though all experiences
are not equally educative. Experience that leads to growth is experience

reflected on, actively considered. In this regard, it is more than random action. To support constructive experience, teachers are expected to play an active role—raising questions, posing problems, bringing new materials to the classroom, and enlarging and enriching the experience levels of students. So often we preempt the experience by our telling. We are so interested in moving on that, rather than let students struggle with a learning task, we intervene and eventually do it for them. In Dewey's terms, experience could be expansive and diverse, or limited and narrow. The more we consciously see, hear, and try out, the richer our experience base; as our experience base expands, the more we have to reflect on and to learn from. Reading about something can be useful, but seeing it, actively observing it, and bringing to bear on it previous experience add another dimension. "To be awake and alive in a world where problems exist," Dewey (1916/1961) noted, "means to be alarmed, on guard, ready to do something." Genuine experience disposes us to be awake to the world, to see what truly matters, and to act.

- *The interests of children and the adult interest in curriculum are reciprocal.* If what is being studied is not interesting to an adult, Dewey would argue, it is not likely to be of interest to children. This is especially clear to a parent. Children's favorite books are books their mothers and fathers also enjoy reading. Moreover, when students in school describe the topics they are particularly enthusiastic about, these are the topics their teachers are also most enthusiastic about. Efforts to simplify the educational exchange, something that is commonplace, are, in Dewey's terms, misguided. Tolstoy tells a marvelous story that exemplifies this idea well. Taking a break from *War and Peace*, he taught peasant children for several years—a task he thought was much more taxing physically and intellectually than writing *War and Peace*. He went through the language curriculum—the Russian equivalent of "hat, cat, sat, and mat" with such stories as "Ivan had a cat who sat on a mat next to a hat." He noted that the children had no energy, their heads down. He then decided to take to the students the complex folk stories of Russia, real literature. He noticed that the heads came up, the eyes widened, and the ears rose to attention. He concluded that "to the teacher, the simplest and most general appears the easiest, whereas for a pupil only the complex and the living appears easy—only that which demands interpretation and provokes thought is easy" (Tolstoy [1862] 1967, p. 289).

- *The development of intelligence and knowledge, whether for an individual or for a culture, grows from cooperative exchange.* Dewey stressed the fact that learning is inherently social, in need of dialogue. Students and teachers need to talk with one another, try out ideas, and work around the edges of a topic.

We can learn in isolation, but our thought is invariably enriched in dialogue. In this regard, Dewey believed that schools would be more likely to prosper if discussions among teachers about teaching and learning were more common. In relation to this concern for interchange, he wrote in regard to the functioning of the lab school that he and his wife, Alice, started at the University of Chicago: "Cooperation must . . . have a marked intellectual quality in the exchange of experience and ideas. Many of our earlier failures were due to the fact that our exchanges were too practical, too much given to matters of immediate import, and not sufficiently intellectual in content" (Mayhew and Edwards [1936] 1966, p. 371). We may need to worry in schools about who will meet the busses or how various classes will be scheduled for lunch, but, if such practical concerns come to dominate the discourse, the quality of life in a school will suffer. The quality of a student's education will also suffer if intellectual exchange is not central.

- *The most effective learning comes from doing, from acting on the world.* We learn baseball by playing baseball. We get better at chess by playing chess. We learn to be historians by engaging in genuine historical problems. Relatedly, our best work usually has multiple audiences and can be thought of as authentic work. It is something we take pride in, that we remember long after its completion. Think about work you did in school that you saw as something special, that you felt was as good as you could do, that provided you with important insights, or that greatly raised your confidence. What surrounded those occasions? Students in woodworking and other vocational fields often construct things that are then used by their mothers, fathers, or grandparents for decades. What they produce is worthy of being honored. Why isn't this kind of treasured work more typical beyond the vocational fields? Further, lest we think only of the usual meaning of *active*, it is important to understand that Dewey also saw thinking in active terms. Physical activities and tasks can never be everything.

- *Education at its best is always about democracy.* That belief dominated Dewey's thought. After all, school was about living in the world, learning to be in a position to remake the society. What good is an education if it doesn't contribute to making one's community a better place to live, if it doesn't enhance the potential for productive relationships, if it doesn't cause us to understand others more constructively, or if it doesn't produce greater integrity? As Elie Weisel points out often, the Nazi SS were graduates of Germany's best universities. What was the quality of their moral education? According to Dewey, education was most productive when its starting point was the needs that existed in the local community—when it was about transformation and improvement of the society. To Dewey, democracy was far more than a political conception; in fact, he was critical of the way American democracy functioned. He noted the scourge of slavery, ongoing discrimination supported by law, the inequalities of income, and the problems of social justice. A particularly important conception to Dewey was "equality of concern." One of his most quoted statements reflects this well: "What the best and wisest parent wants for his own child, that must the community want for all its children." If school **A** isn't good enough for one of our children, it possibly isn't good enough for any child. These ideas should be more central to current practice.

Dewey saw such skills as reading, writing, and arithmetic as understandings derived from needs, not merely as skills to be taught apart from natural inquiry. We read to acquire additional levels of knowledge and for personal enjoyment, we write to share information and refine our thinking, and we use math to solve real problems. It is discouraging to see so much in schools revolve around workbook exercises and simple text, materials that have meaning *only* in school and that are so unrelated to our cultural heritage. In the spirit of Dewey, I resonate with such topics as *whose America is this*? and *why does hunger exist in East Central Africa*? and *how do we create constructive race relations in the United States*? and *why Mars*? Dewey saw curriculum in this way.

Dewey noted early in his writing about schools—regardless of level, whether the primary grades, the middle and secondary schools, or the university—that schools needed to be staffed by scholars and not technicians— persons who are "so full of the spirit of inquiry, so sensitive to every sign of its presence and absence, that no matter what they do, or how they do it, they succeed in awakening and inspiring ardent and intense mental activity in those with whom they come in contact" (Mayhew and Edwards [1936] 1966, p. 265). As teachers, we need to share with our students our genuine love for learning. We need to talk about books and ideas and to share our concerns for the society. Another means is through our authoritativeness in relation to our work as teachers. Dewey used the formulation of teachers as students of teaching to define such authoritative persons, scholars capable of independent action, curriculum makers, and decision makers about practice. It was expected that these teachers would always be at the forefront of changing "the conception of what constitutes education."

Dewey's work, as noted earlier, set off a progressive reformation in the schools in the early decades of this century. While progressivism was never the practice in most schools across the country, there was enough occurring to keep progressivism alive and capable of influencing educational practice in general. Educational historian Lawrence Cremin argues that the schools were never the same after Dewey. The curriculum diversification—to include vocational education, the arts, community studies, extracurricular activities, including sports programs, theater, debate, work study, and community service—is a legacy, if not always carried out in inspiring ways.

I previously introduced teaching for understanding. In many respects, this is a Deweyan formulation. Using what one learns; tying the subject matter to the world; organizing around genuine questions that matter in the world; reading real text and not textbooks; learning actively rather than passively; using community resources; helping students see themselves as poets, writers, historians, mathematicians, scientists, artists, and active citizens in their communities; learning about matters of race and class; and seeing democracy as respectful relationships and dialogue, always related to a seeking of the common good are also closely tied to Dewey's vision of schools and the society.

Although I have discussed high schools, I want to return now to their development. The earliest secondary schools were the Latin schools, classical institutions intended to prepare boys for college. The Boston Latin School, organized in 1635, is the oldest, with many others taking form in the early nineteenth century. To get a feel for these schools, note the following from *The Boston Latin School Bulletin* of 1828: "[Children at age 9 can enroll] providing they can read correctly and with fluency and write running hand [cursive] and know all the steps, marks and abbreviations and have sufficient knowledge of English grammar to parse sentences in prose."

Enrollment in the various Latin schools was exceedingly small. By the middle of the nineteenth century, academies, also known as institutes and seminaries, also sprang up. For the most part, these mostly private ventures (many received some public funds) were not classical, which means that Latin and Greek were not required. Also, many were open to females as well as males. In all, there were approximately 300 public high schools in the United States in 1870, along with close to 1,000 academies.

The big change came after the *Kalamazoo* case in 1872, in which the Michigan Supreme Court affirmed the use of public funds for secondary as well as elementary schools. This understanding became commonly accepted across the country, and secondary schools began their growth spurt. Spurred on by the rapid growth that was also occurring in higher education, there were soon enough secondary schools for educators to believe they needed to define more fully "standards" for a high school education. Through the work of the Committee of Ten (with Charles Eliot, president of Harvard, as the chairman) in 1892 and the Committee on the Reorganization of Secondary Education, which began in 1913 and issued its *Cardinal Principals of Secondary Education* in 1918, many of the secondary school patterns we know so well were clearly laid out.[13]

By the 1920s, most of the curriculum sequences that have become so familiar were well entrenched: it was Algebra 1 in grade 9, Geometry in grade 10, Algebra II in grade 11, Trigonometry and Analysis in grade 12; Civics in grade 9, World History in grade 10, U.S. History in grade 11, and American Government/Economics in grade 12; Physical Science in grade 9, Biology in grade 10, Chemistry in grade 11, and Physics in grade 12. Even as educators over the years have questioned the logic of these sequences and at times have tried to organize in a more interdisciplinary manner, the basic structures have stayed intact.

In terms of growth, by 1890, there were close to 2,500 public high schools and a little over 200,000 students; by 1900, there were more than 6,000 public high schools and 519,000 students. From the post–World War I period into the late 1960s, high school attendance and graduation rates enlarged almost every year.[14] However, accompanying this growth was an ongoing diversification of curriculum. Most of the basic requirements remained intact, but the kinds of educational experiences that came to be accepted for meeting various requirements expanded. The high school diploma did not mean that every student had the same academic experience or had mastered the same skills.[15]

I commented earlier about the victory of a bureaucratic, centralized system of schools. This centralization, which came about through various annexations and consolidations, has continued over the century. In 1920, there were still about 200,000 school districts in the United States. By 1940, the number had shrunk to 140,000. In 1998, there were fewer than 15,000 school districts. Think about the difference in citizen participation in the affairs of schools. In 1920, there were about 1.4 million school board members; in 1998, there were approximately 80,000. Even though the tradition is local control, the "local" has become increasing more ample in scale. One of the criticisms of the growing centralization and greater bureaucratization of schools in the late nineteenth century was that the gap between the people controlling the schools and the students, their families, and local communities was growing out of control. The gap is clearly much greater today.[16]

The progressive reform agenda that had been so prominent at the beginning of the century, certainly influencing pedagogy and helping bring about a more inclusive environment for schools, suffered in the 1930s from the financial and social difficulties of the Great Depression.[17] This was followed by the overwhelming demands of the Second World War, which drew public attention away from the schools.[18] By the 1950s, progressivism had become popularly identified with an approach to learning that gave too little attention to subject matter. In the passing of the Progressive Education Association in 1955, Lawrence Cremin saw the end of this half-century-long progressive reform effort, although he closed his book on progressivism (Cremin 1961) by suggest-

ing that "perhaps . . . [progressivism in education] only awaited the reformu-
lation . . . that would ultimately derive from a larger resurgence of reform in
American life and thought" (p. 253). This may have been prophetic, as the 1960s
brought about a progressive revival in the schools.

In the aftermath of *A Nation at Risk*,[19] the 1950s seemed to be played out
as a sort of golden age for the schools. I was a student and teacher in the schools
at that time. It was a period in which the schools were under severe attack for
not being academic enough or "patriotic" enough.[20] In 1957, for example, the
criticism of the schools reached unparalleled levels as the first Soviet *Sputnik*
orbited the earth. In this cold war climate, the United States had "clearly fallen
behind" in mathematics and science. Comparisons between "Johnny" and
"Ivan" filled the media. Ivan could do everything; Johnny could do little—not
only couldn't he do math and science but he could not even read or write. Out
of the crisis, and after monumental debate in Congress over the merits of the
federal government becoming involved in elementary and secondary education, came a major infusion of federal dollars into the schools through the National Defense Education Act (NDEA).[21]

While, given our more recent experience in the wake of *A Nation at Risk*,
one might have expected the response to this "crisis" to be testing, a process
of "getting tough on teachers and students," the prevailing response was to
put resources into improving the quality of teacher education and instituting
a wide range of curriculum development programs considered to be more academically challenging. At a time when the governance of schools was still understood as local, in the hands of school boards, such a response was natural.
In contrast, the later debates, in the mid to late 1970s and early 1980s, brought
about an emphasis on testing and the retention of students. By that time, considerable authority had moved away from local settings to the state and federal levels. The complexities that surround schools seem to fade a good deal
as the distance grows. In the statehouses, giving all third graders a test seems
like a reasonable way of assuring a higher quality of education, but, in the
schoolhouses, such a direction seems wasteful and distracting.

The 1960s proved to be years of massive social change in the United States.
The civil rights movement, which gained momentum in the late 1950s, was a
fulcrum for social and political reform in the 1960s. The inequities in American life became increasingly apparent and were understood to require a significant public response. The failure of the education system to provide high-
quality schooling on an equal basis to all Americans became a potent public
issue. Support for pluralism, long cast aside in the wake of a longstanding melt-
ing pot theory, grew with the recognition that it was necessary for the creation
of a more workable social democracy.

Depersonalization, generated in part by increasing levels of technology and bureaucratization in virtually all phases of American life, produced a sometimes radical response. Awareness of the rapid depletion and defacement of natural resources stimulated an increased concern for "spaceship earth." And the war in Vietnam, which proved to be more unpopular than any previous U.S. military involvement, brought protest to a high level. This milieu generated a new wave of educational reform that echoed earlier progressive reform efforts.

Some of the 1960s educational reform was characterized in the popular press as "romantic," related to the general questioning in American society about "lifestyle" and "cultural change," but it certainly included serious inquiry into pedagogy around the matter of understanding and helping students make learning their own. Jerome Bruner, in many respects an important inheritor of Dewey's vision of possibility for children and their learning, provided the dominant intellectual influence. Bruner (1962, 1966) advocated an approach to thoughtful subject matter learning that made solid connections to the lives of learners, to their need for understanding the content and not merely an ability to repeat textbook formulations.

Bruner's well-known social studies curriculum, *Man: A Course of Study* (1965), was, for example, designed explicitly to help students think about the world of human beings, both in the United States and in other cultures, in more reflective, analytic ways. This curriculum celebrated complexity and challenged students and teachers alike to think beyond what was presented. Arguing that any subject can be taught in an intellectually responsible way to learners of any age, Bruner directly challenged the popular notion that the early years of education and the early phases of study in a field of inquiry should be dominated by routine skill building.

Just as important as his pedagogical and curricular stance was Bruner's grounding of that posture in the emerging field of cognitive psychology. Bruner made the educational community aware of school learning as a process sensitive to cognitive and developmental factors.[22] He underscored the importance to the learner of gradual mastery of several symbolic systems and modes, and he experimented with ways of representing abstract ideas to learners of different ages.

Along with Bruner's *Man: A Course of Study*, several other experimental curricula of the period were committed to the notion that youngsters could not only learn *about* the important content of the various academic disciplines but could also engage that content in ways significantly parallel to the work of professional practitioners, leading to enhanced levels of understanding. For example, *Science, a Process Approach* (American Association for the Advancement of Science 1962) and *The New Social Studies* (Fenton 1965) sought to introduce students directly to the kinds of inquiry processes scientists and historians exercised. Disciplinary habits of mind were understood to be critical to serious learning— posing problems, interpreting, reflecting, seeking counter evidence, and asking why whatever is studied matters.

Among the various curriculum projects of the period, the *Elementary Science Study* (Guide to the Elementary Science Study 1967) is particularly illustrative of themes that correspond well to many current interests in teaching for understanding. The introduction to this curriculum states

> It is apparent that children are scientists by disposition: They ask questions and use their senses as well as their reasoning powers to explore their physical environments; they derive great satisfaction from finding what makes things tick; they like solving problems; they are challenged by new materials or by new ways of using familiar materials. It is this natural curiosity of children and their freedom from preconceptions of difficulty that ESS tries to cultivate and direct into *deeper* channels. It is our intention to enrich *every* child's understanding. . . . (pp. 1–2)

In regard to teaching strategy, the ESS guide relates

> We want students not only to recognize scientific authority but also to develop both the confidence and the skills to question it intelligently. For this reason we feel it is necessary for the student to confront the real world and its physical materials directly, rather than through intermediaries such as textbooks. . . . We caution teachers against explaining things prematurely and against overdirecting student exploration. (p. 2)

This unprecedented period of curriculum reform reaffirmed inquiry as a model of discourse—questioning, maintaining a healthy skepticism, developing hypotheses, experimenting, examining a range of confirming and disconfirming data, and articulating a variety of possible explanations. An open-endedness was advocated, including the active use of materials and the development of ideas based on careful observation over time. There was talk of the need to "uncover a subject" rather than "cover a subject." The goal was *understanding*, not the amassing of isolated information.

The eventual outcome of this flurry of activity is all too well known: the initiatives foundered and faded into the "back-to-basics" movement of the 1970s and 1980s (Schaffarzick and Sykes 1979). Several forces contributed to a resurgence of less active, less complex paradigms. A fundamentalist backlash, for example, discouraged continuing federal participation in imaginative programs such as *Man: A Course of Study*.[23] Further, the university-based disciplinary scholars who led many curriculum projects of the 1960s often held unrealistic expectations about teachers' comfort with the new, more complex ideas and about the schools' commitment to this more progressive vision of education. In fact, to carry out these various curricular reforms, schools would have had to alter many of their longstanding practices and structures. In addition, the values of progressivism, including skepticism, questioning, challenge, openness, and the seeking of alternatives, have long struggled for acceptance in American society.

It is not surprising, therefore, that they didn't come to dominate the schools.

The federal government's major entry into elementary and secondary education in 1958 was followed in 1965 with the massive Elementary and Secondary Education Act (ESEA). The provisions of ESEA were to push for higher quality and greater equity in the schools. One way of understanding the importance of both the NDEA and the ESEA is to consider that federal expenditures for elementary and secondary schools accounted for little more than 1.5 percent of total expenditures in the schools for most of the period up to 1958, when it doubled with the NDEA. It doubled again in 1965 (with the ESEA). By 1972, federal expenditures accounted for 11 percent of the total funding for elementary and secondary education. It was almost 12 percent in 1979 and then began to decline as an overall percentage of expenditures, falling by 1988 to 6 percent, where it has remained.

Having discussed the civil rights movement, which had many of its high points in the 1960s, it might be useful to discuss the education of African Americans. I focus here on African Americans because of their unique circumstance in this country. It needs noting, however, that Native American populations suffered a disgraceful educational history, as have many non-English-speaking immigrant populations. And those who are economically poor have seldom had the benefit of a high-quality education. In the end, the civil rights movement benefited all of these populations.[24]

In the period before the Common Schools, African Americans in slavery were actively denied schooling. Education was viewed as a direct challenge to the institution of slavery.[25] Those who were free, however, particularly in New England, had some modest educational opportunities. As elementary schools rapidly grew in number prior to the Civil War, small numbers of African Americans, aided by the growing abolition movement, entered the schools in northern cities, although segregation was common.[26]

It was after the Civil War that schools became more common in the South. As part of Reconstruction, schools for freed African Americans were established. By all accounts of this period, African American children and adults were eager for education, and literacy among African Americans grew significantly over the next two decades. While the schools were de facto segregated, it wasn't until the end of Reconstruction, after the 1876 presidential election, that laws were passed in the old confederate states for the creation of dual systems to match the Jim Crow laws and practices that defined race relations. Such laws were not in existence in the North; nonetheless, de facto segregation was the rule. While school participation by African Americans increased greatly as a new century approached, overall education levels were far lower for African Americans than for their non–African American counterparts.[27]

The first big test of the "separate but equal" system of schools established under Jim Crow was settled in 1896 in *Plessy v. Ferguson,* when the Supreme Court upheld the constitutionality of separate systems. This was a severe blow to efforts by African Americans to alter what was clearly an unequal system. It was half a century before a legal case could be mounted again on the issue of inequality in educational practices and opportunities. In 1954, in *Brown v. Board of Education, Topeka,* the Supreme Court argued, in a change from *Plessy,* that "separate schools were inherently unequal," beginning a massive effort to desegregate the schools that continues into the present.

The battles for desegregation, for equality of opportunity, and for a fulfillment of America's longstanding democratic promise, in the 1960s were initially carried out primarily in the South. The integration of the Little Rock schools in 1957, achieved with federal troops, was a symbol of the U.S. government's new determination to enforce the Court orders. In the 1970s, northern cities were also faced with court orders to desegregate their schools. Boston, in 1976, was the literal and figurative battleground for the promise of equal education.

It is not easy to understand the systematic discrimination that has occurred in the schools, that is so undemocratic and so reprehensible morally. African Americans, as a whole, have made considerable educational progress over the past three decades—in high school attendance and graduation, college attendance and graduation, and economic status—yet most African American school-age children remain in schools that are underfunded and provide a less than adequate education. The challenge of equality, of democracy, is still with us.

As the 1960s came to an end, the openness that had existed for more active learning, inquiry, and alternatives to the more standardized approaches to education, essentially a new wave of progressivism, gave way to a political backlash couched in the language of "bringing back educational standards," "back to the basics," and "accountability." It took the form of competency tests used to determine students' suitability for promotion and graduation. Those in the schools tended to see the competency testing movement as limiting educational opportunities, greatly narrowing the curriculum, and negatively affecting those who had long been underserved—African Americans, Hispanics, and the poor. Lawsuits based on discriminatory effects, filed first in Florida, caused many questions about the worth of this testing. By 1977, though, thirty-five states had instituted such tests.[28]

In 1983, the widely publicized report of the National Commission on Excellence in Education, *A Nation at Risk,* was published. Filled with rhetoric about massive failure in the schools, it suggested that standards had fallen and that expectations for serious academic work were limited. Moreover, the implication was that our schools were leading us toward decline as a nation and that it was time for all Americans to demand educational change. No similar report had ever stimulated so much sustained attention or provoked so many legislative bodies to write new education statutes.[29]

Requirements for graduation were increased in almost every state, teacher testing became more common, and new, high-stakes tests were instituted in over half the states—generally, at grades 4, 8, and 11. This was a time of increased state regulatory activity—a forerunner, in many respects, to the new standards, curriculum frameworks, and proposals for testing that are taking form at the end of the twentieth century.

By the mid 1980s, many policy makers were concerned that the high degree of regulatory action that followed *A Nation at Risk* might be discouraging many educators in local schools. They began talking about second wave reform, providing opportunities for teachers and administrators in individual schools to seek waivers from many of the regulations on the promise of even higher-quality work and stronger local accountability. Many of the small school alternatives that gained considerable publicity for their successes—buttressed by interests in choice—were begun in this period. Today, however, these schools are being seen as exceptions, possibly needing to be sacrificed for the sake of a greater standardization, what is being called the "greater good of *all* students." As the tumultuous twentieth century comes to an end, the "reform" rhetoric is about "high standards" and tests for purposes of promotion and graduation. I see little reason to believe that these efforts will cause the schools to be as good as they could be and need to be.

In this historical review, meant to provide a context, much has obviously been passed over. Some aspects of the history will be picked up in other chapters, as historical perspective is brought forward. One issue that needs a fuller historical review is testing. What has been clear over the years is that, while testing has grown enormously and its effects are becoming more palpable, for most teachers its history remains obscure. See Chapter 12 for a historical account of testing.

---

## FOR REFLECTION

Reflect on the best school (elementary, middle, or secondary) that you can imagine. How large is it? How is it organized? How do teachers teach? What kinds of materials dominate? How does assessment proceed? How are parents involved?

How would you respond to those who suggest that the quality of our schools has undergone considerable decline, that they are inferior to the schools in most other industrialized countries?

What would schools have to be like to make a large contribution to democratic life? Should schools be expected to make such a contribution? What would be your most convincing arguments on behalf of such an expectation?

Finally, how would you expect the schools to develop over the next fifty years? Will there be greater centralization or less centralization? Will there be a greater number of private schools or fewer private schools? Will tests play a larger role or a smaller role? Will there be more tracking by judgments of ability and gift or less tracking? Will racial isolation be greater or be on the road to elimination? Will there be greater equity or less equity?

[1]The first time I offered this history was with a large group of experienced teachers. We were engaged in a discussion of "small schools" and the experience of the Central Park East schools as an exemplar of the current interest in small schools. One early question was "Why did schools in urban communities get so large?" This was followed by a variety of questions about schools over time and to a plea for a historical overview of schools in this country. I offered, in response, what I called my "15-minute history of American education." While necessarily cursory, the teachers thought it was extremely helpful. I have presented this short history since to many groups of teachers and administrators, both novice and experienced, as a means of putting current school reform efforts into an understandable context. What I offer in this chapter goes beyond that "15-minute history" but it stays close to the basic outline.

[2]The Massachusetts Bay Colony established in 1647 provisions for townships with 50 households to appoint "one within their town" to teach and for townships with 100 households to provide a grammar school. It wasn't, however, until the early nineteenth century that these "public school" provisions became fairly common.

[3]The major European influences pedagogically came from the work of Friedrich Froebel, Johann Pestalozzi, and Johann Friedric Herbart. I present below some of their ideas, since their educational formulations were widely discussed in relation to the Common Schools in the nineteenth century. That they existed in the language of prominent educators doesn't necessarily mean they existed in practice, but without the language, the practice might have been less constructive than it was. *Friedrich Froebel's* work was especially influential on America's educational reformers, particularly in relation to the earliest years of the school cycle. His garden metaphor—with its sense of unfolding, blooming, and flowering—underscored the developmental quality of learning. For Froebel, educational experiences build on each other and are, therefore, related. In his terms, the more significant various experiences are, the larger their educational potential. Because such continuities were important, Froebel encouraged children to return often to previous experiences, understanding they would bring something different to the experiences each time, thereby enlarging them, imbuing them with new possibilities, and thus extending their understandings. Responding to an educational system that was linear and fact-oriented, *Johann Pestalozzi* eschewed memorization, the verbalization of rules and concepts in the absence of understanding, and all learning activities that could not easily be connected to the learner's life. His pedagogical points of departure were the child and his or her experiences, the concrete materials with which the child worked, and the relationships of these materials and experiences to other objects and ideas, what is essentially the basis for understanding. Student interests were critical, seen as important starting points for learning—especially learning that would be internalized. *Johann Friedric Herbart* viewed all learning as relational, causing him to criticize the isolated learning of disconnected topics that was beginning to shape curriculum in the schools. For him, each new stage of learning had to be integrated with previous learning, the aggregate constituting the base for further learning. His pedagogical approach sought entry points connected to previous learning, strong links to the interests

of students, and consolidation around generalizations or principles to guide ongoing learning in school and in life.

[4]See Cremin (1970, 1983, 1990).

[5]In thinking about this perspective, let's assume that the schools worked very well, as well as we can imagine. Would everyone in America then be employed at high-paying jobs? Would drug problems vanish? Would parents be better? Would child abuse fade? Would communities be healthier? Would the government work better?

[6]See Katz (1968, 1971, 1992); Gintis and Bowles (1976); Spring (1972, 1990); and Karier (1975).

[7]One way for me to think about this is through some contemporary circumstances. Tracking, the process of separating students by judgment about skill or gift, for example, has become conventional in contemporary schools. Virtually *all* the research, over many decades, suggests that tracking doesn't make much difference for those judged most able and is highly detrimental for those judged least able. However, in national polls, almost three-fourths of teachers support tracking, as do most parents. Detracking is the right choice, but it isn't happening.

[8]You might want to read Ted Sizer's three books, *Horace's Compromise, Horace's School,* and *Horace's Hope.* My purpose in raising these contemporary developments is to acknowledge that the nineteenth century debates have re-emerged in almost as vigorous a manner. How long will it take, though, before we read about how decentralization means that students in different schools might be receiving a different education, that we have chaos? The retort, of course, will be that our centralization has brought a more impoverished education. There is still a big debate coming. In fact, the emerging discussions about national standards make this debate inevitable. Decentralization may be the loser again.

[9]In 1900, for example, only 8 percent of the secondary school–age population was actually attending high school. And we need to go to the post–World War II period before the percentage attending high school gets close to anything that can be called universal. It was *1950,* for example, before a majority, 51 percent, of those beginning high school actually completed high school. By then, the high school was different than it had been at the turn of the century.

[10]In many respects, immigration-related conditions today are similar to those at the turn of the century. While we are more supportive of native language today, immigrant students and their families still face considerable discrimination and too limited support.

[11]That concern remains with us. Is the goal in the schools to be coverage or uncoverage? Is teaching less, more deeply, with understanding the goal, or is the acquisition of a large array of information the goal?

[12]Parker's *Talks on Pedagogics* (1894) was particularly popular among teachers, representing in its own way an early progressive tract. If we were to update the language, it would be close to much of the reform literature currently circulating.

[13]The principal discussion surrounding the Committee of Ten was whether there should be a separation of the high school according to goal paths. The agreement was to reject a class-based structure and maintain a common set of requirements for *all* students (in contemporary terms, "high standards for all"). By 1913, when the Committee on the Reorganization of Secondary Education had begun its work, a strong vocational education advocacy had begun, suggesting the possibility of different kinds of high schools (which, by then, had become common in Europe). Essentially the proposals put forward supported the comprehensive high school, with many different programs operating within one building, although containing some common academic requirements. This was considered a democratic solution to the call for different kinds of schools meeting different purposes.

[14]In 1912, there were 1,105,000 students and, by 1920, 2,200,000. By 1930, 47 percent of youths of high school age were attending a high school.

[15]It has become conventional since the 1983 report *A Nation at Risk* to suggest that the high school diploma has *recently* lost its common meaning. The fact is that it has not had a common meaning for most of the century.

[16]Michael Katz (1992) closes his work on "How Urban School Systems Became Bureaucracies" as follows:

> One consequence of bureaucracy . . . is the separation of consumption from control, that is, the increasing divorce of those who are served by an institution from those who control it. In education, this has meant the separation of school and community, signaled

by the increasing ability of school officials to ignore parents, reformers, and others outside the system. Certainly, career educators needed autonomy from uninformed political meddling, but ironically the protection they won contributed to the sterility of urban education. Their isolation lessened their sensitivity to the communities whose children they instructed, to their students, and to the informed, constructive criticism that makes progress possible. In fact the reaction of schoolmen to lay criticism became a defensive reflex as the traditions of resistance forming in the nineteenth century calcified into the responses that often set urban schools and their communities against each other in the 1960s. Bureaucracy's success has also been intellectual, for its triumph has foreclosed the serious consideration of alternatives. Bureaucracy has transcended its mid-nineteenth century standing as one choice among organizational possibilities. Its contingent, historical origins remain buried in the past as its reification has cast the progress of bureaucracy as inexorable, inevitable, and even natural. (109–110)

[17]Even in the face of an economic collapse greater than any in the nation's history, school boards tended to maintain many of the programs begun with progressive impetus—namely, those in the fine and practical arts as well as in extracurricular activities, such as clubs, sports, and theater. Such has not been the case in recent years when school funding has become tight.

[18]One of the genuinely important studies of progressive education, something that educators looked forward to learning more about, was published in 1942 (See Aiken [1942].) It was a story of immense success of the participating schools. The timing couldn't have been worse; the war, not schools, was the preoccupation.

[19]A Nation at Risk was published in April 1983, the work of the National Commission on Excellence in Education. It argued that the country was in jeopardy because the quality of education was not high enough. The public attention to this educational report was unprecedented. It spurred efforts in virtually every state to raise requirements and establish new tests. It also created a climate for enlarging state and local funding to schools, as well as increasing the business community's involvement in schools.

[20]Arthur Bestor, a graduate of the progressive Lincoln School in New York and a historian, was a particularly harsh critic. His Educational Wastelands (1953) was very popular, as was Admiral Hyman Rickover's Education and Freedom (1958), in which he attacked America's educational weakness in the face of Soviet technological developments.

[21]President Eisenhower had to use the considerable prestige of his office in order to get the NDEA through Congress. In a later letter to Life magazine (15 March 1959), he also offered the following advice—his way of focusing blame for the "sorry-state" of the schools: "Educators, parents and students must be continuously stirred up by the defects in our educational system. They must be induced to abandon the educational path that, rather blindly, they have been following as a result of John Dewey's teachings." Unfortunately, John Dewey wasn't alive to respond.

[22]This was also a set of ideas developed much earlier by Piaget. In the 1960s, Piaget's work became well known in the United States, complementing much of Bruner's work.

[23]See Dow (1991) for an interesting story of Man: A Course of Study in the political arena of the time.

[24]The history of African American education is important. I recommend the following as beginning reading: Bullock (1970), Anderson (1985), Bond (1966), and DuBois ([1903] 1969).

[25]In spite of the prohibitions, many slaves learned to read and write. The story of literacy in this period speaks to the tenacity to learn of these African Americans living in slavery.

[26]In 1855, Massachusetts mandated that public schools be integrated. It was 1900 before New York City ended segregated schools (Morison 1965, p. 532).

[27]By the end of the nineteenth century, expenditures in the black schools in the South were four times less than expenditures in the white schools. While elementary enrollment among African American children was relatively high, the number going on to high school was exceedingly small. By 1940, the percentage of children 6–13 enrolled in southern schools was the same for both races; on the other hand, among those 14–17, 28 percent of African Americans were enrolled in school, as compared with 63.9 percent of whites (Pierce et al. [1955]).

[28]Winsor Lott (1977), a New York State Department of Education official responsible for testing, provided the most straightforward response for this testing: "There are probably two reasons for

the current interest in basic competency testing throughout the nation. First, there is concern that schools are awarding high school diplomas to individuals who lack some of the basic skills, who can't read and write, for example. In addition, because of the cost of education, there is a continuing interest in accountability. Here it seems [that] various state legislatures . . . are demanding proof that the schools are doing a good job and that taxpayers are getting something of value for their investment" (p. 84).

[29]Many of the discussions that occurred around this report called on us to believe that there was a time when *all* students could read and write easily and well, studied foreign languages, completed coursework in physics or calculus, understood political processes at relatively high levels, and were steeped in classical literature and American history. Many in the schools were put on the defensive by such unsubstantiated claims.

# CHAPTER 4

# A Philosophical Stance

Teachers need a powerful philosophical base, a compass to guide them in their ongoing work. Without such a base—that provision for a critical stance, a readiness to examine everything, especially what seems most settled—it is easy to accept the many technical formulations of teaching that have become so commonplace in schools and keep students so unengaged—textbooks, wordlists, worksheets, formulas for keeping students under control, tests, a focus on right answers, and simplicity. Such acceptance keeps us away from the better schools and classrooms we need.

For many, a beginning philosophical orientation is rooted in undergraduate coursework in philosophy, an important element of liberal arts education. Not to have read from such works as Aristotle's *Metaphysics,* Plato's "Allegory of the Cave," John Stuart Mill's work on "free will," Catherine MaCauley's *Letters on Education,* Rene Descartes's *Meditations,* John Dewey's *Democracy and Education,* or Alfred North Whitehead's *Aims of Education,* among other philosophical texts, is to miss an important education. However, philosophy of education at its best is more than such readings and the historical relationships growing from them. It is about attitudes and dispositions, the development of a personal orientation toward teaching, a consideration of large purposes for one's work, the possession of powerful ends-in-view, the recognition and understanding of the importance of differences, and decisions about what to teach. It is also about careful thinking, respect for ideas, the challenge of ideas, and healthy skepticism about living in the world. It is about getting close to our own learning and about understanding more fully the ways others think. In these terms, a philosophical stance needs to be fully embedded in *all* the work new teachers do in their preparation for teaching, and it needs to be present in ongoing teaching practice.[1]

We might start with the content of our various teaching fields. Rather than accepting history as one of the required courses in the elementary or secondary curriculum, for example, philosophical thought calls on those preparing to teach history to ask why history *should* be a requirement. What gives it such a claim on young people's time in school? What would be lost if students *were not* to study history?[2] In essence, this is a matter of philosophically engaging their academic fields.

To help my students make an entry to such questions—moving beyond the casual acceptance of these various subject matters as naturally, self-evidently important—I ask them to write a "Why Math (History, Science, English, World Language)?" paper.[3] They are called on to make, in what becomes essentially a letter to their students, as powerful a case as possible for why their students *should* study the subject matters they are teaching—algebra, biology, chemistry, physics, American history, world literature, Spanish.

I pose the question "What would you say to students who ask 'Why are we doing this? What good is it?'" I make clear that they cannot say, "It is required" or "It is a prerequisite" for something else or "You'll need it when you get to college" or "You'll need it when you are a parent." Most of us understand how empty such explanations are. I stress the need for articulateness about such matters, to bring ongoing thoughtfulness about what our students are expected to take away from our various courses and how they will reach that point. Most of the preservice teachers I work with haven't thought about their subject matters in this fashion. Many are troubled, in fact, that they can't easily address the questions. The task, though, gets easier as they begin to reflect on and talk about what originally brought them to a positive connection with their fields or a set of questions within their fields.[4] They also come to understand the importance of carrying with them a powerful language around what they are planning to teach. After all, teaching is partly inspirational.

I also challenge prospective teachers to consider the teaching approaches they use in value terms. Teaching at its best demands consonance with one's philosophical position, a set of carefully reflected-on beliefs. Otherwise, it lacks any real passion or inspiration. For example, will the approaches used empower or disempower the students, lead them to greater independence or more dependence, give them the means for expanding their learning (in this sense adding complexity and flexibility) or keep them where they are? Thinking about teaching in these terms also makes testing, tracking, mainstreaming, retention and choice—among the issues that are currently under discussion in and around schools—subjects of critical inquiry, needing careful thought.

Israel Scheffler (1991) suggests that "philosophy brings to education characteristic emphases upon clarity, purpose and warrant. It challenges us to be clearer in our thinking, more responsible in our beliefs and more alive to the aims and consequences of our actions"[5] (p. ix). It is an active stance on teaching, a matter of bringing clear and critical thought to our lives as teachers, understanding that we can't ever just "go through the motions." This is what John Dewey had in mind with his acknowledgment that teachers needed to be students of teaching, persons who reflect on their practice and who are always prepared to ask, "Why this and not that?"[6]

Among the many philosophers who have written about education, none has been as influential as John Dewey, who took philosophy fully *into* the world, making it a central and intellectual force for teachers. Dewey saw philosophy as useful, a means of helping people face the world and contend with its problems, understanding that change is fully possible. In these terms, philosophy also represents a disposition, an important mode of reflective thought.[7]

In a late-nineteenth-century text, *Modern Philosophy,* Arthur Rogers (1899) suggested that "philosophy . . . is nothing but an attempt in a reasoned and comprehensive way to answer the question, 'what is the meaning of life?'" (p. 3). That kind of question, although sometimes ill-defined or only partially articulated, is always with us. In their own ways, children and young people in the schools ask teachers that question daily. It is another reason for teachers to think philosophically; it keeps before us an understanding that teaching always goes beyond subject matter and books.[8] As a way of considering philosophy in these terms, I offer a point of view about the importance of establishing thoughtful purposes for our work as teachers, suggesting in the process a *use* of philosophy, an actual entry into philosophical discourse.[9]

It is out of thought about large purposes, the important ends we envision, for example, that a genuine conversation about schools, teaching, and learning is possible. Other starting points keep teachers absorbed by fads and searches for a fabled "one best system."[10] In this regard, a philosophical stance assures that complexity remains paramount, that the technical solutions that abound for every aspect of schooling receive the ongoing challenge they deserve.[11]

At its best, teaching is first and foremost a moral and an intellectual undertaking, always beginning with children and young people and their intentions and needs, always rooted in powerful purposes. Unfortunately, the understanding that the educational enterprise is about big ideas, inspirational hopes, and generative conceptions is not sufficiently the preoccupation. We aren't close enough to Emily Dickinson's evocative lines "I dwell in possibilities" and "not wishing to miss the dawn, I open every door . . . " Being prepared to open every door, to consider the fullest of possibilities, is an important aspect of philosophical thought. It suggests a need to keep close by a continuing set of "what if?" questions.

In reflecting on the schools, there is more concern about whether children learn the mechanics of reading and writing than grow to love reading and writing; learn *about* democratic practice rather than have practice in democracy; hear about knowledge, essentially being in settings where knowledge is dispensed, rather than gain experience in personally constructing knowledge; engage in competition rather than learn the power of cooperation and collaborative thought; see the world narrowly, as simple and ordered rather than as broad, complex, and uncertain; and come to accept the vested authority that exists around them in organizational structures and text rather than be helped to challenge such authority, and to bring a healthy skepticism to the world.

I understand that I have posed the foregoing in oppositional terms. While these tasks are likely never so mutually exclusive, it is by placing the claims up front and in such terms that we can begin a genuine conversation about them.

For example, if a "genuine love for reading" were to matter, whatever we did in the teaching of reading would reflect an enthusiasm for language, and the rooms in which we teach would be full of books. Our language would flow with references to books, and libraries would be well integrated into our ongoing work. As it is, we are not sufficiently engaged in our schools around the meaning of or possibilities in our work. We may be keeping students busy, but that isn't good enough. We may even get high average scores on one or another test, but that also isn't good enough. It doesn't provide a large enough story about the depth of anyone's engagement. It doesn't address the moral and intellectual issues.

What ought to guide us as we consider the schools in relation to large purposes? Very little of what I offer will be new, but possibly in the stating there will be a renewed basis for reflection and action in intellectual and moral rather than technical terms.

What we know most about children and young people is that they are *always* learning. That is their nature. As they touch the earth, observe the culture that surrounds them, listen to stories, and speak, they are gaining a personal relationship with the world, which Jean Piaget calls a balance between changing the world and changing themselves. If we were to keep such a view about our students constantly before us, we wouldn't be so quick to assume clinical approaches to education, full of so many labels that imply deficits in children. Not to begin our work by acknowledging the natural strengths and energy of our students is to limit the possibilities, to assume for too many an education with too little power. It keeps the school as an institution and its structures and central mechanisms so dominant that the interests of the schools often overshadow the child. All of our efforts to standardize the schools, for example, tend to put the students in a secondary place.[12] We need more trust in our students.

In the schools over the past decade, we have been called to see our world through a lens of economic competitiveness, with the principal focus on Japan and Germany, with Korea, Taiwan, China, and Singapore close at hand.[13] We need educational settings that challenge young people intellectually and morally, that provide the skills and understandings that are generative of ongoing learning in the schools and in the world. We must want for our children and young people the best education we can imagine. However, placing so much stress on economic competitiveness—stronger math and science programs to win the war of technology, to maintain a level of economic superiority, for example—is distracting, even as it is distressingly accepted by schools of all kinds, even those of progressive persuasion. It is a formulation that too often prevents us from seeing the world as fully connected and its people as having mutual needs, with growth a matter for celebration. The zero sum formulations associated with competition—gains in Japan meaning necessary losses in the United States—are also self-defeating. Representing the world in these terms masks the inequities that exist and the imperatives to work actively toward their redress. This view also has a moral dimension, which needs to be addressed. Is hunger in Africa acceptable? Is the burden of debt carried by so many developing countries their just due? Is that where competitiveness leads? It has that potential. Whenever I think about the economic competitiveness argument, I have in mind an educational discourse that passes right over the heads of our students who sit in front of us each day—almost as if they aren't there. I see students asking about the construction of positive personal relationships or the reasons for continuing inequities in their communities and the schools wanting the students to outscore Japanese students on the next international test. It seems so wasteful, so disrespectful.

To speak of economic competitiveness in relation to the world also has an impact at the level of the school and classroom. Must our goal in the schools also be rooted in competition, or can cooperation be a principal objective? What are some of the ways to think about this? Shall we, for example, track students, provide challenge for some and little for others, place limits on the possibilities for some and open the world to others, perpetuate inequities or work toward their eradication, and clutter our discourse with labels that pit students against each other by race, class, perceptions of intelligence, or gift? Shall we accept the message of test scores or go beyond them, or come to see retention of students as necessary or question such thinking? How many of us are prepared to challenge the various ways schools separate students, to speak about the inequities that exist in the schools as well as in the world? As it is, the inequities are becoming more pronounced and more devastating.

What if we were to spend time on this question: what do we most want our students to come to understand as a result of their schooling?[14] What if our students learn to read and write but don't like to and don't? What if they don't read the newspapers and magazines or can't find beauty in a poem or love story? What if they don't go as adults to artistic events, don't listen to a broad range of music, aren't optimistic about the world and their place in it, don't notice the trees and the sunset, don't look at the stars, are indifferent to older citizens, don't participate in politics or community life, and are physically and psychologically abusive to themselves? And what if they leave us intolerant, lacking in respect for others who come from different racial and social backgrounds, speak another language, and have different ideas or aspirations? Should any of this worry us? Should such questions be more dominant in the schools? Obviously, I think so. In fact, if we were to focus attention here, much might change. The schools might, in fact, be different places.

They would likely be settings in which performance is dominant, a wider range of materials is present, and students make greater use of resources beyond the school. People in the community beyond the school would also be more involved with young people and their education.

We often speak about children in our society as "the future." What do we imply by such a belief? Does it mean ensuring that young people can live in the world as it is, or ensuring the skills, knowledge, and dispositions that will enable them to *change* the world, to construct on their terms new possibilities? What we think about that will say a lot about what we do in our schools, the ideas we explore, the questions we raise, the books we read, and the experiences we provide. What if we were to ask in regard to everything we did how these things will help our students be in a position to change the world? To do so would raise the stakes greatly. We would likely find ourselves discarding much that is typically taught.[15]

I often ask if our children are being provided a basis for active participation in their communities. Are they learning the meaning of social responsibility, of citizenship in the broadest sense? Are they gaining ongoing experience in helping make their communities better places to live? Are they adding something important, something lasting to the life of their communities? When we aren't clear about such questions or are not keeping them in mind or making them a part of our ongoing discourse, we tend to fill our schools with contradictions, which tend over time to foster cynicism and limited support— hardly the basis for making them the centers for inquiry, authority, and change that they need to be.

We are being flooded in our society with concerns about values. What are adults committed to? While I am not particularly enamored with school-based programs for enhancing character development, primarily because they seem contrived, children and young people need to know that their parents and teachers *have* important values. Those beliefs and values come through in many ways. What kinds of values do we present as educators? How do we express caring deeply about the students and about the society? How do we act out our citizenship and show our love for learning? Do we ask often about events being examined, what do they mean, and why should they matter? Do we engage each other about such things?[16]

Friedrich Froebel, a theoretical and practical giant in the early childhood field, used the garden metaphor extensively in his writing about children— a sense of unfolding, blooming, and flowering. His metaphor is worth serious reflection. It is a conception to come back to often. As Froebel suggested, experiences do build on each other; the more powerful they are, the greater their potential for being fully educative and fully generative. While each stage of life and each experience are important in their own right, they are also integrally connected to what precedes and follows them. Such an understanding should always cause us to ask about continuities between the experience and content of the preschools and the primary grades, the primary and intermediate grades, and the intermediate grades and the middle/junior high schools and middle schools and high schools, as well as the importance of returning to earlier themes at each level. Is it possible, for example, to go to Chicago's Field Museum of Natural History or the Smithsonian too many times, to reread particular books too many times, or to revisit Martin Luther King's or Dorothy Day's life too many times? Everywhere, though, primary children are told, "You don't want to read that book again," or "You will learn about that when you get to the fifth grade." Analogous refrains are replayed often along the schooling track. That, by the way, is one of the means by which difficult questions are set aside. One of the stated purposes of current specifications of curriculum content being carried out by various states and school districts is to limit the overlap. This represents a concern for coverage, not necessarily a concern for genuine understanding of critical ideas or the development of expertness.

Further, such understandings about continuities should help us understand what we lose—in fact close off—when we consider curriculum narrowly and in terms of isolated, disconnected studies. Separating learning, as we tend to do, typically leads to less understanding, not more. Can we possibly get intensity with six or seven separate, generally unrelated, nonthematic subject matters a day or when we feel we must get through everything so quickly? We often lament the poor quality of children's work but typically don't work long enough at anything to ensure it is of high quality. How many of us do our best writing when we are provided ten minutes, or thirty minutes, or a day to complete the task? What do we really expect from our students? A critical philosophical stance asks us to put ourselves in our students' shoes.

Returning to the question of large purposes, if we were to see the development of active inquiry as a major goal, much that now exists—workbooks and textbooks, predetermined curriculum, reductionism—would begin to fade. Teachers would be free to make living in the world an integral part of the curriculum. By taking this formulation seriously, we would be more attentive to students' inclinations and values. To do otherwise, Patricia Carini (1995) suggests, is "to rest content with the appearance of knowledge and forfeit all pretense of educating responsible thinkers, capable of forming opinions and taking actions" (p. 23).

It is out of this personal intention and personal knowledge, not those small pieces of disconnected knowledge, that bridges to extended learning are constructed. An education that builds bridges, makes fuller learning more possible, and expands a young person's potential for independence is an "empowering education." That is a goal worth striving for. It is also an education that is possible.

Another way to conceptualize continuities and bridges, keeping learning possibilities open, is to consider, as philosopher Mary Warnock puts it, that "the cultivation of imagination . . . should be our chief aim in education" (Lazerson et al. 1985, p. 70). In essence, imagination is a perspective, a way of seeing connections and meanings beyond the routine and the commonplace. Such a perspective demands a curriculum that truly challenges young people and that is laden with questions and multiple possibilities for entry and for active learning. It also suggests time to observe, sit, think, and rework ideas.

In this regard, Tolstoy (1967) noted, on the basis of his work with peasant children, that "to the teacher, the simplest and most general appears the easiest, whereas for a pupil only the complex and the living appears easy—only that which demands interpretation and provokes thought is easy" (p. 289). He didn't view ambiguity and uncertainty as something to remedy but as the soil for deep learning. We would do well to keep such a perspective in mind. The simple and the certain are not the roads to democracy in our contemporary age; they also provide no basis for optimism.

Eleanor Duckworth, a former Piaget collaborator, provides us with yet another way to think about purposes. She equates the essence of intellectual development with the "having of wonderful ideas," which she defines as those occasions when a student, on his or her own, comes to understand a relationship, or how something works. Duckworth reminds us: "There is no difference between wonderful ideas which many people have already had and wonderful ideas which nobody has happened on before . . . in each case, it is a matter of making new connections between things already mastered" (p. 231). This is a formulation we should make more central to our work.

A school committed to supporting "the having of wonderful ideas" is establishing for itself the goal of getting all young people as close as possible to their upper limits of learning potentialities. As it is, most don't come very close to that upper limit. The expectations aren't high enough, the environments for learning are too sparse, the questions asked are too small, and the resources are too limited. Inevitably, as well, powerful purposes have been absent.

In thinking about schools in general—as well as our own schools, those in which we live much of our lives or to which we are most committed—we always need to reach back to first things, to guiding purposes, and to our richest, most powerful, most generative conceptions of education and to work toward them. Such purposes need to be a part of our common language; thus, our practice would likely assume some different and more consonant directions.

A philosophical disposition pushes us toward the more thoughtful purposes that keep our practice alive. It keeps us immersed in ongoing reflection, in a world guided more by questions than by answers. It is important to enter teaching out of a powerful philosophical base, and it is important to keep that base vital throughout one's practice.

---

ॐ

## FOR REFLECTION

Why should children and young people study the subject matter you most care about—whether history, math, science, or literature? What is most important about it? Also, as you think about this subject matter, what are the ideas, topics, and texts you believe are most critical for children and young people to understand?

As you think about your students, what would you most want to be able to say about them when they leave you?

Finally, what if the purpose of schools was to help children and young people be in a position to change the world, to make it a better place in which to live economically, socially, aesthetically, environmentally, and culturally? What would the schools have to do more of and less of?

---

[1]For me, this means more than an exercise called "My Philosophy of Education," which has become a mainstay in teacher education programs. It is not a one-time event, a paper to fulfill a requirement. It must be seen as a living work, returned to often.

[2]While I raise here the importance of posing such questions at the preservice level, they need to be revisited from time to time as teachers engage in their long-term professional practice. Nothing should be taken for granted.

[3]Through this description, I am also inviting readers to try the exercises, to work through similar questions.

[4]I push very hard on personal experience and the meanings surrounding that experience. I want students preparing to teach to understand that they have resources on which to draw.

[5]Scheffler (1973). For a fuller discussion of Scheffler's perspective on the role of philosophy in teaching, see Scheffler (1973).

[6]I ask students preparing to teach to maintain a reflective journal, which I relate to Dewey's understanding of the importance of helping teachers become students of teaching. Many of the entries are rooted in things being wondered about—it is a way of making greater sense of this world of schools, classroom practices, teaching, and learning. My students come to value this journal writing (often several hundred pages by the end of a year). They often continue to be journal writers in their teaching years, finding the writing a way of keeping their critical stance intact and enlarging their ongoing understandings of teaching and learning. See the Appendix for a guide to journal writing.

[7]I discussed Dewey and his educational contributions more fully in Chapter 3.

[8]It is not my intention in this discussion of the importance of a philosophical stance on education to describe the various schools of philosophical thought or the major philosophical ideas that have guided educational practices over the years. There are a number of texts that preserve and

inservice teachers might find useful that provide such a background : Cahn (1997), Heslep (1997), Hirst and White (1993), Kohli (1995), McKenna (1995), Noddings (1995), Pratte (1992), and Rorty (1998). Some of the following might also prove illuminating: Apple (1993), Ayers and Miller (1998), Bridges (1997), Eisner (1998), Martin (1994), Noblit and Dempsey (1996), and Power and Lapsley (1992).

[9]I draw for this discussion from "Toward Large Purposes" in my book, *A Letter to Teachers*, Jossey-Bass, 1991.

[10]David Tyack (1974) has written about this continuing search for the one best system that "will make everything work perfectly."

[11]One of the currently popular solutions for raising academic achievement is to retain students, beginning at grade 2, on the basis of a score on a standardized test and to determine graduation on yet another test. I discuss this issue more fully in Chapter 12 but will note here that such a solution has been tried before, with disastrous results.

[12]As we close out the twentieth century, the pressures for standardization in the schools are overwhelming. This re-emerging standardization is enormously limiting.

[13]It will be interesting to see where the discourse goes in light of the economic collapse in the various Asian countries and the stagnation of the German economy.

[14]I ask often of both preservice and inservice teachers what do you most want your students to take away from a semester/year with you? What will they walk away with, understand, be confident about? What connections will they make between what they are learning and the world? Such questions keep us focused on the large purposes.

[15]Once more, I know that I have raised the stakes, suggesting that schools can be more than they are. While I understand the constraints, I also believe, as I have stated earlier and will return to at various points, that, without engaging the larger set of ideas, we won't move toward the better circumstances for children and young people.

[16]Classrooms and schools need to be civil places in which mutual respect abounds. Students and teachers need to build that civil environment. Doing so, however, is always more than teacher homilies and signs with rules or aphorisms. It comes from what we do and how we carry out our commitments.

# CHAPTER 5

# A Place for Passion

I have already suggested the role of our own biographies in teaching—that connection to our personal histories as learners and as students in schools. In this chapter, I will make this conception more concrete. We know, for example, that our learning was enhanced when we had opportunities to choose the learning tasks, when what we were learning related to things that mattered to us. Keeping that understanding in mind in our teaching ought to suggest that we should make such opportunities and conditions as prominent as possible in our classrooms. Likewise, remembering all the things teachers did that got in the way of our learning—not being prepared, being judgmental, not being clear about expectations—should help us reject such practices in our own teaching. This kind of reflection is *one* way of making constructive use of our biographies as students in schools. It is also the most conventional use of our experience.

Getting close to our biographies is, as well, a matter of retracing our various intellectual passions, a means of getting closer to the learning that we have come to value. It is, of course, learning that we want to promote in our work as teachers. To speak of passion in teaching is to recognize how important it is to make connections to what truly matters to us, as well as to our students. It is an acknowledgment that we teach best and our students learn best what we and they most care about. What are some ways for us to get closer to our own learning and to our deepest intellectual passions?

I most often begin my work with preservice and inservice teachers with what I call the "Intellectual Passion Paper." It is one of the most productive, most generative activities we engage in together. I will outline here the activity in detail, with the understanding that it can be a useful task for *all* teachers, regardless of where they are in their careers. It might be something to write and share with a small group of other teachers. In such an environment, it could stimulate an important and ongoing conversation about ways of using the collective insights about various passions in ongoing classroom work. (I encourage readers to try the paper.)

Tying *passion* with *intellectual* might seem initially problematic, primarily because of the way *passion* has been used in our recent cultural milieu. *Passion* has come to mean an "emotion or a feeling." At an earlier time, it was most closely connected to its Latin root meaning, which is *suffering*, generally tied to New Testament accounts of "the suffering of Christ." I will use *passion* here as "something cared about deeply," an "enthusiasm for something," meanings which also have historical roots. For those who continue to have difficulty linking *passion* with *intellectual*, I suggest using *interest*.

Inevitably, when introducing this activity, I get such questions as "What if my deepest passion or interest is cooking, hiking, surfing, or baseball?" In fact, over the years preservice and inservice teachers have written about all of these.

When a person truly cares about such things, they assume many intellectual aspects. The person with a passion for cooking begins, for example, to read about the history of various ingredients and the cultures related to particular dishes, comes to understand the ways various ingredients interact, can discuss foods in a variety of ways, and is able to connect cooking with other subject matters. It is not surprising that many of "the cooks" in this exercise have been chemists. Others have been in English and are attracted to literature and film in which food plays a large role. They also make considerable use of food metaphors.

As a means of identifying this "deepest intellectual passion," I ask teachers to consider "something you understand well, think about a great deal, can talk about easily, and feel you have under control. It might be history, the growth of American labor or the civil rights movement; it might be a good story, books, reading, or Shakespeare; it could be inquiry, sports, animals, or new people; it might be matters of justice, concern for the environment, or human relationships; it might be music, New Orleans jazz, mathematical probabilities, the solar system, or the moon." I also suggest they consider the following: "What would people who know you well identify about you? What would stand out? It might be 'He loves to read.' 'He's always carrying a book.' 'If you want to know how to tell a good story, ask Mary.' If you have time on your hands, how are you likely to use it? Will you visit an art gallery, sit and read mysteries, bake a cake, go to the local mountains to hike, or write?" These prompts seem sufficient to get people thinking.

I then provide the fuller dimensions of the paper: "The first task is to identify and describe your passion. You are then to write to the following: Where did this passion come from? What was the first instance that you remember? How was the passion sustained over time?" There is usually a gasp when I note that the paper should *not* be over eight pages. The first response is "I'm not sure I can get three paragraphs, let alone eight pages." I suggest that, once they get into this reflection, they will likely be hard pressed to stay within eight pages. Of course, I have a long history of these papers as my base (and I have written several such papers). I also offer the following array of possibilities with regard to the paper segments: "For some of you, the origin of your passion can be traced to childhood, but for others it may have come later, while you were in high school, even college. It may be related to family members, but it could have come from other associations. It might be school-related, although it could be fully outside of school." I typically relate segments of various intellectual passion papers written earlier, primarily to help set a tone for this work. While these stories vary considerably year by year, one that I usually tell is as follows: "Several years ago, one of the teachers traced her pas-

sion—reading—to her infancy. She could read, she was told by her grandmother, at the age of 7 months. While being walked by her grandmother in a
stroller, she pointed to a McDonald's sign and said what her grandmother believed to be 'McDonald's.' Her grandmother told everyone in sight for many,
many years that her granddaughter could read when she was 7 months old
and would, therefore, surely 'go to Harvard College.' This meant many books.
Her grandmother brought books to her for every special occasion. This teacher
remembers her grandmother asking whenever they met, 'What are you reading today?' She became a *passionate reader*."

I stress that our purpose in this paper is to "move you toward your own
learning of things that matter to you as well as provide a base for addressing
the importance of passion in teaching." I also make clear that I will ask everyone, in small groups, to read the papers, to use the occasion for collective thinking and to learn more about one another.

In all the years I have used this activity, I have seldom seen an unengag-
ing, uninteresting paper. Moreover, the variety is always large. This speaks to
the power of the activity. Usually, participants describe how good it was to
think about their learning in this way, to recapture what matters to them, and
to understand more about its many dimensions. They also come to understand
more fully the potential for reconsidering their understandings of good classroom practice. It has long been clear to me how important it is to retrace our
own learning of what matters to us. It represents a base for us as we work out
for ourselves constructive approaches to teaching. As important, however, is
that it helps us make better connections to our students, understanding that
they are likely similar to us in their patterns of learning.

Not surprisingly, many of the themes and patterns in the personal biographies have grown out of family relationships. As teachers, we need to think
more about the importance of families (a topic I raise more fully in Chapter
11). Passions also emerge from supportive environments, opportunities for personal exploration and cooperative relationships. They also come about through
diverse resources, powerful questions, opportunities to take risks and be supported, real text (rather than textbooks), involvement in the world, social commitments, awareness of diversity, open-endedness, close observation, curiosity, pursuit of personal questions, chances to take some things slowly, and
travel. The foregoing are essentially important contexts, conditions that promote learning, to be taken seriously as we think about our teaching. Most are
related to experience outside schools. What would it mean for us as teachers
to take them seriously *in* our schools?[1]

While many of the passions described in these papers developed beyond
school, all *could* have received important support, some nurturance, in school.

All the conditions that contributed to memorable work could be the principal conditions within schools. Why should we not want to assure that such circumstances prevail? Schools should, of course, be about powerful learning—the kind of learning individuals remember and make their own. [2]

Another lesson is that, in any classroom, regardless of setting, there is likely to be a similar range of interests waiting to be extended, serving as critical starting points for learning, that are able to enrich the classroom in important ways. Preservice and inservice teachers are overwhelmed by the array of passions of those participating in this activity. They readily acknowledge that it is likely as broad in any classroom (although most have never tested the assumption), even though the passions may not be as fully developed. It is important for us to see such possibilities in our work in schools, to think of these various passions as points of beginning expertise, and to understand that we have many resources available to us in the classroom. This is another means of being ready to begin *with* our students. This is especially important, a basis for a genuine community of learning in which every person has a genuine contribution to make.

What makes the interests memorable, an important part of our lives, is that we have come to possess some reasonable mastery with and around them. We have something we can honor. One of our tasks as teachers is to assure that our students leave us with a similar sense of mastery or at least the beginnings of such mastery. Think about what it means to have something to honor—something that matters. To get there, it means getting close to what our students care about and have beginning interests in. Like many other teachers, I have made use of autobiographical-like writing in school classrooms as an entry to such knowledge. Knowing our students well means having opportunities for extending their learning, for making learning more intensive. That is the teaching-learning exchange at its best.

What follows are some thoughts about the ties between the various biographies that are produced in the "Intellectual Passion" exercise and ways we might assure support for these kinds of passions. They are meant to help us consider practices that contributed to our own deep interests in learning. The ideas have come from ongoing class discussions about the relationships of the various passions with classroom practice. You can and should add to the list. Reflect on what would have helped you as a student extend even further the learning that *really* mattered to you.

- *Use the outside environment:* field trips to historical and literary sites, museums, and various language and cultural communities (e.g., German, Italian, Hispanic, Native American or Chinese). Let the experiences students have had beyond school become more integral to the ongoing curriculum.

Students' interests can be important starting points; remember that starting points are seldom ending points.

- *Make use of oral histories:* the ongoing stories of real people. Raising such stories to greater prominence also makes the students' stories more important, more apt to surface.
- *Provide opportunities for students to share their interests and ideas.* Make sure students have occasions to teach one another. What if every student were to become an "expert" on one aspect of the subjects we teach? It would then seem natural for them to assume an important teaching role.
- *Use primary documents:* real materials (including art, music, and material culture). As an alternative to textbooks, primary sources often are more "alive." They demand interpretation, giving students more opportunity to use their personal knowledge.
- *Make ample use of what students already know* as a way to approach what they do not know or lack experience with. Acknowledge that students have considerable knowledge about the world. Moreover, it is often unique.
- *Use/organize cultural ceremonies.* Foods are always popular. This represents another tie to the students' lives. Consider more fully the community that surrounds the school as the critical text, a possible starting point for most of the curriculum. (It is often surprising to me that students tend to know more about exotic places in the world than about their own locales.)
- *Bring literature to life* or bring out the life that exists in literature. Recognize in literature such universal elements as emotions, relationships, and contexts, which can be brought to life in the classroom through plays, writing, and discussion. Create (or recreate) a context in which these are alive. Consider the oral aspects of literature—dramatizations and other activities in which the students talk and work with each other.
- *Reflect on the assumptions we make* and on the ways in which these can stop the process of communication. Reflect on the definitions of the content being explored. (I think of the teacher teaching about *The Old Man and the Sea* who assumed all the students had been to the ocean.)
- *Develop activities in which the students choose topics surrounding their own interests* and give them time to prepare a presentation on the topic. They do the research and some write-up with help from the teacher. The students present as they feel they are ready to do so. Help with questions and suggest places where the students can find more information.
- *Create a "human" environment in terms of the tone or atmosphere of the classroom.* Make space for student participation, learning, and contact with people in the community through the materials of the community and through people who visit the classroom.

- *Develop mail and computer networks with others in other settings, even other countries.* Building relations with others with different experiences can be illuminating. A genuine audience for students' work often enlarges their sense of seriousness.
- *Create a classroom environment that stimulates learning.* Use posters and pictures as "windows to the world."
- *Do "things" that personally touch the young people,* things that are relevant to them and that they care about.
- *Visit places (actual or similar) (e.g., Walden Pond) that inspired the writer or scientist whose work is being examined.* Discuss how people lived at that time.
- *Keep a visible stance as a teacher,* as an active and a passionate learner who is truly interested in new questions and different approaches, and is remaining fully conscious of the world.
- *Focus on big questions.* It isn't necessary to cover everything. Having to cover forty chapters is not the way to sustain "romance."[3]

This focus on intellectual passion can also be an important entry point for teachers. Each of us teaches best what we have the most interest in, the greatest passion for. It is important that we draw heavily on that passion as we develop curriculum. Our passion for learning must be especially visible to our students. We express that passion with our enthusiasm for students' ideas, for work well done, and for books and ideas, as well as with our ongoing questions—"Why is that?" "What if you were to do that another way?" We also express it by maintaining a dialogue with our students, being ready to go many extra miles on their behalf. In this regard, passion is related to commitment. It has a connection to large purposes. It is another central aspect of our work as teachers.

## FOR REFLECTION

You might consider writing an "Intellectual Passion Paper" using the following outline: describe your deepest intellectual passion—something you understand well and feel you have under control (a subject matter, a particular event or series of events, or an author—it might be travel, books, inquiry, new people, a good story, or the stars); then ask yourself, and write about, where this passion came from, its first instance, and how it has been sustained over time.

Assuming that your experience can be related to the experience of or the possibilities for your students, what will you be sure to bring to your classroom in terms of questions, materials, activities, and experiences?

Finally, what are some of the ways you can get closer to your students, their interests, and what they care about? Why should this matter?

[1]Those with whom I work at both the preservice and inservice levels ask why schools can't be places that support such learning conditions. This very quickly gets us into discussions of the history of schools and matters of size and scale. It seems clear that the possibilities are far greater in small schools, in which control issues diminish in importance, students can be well known, families can be more easily active participants, interdisciplinary work is more possible, time can be more easily controlled, changes can be more easily made, and all students are needed for everything that goes on.

[2]In a school closely tied to Ted Sizer, the initiator of the Coalition of Essential Schools, in which I met with students, discussing the school and its meanings, a student told me that what she does in this school "has memorable qualities." Given the quality of what teachers asked students to do and the quality of work students produced, I had to concur.

[3]Alfred North Whitehead (1929) uses the conception of "romance" as the critical base for learning, the sustaining element for all learning that matters. See "The Rhythmic Claims of Freedom and Discipline" in *Aims of Education*.

# Approaches to Teaching

Many of the students who enter teacher education programs want to know explicitly *how* to teach, assuming that there is a precise science of teaching that must be learned—at least that is what they say. Many see this science in technical terms and have little patience with everything else, which they often disparagingly call "theory." Getting beyond such a view is important. I argue that teaching is almost never technical, that a philosophical grounding is, in the end, eminently practical. The questions we raise matter. How we think about teaching, the approaches we take, ultimately grows from our thinking about purposes. That point will be central in this chapter.

There are entire textbooks written about various approaches to teaching, although they are most often called "Methods and Materials for the Teaching of Social Studies" (or science, mathematics, world languages, English, and so on.) They begin from the premise that there *are* particular procedures that will, if followed, lead to successful practice. Such directions tend, though, to have an external quality, with the teacher being seen as an intermediary between knowledge about teaching and the students. These texts might be useful later, after a teacher has begun more personal explorations about teaching and has gained some experience. At that time, such texts can more easily be seen as sets of ideas, other possibilities, and not as guides.

While there is much to learn from the experience of others, from generalizations growing out of focused, classroom-based research (which is often the base of methods texts), ultimately teachers must find for themselves approaches that work for them and enable them to feel confident about helping their students learn most productively. I have over the years seen many interesting practices that seem to work for the teachers involved. They might not work as well for others. In the end, the approaches we adopt as teachers need to be compatible with our philosophical stance, our beliefs about teaching and learning.[1]

I begin my "teaching approaches" work with preservice students by asking them to observe classroom practices carefully. Their first focused observations and reflections are organized, for example, around how teachers open and close their classes. Are the teachers present in the classroom? How do they greet students as they enter? Is there an opening ritual? How do they signal a beginning? What do they do and say? Are the purposes for what follows clear? How does the opening contribute to the success or lack of success of the class? How is the work of the class brought together at the end? Is there a summary, and who makes it—the teacher or the students? Do students know what is to follow? Is there a homework assignment? Is it clearly defined? Do students know what is to happen when the class meets next? Do students leave with a question, something to continue thinking about?

There is considerable variety in what the students observe in the class-rooms. Teachers, for example, are often not in the classroom before class, or, if in the classroom, they are at their desks reading or writing, rather than at-tending to the students. They make no acknowledgment of students as they enter. There are also teachers who greet students as they enter, shake hands with many, ask a question, or respond to questions. My students notice the dif-ference. They understand the importance of being fully present, of the personal exchange at this transitional time.

Some teachers take a long time to get started, spend a lot of time getting students' attention, and provide little direction about what is to happen. Some begin with a question—part of the ritual students understand to connote the formal beginning of class. In some classrooms, students know they are to write in their journals for the initial five minutes, another opening ritual. There are teachers who have the class agenda on the board, so students know what is to happen, and there are teachers who don't provide any information about how class time will be used. Again, my students notice the differences and how the productivity of classes is affected.

We tend to pull our own generalizations from these opening and closing observations. Consider the following:

- Greet the students as they enter the classroom. While it isn't possible to make contact with *each* student, an acknowledgment *of* the students is im-portant. Transition rituals that get the students involved quickly, that place more responsibility on them, can be useful.
- Administrative tasks—attendance taking—need to be handled quickly and efficiently. In some classes, this can take ten to fifteen minutes and make it very difficult to proceed.
- Clarity about what is to happen is important. This relates to the need for good planning. Some teachers have an outline on the board, showing the tentative flow of the class period. Some classes have helpful routines. Stu-dents know what to expect. Alongside this principle, though, is the need for flexibility.
- Recapping from the previous day, keeping the work connected, is useful.
- Good focus at the beginning—clarity about how the class will proceed—and at the end—a recapping and a direction for the next day—is useful.
- Clarity about homework is useful. Many teachers put the homework as-signment on the board to avoid the rush at the end of the period.
- Demonstrate a genuine interest in the students. Such an interest comes through in successful classrooms.
- Knowing the students is important. It is also desirable for the students to know the teacher.

Our focused observations take up other matters as well—the kinds of questions posed, the tasks students are asked to complete, the amount of performance activity, the nature of student writing, the materials used, the role of technology, the uses of resources beyond the classroom, the nature of teacher planning, and the use of student interests and intentions. The purpose of all these observations, reflective inquiries, and writing (I ask students, as I noted earlier, to maintain reflective journals) is to consider teaching-learning generalizations and to begin the process of formulating our own views of good practice. I find such inductive activities far more productive than reading a text that offers already distilled formulations. The following are some of the generalizations from my classes:

- The physical arrangement of the classroom *matters*. The teacher needs to find a way to remain physically close to the students.
- Students need to play an *active* role in the classroom. It can't be *all* teacher. (Teachers can learn from the students.)
- There needs to be clarity about boundaries for behavior.
- Interaction makes for a more productive classroom.
- Teacher expectations need to be high and demonstrated all the time. This implies care with what is said and done, what students are asked to do, and how students are responded to. (Simple work is not particularly engaging.)
- At least most of the time, what is being taught needs to have a connection to student interests and intentions. It is important to draw on students' experiences—not just on what is in the book.
- Mutual respect is important.
- Classrooms are more successful when teachers enjoy the students, trust the students, and have a sense of humor.
- Good questions, those that invite participation, are helpful. Classrooms full of answers tend not to work well.
- Teachers need to express a seriousness of purpose—a belief that what is being studied really matters. Teachers also need to express hopefulness.
- The materials used make a difference. Good materials invite participation.
- It is important for students to know *why* they are being asked to do things. Teachers should be careful to help students understand the various assignments.

As I have noted earlier, the kinds of observations made by my students preparing for teaching would be useful for experienced teachers as well. I believe inservice teachers would profit from observing each other's classrooms, discussing openings and closings, rituals, materials, student projects, student writing, and questions posed. The possibilities for reaffirming good practices and extending learning are extensive.

What have I learned over the years about various approaches to teaching? I now offer some thoughts about the most common approaches, not as methods to follow but as ideas for ongoing consideration and continuing reflection on what we observe or are trying out in our own classrooms.[2]

Teaching is about helping students become and maintain themselves as learners, not just in relation to a specific content but more broadly to include the development of positive dispositions and attitudes that support and sustain learning. Many Coalition schools use the language of "habits of mind," a perspective I consider important.[3]

How we as teachers think about and approach our teaching matters greatly. If our purposes are not potent, the possibilities for student learning lessen. If we don't take into account students' interests and intentions, their commitments to learning are diminished. If we don't view performance as central, what students do is likely to be limited in quality and the potential for extended learning less probable. If we don't provide the time and scaffolding necessary for students to complete work they can honor, there will be too little intensity in the teaching-learning exchange.[4]

One of the oldest approaches to teaching is the *lecture*—an occasion when the teacher tells, explains, reads, or interprets something. Its beginnings go back to a time when books were not easily accessible and information had to be provided through such a teacher-telling process. The lecture was also closely connected, at least in the West, to the religious homily and Bible readings. And, of course, early schools had religious origins.

Many of the conditions that gave rise to the *dominance* of the lecture, however, no longer exist. Reading materials are readily available, as are videos, audiotapes, photographs, and computer programs. The fact that students have access to so much learning material makes the teacher's work different, less dependent on lectures (although *not less important*). Lectures should no longer assume a dominant place in the schools, primarily because they tend to leave students too unengaged in the learning process. Nonetheless, used *selectively* and *purposefully*, lectures can be genuinely useful. For example, a lecture can be used constructively to introduce a book, subject, concept, or particular country or region of the world—essentially providing a context and generating interest; summarizing divergent points of view; providing an interpretation or a synthesis of dominant historical, literary, language, scientific, mathematical, aesthetic, and philosophical themes; explaining with multiple examples complex ideas and unfamiliar language; filling in pieces that *surround* the particular topics, ideas or formulations being studied; and providing specific instructions. As schools are now organized, *some* lectures, at least at the secondary level, might take up an entire period (forty to fifty minutes) but most would be more effective if they were shorter (ten to twenty minutes). In the elementary schools, lectures should not be more than ten to fifteen minutes.

Some of the components of a good classroom lecture are clarity of purpose, coherence in its outline, an ability to be followed, and a connection to what is already understood by the students, while being more than a report of what has already been read and understood. To keep students' attention, it must be engaging, calling for *active* listening; intrinsically interesting; and cared about and communicated by the lecturer to be *very* important. Our personal experience should be helpful here. As students, what made an engaging lecture for us? What do we remember as being particularly useful?[5]

The most natural and most frequent approach to teaching is *discussion*. It is the process most students and teachers remember as particularly fruitful in their learning outside of school. Everyone converses to gain information, clarify decisions, and consider next steps. Nonetheless, discussion in a classroom must assume a more formal structure, as the time is short and the numbers of students involved are most often large.

At its best, a classroom discussion is *not* a question-answer dialogue between the teacher and students. It needs to flow *among* members of the class. Most of what are called "discussions" in the schools are of the question-answer variety:

T: Who was Benjamin Franklin?
S: An inventor.
T: Good. Any other answers?
S: He was at the Constitutional Convention.

It is probably best if these kinds of question-answer activities are *not* seen as discussions. There may be a time and place to go through question-answer exercises—possibly for a review or as an occasion to learn about students' beginning understandings related to a topic of study—but they should not occur as a staple.

Discussions that make a difference begin with genuine questions—those for which there is some uncertainty, room for interpretation, and multiple answers—"How else could the story have ended?" "Why was the Revolution fought in 1776, when Americans were, in comparison with those in England, paying virtually no tax and living so well?" If there *is* a single right answer to the questions we pose, the questions are not particularly educative. If the teacher is leading the discussion (students can also lead discussions of the entire class or within a small group), his or her task is to get everyone involved and to assure that opposing points of view are considered, various opinions are valued and respected, and the focus is maintained. That is what makes it a classroom discussion, not a coffeehouse or kitchen table conversation.

A discussion should have a *purpose*—it should lead to generalizations, possible conclusions, enlarged understandings, and a different inquiry. For this to occur, however, there needs to be valid information available around a subject of importance to the students. This suggests that students would have done some reading, engaged in inquiry, been asked to think about something, and write about something before the discussion. During the discussion, concepts can be clarified, positions challenged, and new understandings formed. Certain skills—listening, posing questions, building relationships among ideas, making ideas and not persons central—can also be taught and learned through a discussion.

For a discussion leader, it is always good to have thought through the important issues, central questions, possible entry points, and possible responses, to have some clarity about what might occur. There will still be surprises, but it can be helpful to have considered some of the questions likely to come up. I think about this as "rehearsing possibilities," having other questions and resources in mind that might extend the students' thinking. Good discussions are more apt to occur *after* good preparation.

*Why* and *how* questions tend to work better than *what*, *when* or *where* questions, primarily because they keep issues open. Moreover, it is generally better to refer questions asked to someone in the group. Finally, it is helpful to summarize occasionally, making sure the central ideas and the various viewpoints are in view. The following discussion transcript comes from a ninth/tenth grade humanities class in a secondary school and may prove instructive. (The discussion grows out of a reading of Lorraine Hansberry's play *Raisin in the Sun* and several biographic articles about Hansberry. At the previous meeting of the class, the teacher had asked students to think about the "American Dream," as raised in the play and as it exists in our culture.)[6]

Teacher: Is there anything in the play that suggests a deeper connection to the American Dream?

S1:   I just wanted to say that you were talking earlier about the issue of respect . . . and material things. I think a lot of people seek only material things, comfort. That is their American Dream. . . .

S2:   But I don't think it will ever be different. Why would it be different?

T:    . . . So in the search for the American Dream, to go back to Lorraine Hansberry and what her story is about, you are saying that things have changed.

S3:   The search for the American Dream is mostly about material goods and it is destroying everything.

T:   So the search for the American Dream is destroying everything. Is that Hansberry's statement or is it ours? This play takes place in the 1950s and she died in 1965. Now a number of years have passed. . . .

S1:   It seems, going back to the play, that money almost destroyed his family and his dignity. . . . He was going to take the money and not stand up for himself.

T:   O.K., now it's 27 years later and some of you are saying that the search for the American Dream has had some negative effects.

S2:   It *is* negative. . . . What do people think it is? It seems to be described often as a family and house and white picket fence and a dog. That's just not how things are. Things *have* changed.

S4:   I think the American Dream has changed. When the country began, the American Dream meant freedom of religion, practice what you wanted and be free from persecution. And then the American Dream became money and to have the life you want. So to get a white picket fence and a new house and a dog, you need money. . . . To get your freedom if you were a slave, you needed money. To get land to farm, you needed money.

T:   And today?

S4:   Today, today it's pretty much money.

S5:   Greed is dominant today.

T:   I have heard power and money and greed. . . . So what is it? Is that what the American Dream has become?

S6:   If you have a lot of money, you have power. Money and power have become the same.

T:   So how does it influence the dream?

S3:   You need money to pursue the dream.

S5:   Without money today, you have almost nothing. And you are a nobody.

T:   So how does all this fit—the search for the American Dream has negative effects?

S7:   Everyone thinks without money, you have nothing—but it's not really money, it's what money represents—that sometimes makes it evil.

S4:   But money is the door to dreams. The more money you have, the more you can have.

S8:   People think it matters more. Drug dealers sell and make money and have people killed because they want even more money. Even corporations mess up the environment so they can make more money.

T:   So where does dignity come in—the dignity that we talked about with *Raisin in the Sun*?

S11:  Few people care about dignity anymore. When you have money, you are looked up to, worshipped.

T:    Then dignity doesn't matter? Is it possible that pursuing the American Dream is never finished?

S7:   I think being happy is the American Dream. It is about living comfortably.

S1:   But being happy and comfortable isn't the American Dream. It has to be more.

S3:   To do what you really want to do and also have a family is the American Dream.

S6:   Just because you don't have a family doesn't mean you don't have the American Dream. What about having peace within yourself?

S4:   The American Dream today is not to have a family—it is *what* you *want*.

S9:   There can't be just one American Dream. That is too individualized.

S4:   There isn't a standard which everyone has in their head. . . . You have the right to disagree and you have the right to have a different dream from your neighbor. Your neighbor might want money but you might want peace and quiet. In that respect, I change my mind. I don't think there is one American Dream anymore. I think it is just what you want—*that* is the American Dream.

S10:  Anyway you want to live your life, that's the American Dream right there.

S11:  Today, because everyone has their own ideas, we tend to be selfish and think only of ourselves. That's the way the world is.

S4:   That's why the hairspray analogy fits into that. If you buy hairspray, you don't think about the ozone, you just think about your hair. If you want a job, you don't care about all the other people who apply for the job, you want that job and if you are a determined person, you might do almost anything to get that job.

Good discussions don't just happen in a classroom. Teachers have much more success when they prepare the students early in the school year to participate successfully in discussions. They do this by describing the kinds of questions that are most productive in guiding discussion, defining the rules for speaking, stressing the need for civility, and outlining how diverse points of view can be reconciled. They also engage in practice discussions. Further, asking early how the discussion is going, in relation to criteria the teacher and students define, is helpful in moving the discussion format to a higher level of quality. As is true for all approaches to teaching, thoughtfulness needs to be brought to bear on this instructional approach.[7]

*Cooperative learning*, a mainstay in the progressive schools early in the twentieth century, has had a large-scale revival, being seen as a means of helping students develop a sense of responsibility and interdependence, enlarging learning and supporting efforts to move toward mainstreaming and away from tracking.[8] It is also a direction that matches the growing interest in performance assessment.

Teachers have found that cooperative learning is much more than putting students into groups and expecting them to do well. (I have heard often "I tried cooperative learning, but it just doesn't work for me.") Teachers have come to understand that cooperative learning groups do not naturally work. Students need to learn the skills and procedures that facilitate group interaction. Time spent early in a school year on such learning makes a huge difference.[9] For example, becoming thoughtful about sharing and listening, learning how to clarify ideas and accept different points of view, and becoming proficient in the use of brainstorming procedures and in leading a discussion are important to the success of cooperative learning groups. With practice, students focus on ideas, not on personalities. They learn to disagree without discouraging ongoing discussion. They become better sharers of materials, more sensitive to the importance of getting everyone involved. It is, of course, helpful when teachers model these skills in the ongoing work of the classroom.

Practice with generic problems—from the newspaper or issues in the school and community—is a good place to begin. Using some self-evaluation exercises alongside can also be productive: "How did we do as a group?" "Did everyone participate?" "Did we remain focused?" When cooperative groups fail, it is usually related to lack of preparation.

It is also helpful for students in the groups to take turns with various roles—moderator, recorder, courier (the person who goes to the teacher with questions), process observer (the person who pays attention to time, whether everyone participates, and the groups' productiveness). Early on, discussions about these roles and the criteria for their successful development are important. Again, good preparation makes a difference.

Further, the activities the groups work on have to be carefully constructed, involving individual effort along with group activity. Moreover, they need to be reasonably complex. If they demand a single response—one answer, for example—they do not need the efforts of a group. Uncertainty about an issue is a good starting point for group work. Working on different aspects of a complex problem or issue makes group work useful—the whole then becomes much larger than would otherwise ever be possible.

A question teachers often ask is "What size should groups be and how should they be formed?" The research on cooperative learning suggests that groups should not exceed five students. Groups of three to five seem particularly appropriate for most tasks. While some tasks are done easily by merely asking students to join the person or persons sitting next to them, it is best to intentionally organize working groups on a monthly or semester basis—even though some members might be shifted occasionally.[10] When those in a group are used to working with one another, they are typically more productive.

Another popular approach to teaching that is re-emerging is *The Project*—which, at its best, is closely aligned with cooperative learning.[11] Projects are often selected by a class, with various groups working on different aspects, depending on the interests of the students in the group. They are also generated from lists of possibilities outlined by teachers. A project is typically seen as a long-term activity—several weeks, possibly a semester in middle and secondary schools, and several days to a week in the elementary schools. The reason for the longer time frame is to assure that the project can be done well, that students will emerge with a reasonable degree of expert knowledge and skill and an ability to take pride in the product. The longer period of time devoted to the work also provides opportunities for scaffolding understanding performances (demonstrations of progress) along the way and ongoing assessment (response by peers and by the teacher).

In settings in which teachers make use of projects, time is spent on how to engage in research, do surveys, use graphics for presenting data, use video equipment, interview others, and design experiments. In fact, a natural question to ask after a project is identified is "What do we need to know how to do to complete this project at a high level?"[12] There must also be a wide assortment of materials available to students (a gathering task that project work implies for teachers), and teachers must be able to spend time in small-group conversations and ongoing *coaching*.[13] Starting the year with a project around such questions as those that follow can be helpful, providing practice with various research skills: "Can the city be made more livable?" "How has the neighborhood surrounding the school changed over the past 100 years?" "How safe is the drinking water in our school, neighborhood?"

Students tend to find project work challenging and engaging, especially when they have a role in selecting what is to be done. They appreciate being able to do something they can honor, that they can call their own. It is the special projects they completed that my students remember most fully from their school experiences.

*Inquiry teaching* is closely related to project work, although it can also guide discussions, various presentations, and cooperative learning activities. The work of Ann Cook and Herb Mack and their Inquiry Demonstration Project in New York City is a good representation of inquiry in action.[14]

As developed in the Inquiry Demonstration Project, the inquiry process is relatively complex and requires the acquisition of skills in four key areas. The project asks students to

- *Become familiar with concepts of logic*—be able to discuss ideas and analyze assertions logically and able to apply such skills meaningfully in a variety of situations
- *Examine their own experiences in reaching conclusions*—be able to understand their experiences within a broader context and able to listen to others and research the available literature
- *Become aware of the complexity inherent in issues and arguments*—come to deal with ambiguity, to understand that in many cases there is no "correct" answer. They need to realize that, given the same starting point, reasonable individuals can and do reach a variety of differing conclusions. Respect for divergence and an ability to analyze differences while accepting diversity are important understandings to be addressed.
- *Discuss ideas; conduct interviews, surveys, or experiments; or present written analyses of issues*—students need support to refine their thinking, to interpret the data they collect. They need to be challenged to produce work that they recognize as the best they can do.[15]

These skills, carried out through encounters with important content in the various subject matters, can be related to what the Coalition of Essential Schools defines as "Habits of Mind" or "Intellectual Dispositions." Teachers engaged in inquiry focus on challenging students to think and rethink, write, revise and edit written work, question, formulate, and analyze. It is the kind of intellectual intensity we need in the schools. One of the most visible outcomes is the publication of student work. With student assistance, teachers *reproduce* work resulting from student investigations, believing that the topics explored are of interest to a wider-than-classroom audience, and the various sources students used often seem unusual and worth wider exposure. Moreover, teachers find that the act of preparing materials for others to view frequently provides a significant incentive for students to edit and rework their original efforts.[16] Such published works are also demonstrations that such complex work *can* be done, providing a basis for more such work. They also tend to inspire the *next* group of students beginning their first large projects.

In inquiry projects, students come to understand that they don't need to interview persons of great prominence in order to produce interesting results, that what may initially appear to be little more than stories from their everyday lives or from the lives of their neighbors take on new significance and value when collected and presented well. Moreover, their experiments can relate to local matters—the local pond water, common products from local stores, local health conditions, or local housing issues.[17]

This attention to details also holds true for other aspects of student investigations prepared for publication. For example, in compiling statistical data resulting from student-designed questionnaires, students debate the validity of the results, often arguing about the clarity of the questions; they discuss the various interpretations to be drawn from the same set of facts; and they determine how to present the conclusions in ways that encourage others to read and make meaning from the findings.

Essentially, this kind of inquiry work begins from the premise that students are capable of handling complex content, constructing consequential arguments around that content, becoming expert in an aspect of the content, and clearly presenting their understandings. This should be a common premise for all of our work as teachers.

A good example of inquiry teaching is included in the report of the National Committee on Science Education of the National Research Council, American Academy of Sciences (1996). It shows the use of inquiry skills, as well as the use of groups in a biological science activity. It is a lengthy quotation but is emblematic of how many prominent scientists believe learning in schools should proceed.

### Preparing for the Activity

The teacher raises the question, "What are the effects of acid rain on organisms?" The class discusses the relevance and importance of the question and reviews what it knows and has heard about acid rain.

In their small groups, students generate some possible investigations that could help them tackle this broad question about the effect of acid rain on organisms. The teacher explains to the students that materials associated with a more focused question are available to them. The more focused question is, "What is the effect of pH on the eggs, larvae, and pupae of fruit flies?"

### The Activity

Students return to their small groups to plan their investigation to address the question. Each group will work on a different experiment and use a different experimental design. One team of students may choose to look at the effect of pH on the three separate stages of the fruit fly. In the first sample, the eggs will receive a single exposure of acid rain. In the second sample, the eggs will not be exposed to acid rain but the larvae will receive the exposure. In the third sample, the egg state and the larva stage will not receive the exposure, but the pupa state will. The same group will provide an exposure of acid rain to the egg, larva, and pupa stages. This group may give each stage one third of the acid exposure during each phase or may give a full exposure three times.

A second team of students may decide to focus on the effect of pH changes. A third team may concentrate on the frequency of exposure to the acid during each stage. A fourth group may decide to design an ambitious experiment that takes into account several of these variables.

Different groups will also have to decide what the output variable will be. For instance, one team may look at the survival of the fruit fly. Another team may focus on the fertility of the surviving fruit flies. Completion of the inquiry will require students to review (or learn about) pH, statistical significance, and other areas of the science and mathematics curricula.

Students keep journals of their investigations, which include decisions, observations, data, analyses, conclusions, and proposals for further investigations. The class is responsible for evaluating each group's work. Students discuss with the presenting team their systematic observations (including the organization and interpretation of data), and their drawing of conclusions (including the syntheses of ideas) and offer suggestions for improvement.

### Representative Inquiry

If students are regarded as members of a community of learners, the next step would be for different classes in the same school to share the results of parallel studies on, say, fruit flies, daphnia, and beetles. Different classes in different schools also might share and compare results with other schools through the use of telecommunications. The different schools might compose and publish a science journal as a final report.

The foregoing is, in many respects, a shift in direction for the teaching of science. But it represents an approach that should lead to understanding science. That should give us encouragement.

*Literacy*, certainly stressed in the project- and inquiry-oriented classroom, should be a universal concern for all teachers. Regardless of their academic fields or levels, teachers need to see themselves as *reading* and *writing* teachers. This suggests yet another kind of thoughtfulness about the teaching-learning exchange. It means, at the very least, that all teachers will talk about books and draw frequent attention to articles in newspapers and magazines. It also means that teachers will assist students in entering unfamiliar texts through a variety of prereading exercises, such as drawing attention to new words and concepts and highlighting what to look for. Classrooms that take literacy seriously will be full of print materials, displayed as colorfully and accessibly as possible. Writing, thoughtfully responded to, will be particularly important.[18] As teachers have come to understand more firmly that thinking and writing are connected, students are being asked to do considerable writing in math and science classes, as well as English and social studies classes. With regard to writing, many teachers now use journals regularly as a means of promoting and clarifying thought, as another opportunity for students to describe, record observations, note questions, keep track of their work, and engage in self-evaluation.

The dilemma for most teachers who make use of journals, as well as most other forms of writing, is "how to read them all." Some try to read through the journals on a weekly basis, picking particular entries to respond to, usually through questions; by offering a similar or different perspective; or by suggesting some different lines of thought or alternative possibilities. Others ask students to note sections they wish to have read and responded to, as well as sections they do not want read. In yet other settings, teachers ask students to engage in peer responses—providing the students another reading, writing, thinking experience.

A process for peer review I have found useful in middle and secondary schools (and which could be modified for use with younger students) as well as in the university is the following—set forth as instructions:

1. Exchange journals—work with a person with whom you feel comfortable. Read the journal you have been given with the following questions in mind:
   a. What seems to be a dominant theme?
   b. What questions and ideas most engage you?
   c. What do you wonder most about as you read the entries?
   Do you have an alternative response to anything in the journal—another way of responding that you feel might be useful?
2. You should write a response (no more than one page) to give back with the journal. After you have read the response to *your* journal, you should take time discussing the response with the person who wrote it. (The two of you should get together to discuss each other's response.)
3. After reading the response to your journal and participating in a discussion, write a one-page statement to be given to the teacher. The following questions might guide this statement:
   a. What was most interesting about the response? Was there anything you didn't think about?
   b. How are you thinking about the principal issues you raised in the journal? Where has your thinking arrived? What questions still remain?

*Homework* is one of the staples of schools. Its purpose, though, is not always so clear. Teachers with whom I work understand it is important but struggle with questions of "how much?" and "for what purpose?"

Historically, homework has been seen as an extension of school—a means of supporting what is being learned in school and of providing practice. It has also been imbued with the language of virtue—the learning of self-discipline and hard work. Additionally, it has been tied to such religious aphorisms as "idle hands . . . ." By the end of the nineteenth century and influenced by the progressivism of the period, there were concerns about homework interfering with what were seen as more compelling needs to have a childhood—time for playing, exploring, talking, and going to museums and libraries. Many school districts, in fact, abolished homework for the elementary years of schooling (K–8). Today, with our *extreme* concerns about children and young people and the quality of their education, homework is seen as essential.[19]

While I will offer a perspective on homework that I trust will be useful, I should note that *homework* may not be our best term. Much of what is imagined by teachers is as likely to be done outside of home as at home. I suspect, though, how we label it isn't an issue to devote much energy to. Our energy should go, instead, toward questions of purpose and thoughtfulness about what we ask students to do beyond class time.

Many of my beginning teachers indicate that students don't regularly do the homework that is assigned and that class often proceeds with the assumption that homework will not be done. As for most approaches to instruction, we have to work at the ends we most desire. We have to work at creating a culture of homework, by "teaching" our students to *do* homework. This likely means starting in small steps, being very precise about what is to be done. I might begin by asking students to write one line—a response to something—that will be the starting point for the next day. It might be to look at one structure on the way home and be prepared to offer one observation. It might be asking a mother/father/guardian/older brother/sister one question that relates to an aspect of what is being studied—Vietnam, favorite music, heroes, space exploration, race relations, employment, or particular parts of the world—as a lead in to the next day's discussion. It could be selecting one line of text to read in class the next day. These kinds of beginnings can be enlarged over time, becoming more extensive and complex.

Homework should *extend* work in the classroom. It should make the next day's classwork more productive and help move a project along. Too often, homework is busywork, repetition from class. It *doesn't* extend the work and add other dimensions. The following homework assignments are ways to think about this issue more fully. (The assignments on the left are far less interesting than the assignments on the right.)

Complete the following problems:

$42 \times 27 =$
$142 \times 21 =$
$42 \times 26 =$
$14 \times 12 =$
$37 \times 26 =$
$37 \times 27 =$

Think about and describe two ways to do an estimate of the area of your living room. Then describe three ways you can determine the size without putting a tape measure on the floor.

Answer the following questions (using your textbook):

1. The two most important buildings in Boston are _____ and _____.

2. Who was the architect of these two buildings?

3. What is the architecture of these two buildings called?

4. How old are these two buildings?

What do you believe are the two most important buildings in your community?

Why are they the most important?

Describe one building in as much detail as you can.

How old do you think the building is? How can you tell?

Beyond the foregoing approaches to teaching—which are fairly traditional, have been around a long time, are used by many teachers, and are easily understood by teachers and students alike—teaching and learning can be enhanced by *making use of resources beyond the school*. Museums and art galleries are particularly stimulating classrooms, as are governmental settings, such as courtrooms, legislative chambers, libraries, and records' depositories. Research laboratories, business establishments, parks, churches, senior centers, and day care facilities also hold considerable potential. And most communities have many interesting people who could share their expertise and experiences with students. Not to make use of the rich and varied resources that exist beyond the school is to limit the learning possibilities for students, to keep school learning too separate from learning in the world. Students often express the view that their education makes few connections to what they see day in and day out. They learn more about exotic parts of the world than their local environment. They are given little reason to believe that they can be major decision makers about what happens around them. That needs to change. Civic engagement, that sense of commonwealth, is important. It needs to begin in the schools.

*Technology* also offers a particularly important means of learning that tends to be underused in schools, even as the discourse about technology suggests otherwise. The VCR and CD-ROM technologies are especially well developed and are rich in their potential; they are able to take students to all parts of the world, into the world's great museums, even into outer space. Students can see physical and biological specimens in forms not available without the use of these advanced technologies. And they can interact with students in other parts of the United States and the world, sharing their work and posing questions. I don't typically see students engaged with technology in these ways. Most use seems directed at word processing. If we were to tie the technologies more to projects and inquiry, understanding that time is necessary, we would move to a more constructive level of technology use.

As I think about various approaches to teaching, I am reminded of a Foxfire project carried out by ninth and tenth grade students at Rabun County High School in Georgia around the question "What motivates students?" The students came to a consensus on the following teacher behaviors that they believed contribute to motivating students:

- Teachers should not embarrass students in class.
- They should have a high interest in their students.
- They should have a sense of humor and be energetic.
- They should conduct class discussions and debates sensitively.
- They should foster a cooperative class atmosphere.

- They should vary the classwork so it doesn't become routine, and they should have lots of supplementary books and articles and artifacts pertaining to the subject.
- They should allow or encourage student decisions in the classroom and student evaluations of their work.

They then developed a list of the ingredients that they believed produced successful teaching-learning activities in their classroom:

- Students got to choose their own projects to conduct.
- Each project resulted in a tangible end product. The product was a challenge to produce, and it made them want to work on it, want to think, and want to make it the best they could do.
- The products had an audience, and knowing they would be showcased and presented to other people, either in or out of school, was a main factor in making the students want to work hard and meet deadlines.
- They weren't afraid to try things they didn't know how to do, because the teacher made sure they wouldn't fail; and if they made mistakes, they could do things over until they got them right. The teachers made sure the students were supported, and knowing there wasn't any way to fail motivated them to give their projects their best shot.
- Every student felt needed, and, when the products were finished, every student could see his or her work and point to his or her part. Nobody was left out.
- The work was different from the routine. Students didn't need to use the texts, they were actively doing something, the tasks pertained to the academic work, and the students knew they were learning something.
- The students knew they were using skills they would need in their jobs, such as using time wisely, exercising responsibility, and not letting the group down.

Some of these forementioned ingredients can be seen in the examples that follow. The first comes from a public primary school teacher's journal account of her growing confidence in the arena of science (Traught et al. 1986).

> One day I walked into Rhonda's [classroom] and saw these silkworms. She asked me if I wanted some and told me that these were the best pets for a classroom. You didn't get allergic to them and they never would crawl out of the box. They were very easy to take care of. All you had to do was to give them fresh mulberry leaves every day. Of course that is easy because of the mulberry tree in the yard. There was so much excitement that developed around those silkworms. Every day I was excited to come to school in the morning and see how they were. I was drawn to them. It was so interesting to see how

they grew. And the children were fascinated watching them every day and feeding them. It opened up such fascinating questions for me. How did it come to be that silkworms don't crawl away? I thought that was such a wonderful thing that this could have developed so that the caterpillars stayed in the box and the moths don't fly away either.

We learned so much about them. And whenever I had a question, I could just ask Rhonda and she would tell me to do this or that, and not to worry, they were doing fine.

Then one day the kids noticed that ten caterpillars were in the mulberry tree. It became a natural extension of the silkworm experience. The kids wanted to know how they were different, and how they were the same as the silkworm caterpillars. They all wanted to catch them and put them into containers. We had to scrounge around to find every plastic container in the school so that each one could have a caterpillar to watch and take care of. They were so attentive. Then they talked about them and drew pictures and wrote about them for many days.

Then we were studying Chinese mythology and we were in a back yard. The children dug a deep large hole and it reminded me that when I was little I used to love to dig too. I told them that I used to think that I could dig all the way to China. They thought this was amazing. That you could dig all the way to China. Well they knew all about China. They kept talking about how wonderful it would be to get there. This talking about China really pulled things together: the silkworms, and the caterpillars, and the stories from China. Then the holes got deeper. They started making comments about how the soil looked different at different levels.

This got us into a study of the soil and why there would be differences in it. One thing just led to another. I was glad that something I had thought to share from my childhood had meant so much to them. All of these activities felt so connected and whole to me and to the children. (pp. 17–18)

The learning activities in this example have a natural flow. That the learning activities are connected makes them all the more potent. The teacher's interest, her willingness to be a learner, is also a striking element in the account.

Many teachers at all levels have sought to assure connections across various fields of inquiry by using themes as organizing frameworks. The work of 8- and 9-year-olds in the Dewey School of 1898 is a good example of organizing around a theme. I share it as a way to suggest that thematic, integrated curriculum ideas have been with us for a long time but also to acknowledge its ongoing potential. John Dewey (Mayhew and Edwards [1936] 1962) wrote

[By following] a few of the great migrations and explorations that opened up the continents of the world, the children built up an idea of the world as a whole, both racially and geographically. In their imaginary travels, they acquired knowledge of the place of the earth in the universe and its larger physical forces and of the means that man has used to meet or employ them. They then settled down to the study of a specific people in a specific way and learned how, through the agency of individuals, groups of persons have subdued the

untoward elements of their physical environments and have utilized the fa-
vorable ones. (pp. 164–165)

He noted further,

> When the question in a child's mind was formulated by himself, was his own
> question, it became a doubt that needed his reflective attention. . . . enlisted
> his undivided attention. He needed no prod or spur. . . . no ready made
> answers. He actively sought and chose relevant material with which to answer
> it. . . . The problem was his own, hence the training secured by working out
> its solution became his own. (p. 184)

The young children in the Dewey School spent an entire year on this study of
worldwide migrations. In a sense, they were reliving the accomplishments of
others, making them their own. What passes for curriculum in most schools
today is only a pale reflection, barely touching the surface of the important
knowledge that exists to be learned for understanding.

Reflecting on the intensity of the Dewey School curriculum, I am also reminded of May Sarton's *I Knew a Phoenix,* in which she provided an account
of her early schooling at the Shady Hill School in Cambridge, Massachusetts,
in the 1930s. She suggests that her sedentary adult life may stem from a school
environment in which she traveled for days along the dusty roads of Athens,
spent months climbing the Himalayas, and painted the great landscapes of the
world—using up so much of her energy, her whole being, that she had to sit
and rest in adulthood. Her school experience had power, leaving something
to remember. In much of today's curriculum, there is so little in the school
lives of most children that has a potential for powerful remembrance.

Finally, I want to share some of University of Chicago historian Tom Holt's
(1991) approach to teaching a history course. In an undergraduate course at the
University of Chicago, he argues that history teaching is much the same, whatever the level. It is always, he says, about "going beyond the facts toward the
making of a narrative, with all the selection, empathy and risk of a point of
view that this implies (p. xi). Finding a problem that is worth solving or a question worth pursuing, Holt suggests, is the teacher's critical task with any subject matter.[20] He understands that teachers must be decision makers about what
and how they teach. Holt organized the Reconstruction unit, which is critical
to his essay "Historical Thinking," around the issue of what freedom means
by examining the Freedman's Bureau and sharecropping.

As a means of contrast to what he does, Holt shared the account of the
Freedman's Bureau and sharecropping in a popular secondary school textbook.
Needless to say, he believes that what students have before them to read matters greatly. There is certainly a narrative in the secondary textbook descriptions he quotes, but there is little to suggest that there are competing narratives

or more vivid, personal narratives about the people who lived at that time. What was an extremely dynamic period in our nation's history comes off as static, in many ways stunted. And the questions posed to students in the text suggest that learning history is mostly a matter of memorization.

Given Holt's view that history is about people, rich and poor, men and women, he writes, "[The classroom] should be the place to examine many of the fundamental continuing questions of everyday life. The choices and struggles faced by black ex-slaves are not mere fodder for memorization but fields of inquiry to be examined and pondered for their larger meanings for human experience" (p. 18). All subject matter should be entered with such an understanding.

Holt began his course by asking students to write on what freedom means to them. It was part of his need to begin with students' understandings of central conceptions important to the work to be undertaken. Teachers often forget that students are not empty vessels, that they have many different understandings—some quite sophisticated, others naïve (although not unimportant). After exploring these understandings, the work proceeded with documents from the period. The first was the Emancipation Proclamation, with a focus on such questions as "What were its terms?" "What were the limitations?" and "What do you imagine its impact was in the context of a revolutionary conflict?" He wanted students to read between the lines, to understand that the study of history is mostly about questioning and imagining. A second set of examined documents related to land given to former slaves by General Sherman. One was a letter, written by freedmen, that outlined what they expected freedom to mean; the second was a statement, written by a Freedmen's Bureau agent, that could almost be interpreted as a reply. A third document was a report on the views of an African American Freedmen's Bureau agent, who assumed a "radical" view of freedom. The documents were selected, Holt says, "to help students understand one moment of history as the interplay of many lines of action, conflicting desires, and dramatically different conceptions of what freedom should bring" (p. 19). He notes that, even with his predispositions toward the documents and their meanings, "the most successful discussions are neither predictable, controllable, nor closeable. And that is as it should be" (p. 19).

Throughout this history course, Holt stressed the idea of thinking historically. "Mid-terms and finals were not tests in the traditional sense," Holt writes, "rather, they were occasions for students to perform as historians . . . On their take-home midterm examination, for example, I gave my students three labor contracts from different periods and asked them to act as curators preparing an annotation of the documents to accompany a display in a museum" (p. 29).

What should be of particular interest to teachers in Holt's essay is his discussion of a high school student dealing with the *Letter from Edisto Island* (essentially a petition to the government about land). The student's transformation from being "unwilling to imagine his way into the letter" to using considerable imagination and building a rich narrative is fascinating. Enjoying a historical work in this fashion takes time, but the time spent generates many ongoing possibilities.

In sum, there are many ways to approach teaching, but, in the end, virtually all approaches have to be transformed to fit the particular teacher's understandings and dispositions. We must find our own ways of working, even though several broad principles remain before us. Finally, whatever we do must be thoughtful and directed at powerful student learning.

---

## FOR REFLECTION

You might make a number of focused observations in various classrooms. Note how different teachers open and close periods and lessons. What are the questions they pose? How do they introduce new materials and ideas? How have they organized the classroom physically? When the classes work well, what has made the difference?

Draw your ideal classroom. What kinds of furniture exist? What are the seating arrangements? What is on the walls? What kinds of materials are dominant?

Think about the kinds of school-related settings you find most comfortable as a learner. What kinds of things does the teacher do? What are the students' expectations?

Finally, as you think about yourself as a teacher, how would you like your classroom to function? What are the rituals you would like to establish? What do you see yourself doing most of the time? at other times? What approaches to teaching do you find most suitable—which best match your dispositions? What do you understand to be your largest purposes?

---

[1]This conception becomes especially apparent when observing settings in which teachers are mandated to follow closely a *particular* approach to teaching subject matter. (Many behavioristic teacher models, for example, give very precise directions.) Some find the approach natural and do well with it; others look very uncomfortable and don't do very well with the process. It seems clear that teachers need to *be themselves* in a classroom.

[2]I also ask students to reflect on approaches they found productive as students. We need to acknowledge that preservice teachers have been in many classrooms over the years as students and

have observed large numbers of teachers. In elementary and secondary school, for example, I had experience with sixty-six teachers. I witnessed *many* different approaches to teaching, some much more productive than others.

[3]The Fenway Middle College High School in Boston, one of the early schools within the Coalition of Essential Schools, outlines the following "Habits of Mind" as critical: *Perspective/Viewpoint:* What viewpoint are we hearing/seeing/reading? Who is the author? What is his/her intention? Are there other ways of looking at this? *Evidence:* How do we know what we know? What's the evidence? Is the evidence credible? *Connection:* Where have I seen this before? How are things connected to one another? *Relevance:* Why is this important? What difference does this make? Who cares? *Supposition:* What if . . . ? Can we imagine alternatives? Suppose that . . . .

[4]The conception of *scaffolding* is, I believe, particularly important, especially in settings in which students are asked to engage in complex tasks and to complete high-quality work. If, for example, we want students to take meaning from, give an interpretation of primary source materials, we will need to teach them *how* to read primary documents and provide some practice (which is a form of scaffolding). If we want students to write an essay that includes a strong thesis statement and multiple, contesting arguments, we will likely have to teach them how to do the various steps and to work at the task in stages, with ongoing assessment close at hand. In performance terms, it is a matter of considering what we expect at the end in terms of a product for exhibition and then asking what we and the students need to do to get there (what is called within the Coalition of Essential Schools "planning backwards").

[5]I recall large numbers of lectures that were little more than summaries of the readings. I often felt I would rather read the material on my own. When lectures worked, they were interpretive, were developed around sets of questions, and didn't provide definitive answers.

[6]The transcript represents approximately fifteen minutes of discussion. You will notice that the teacher does not speak often or extensively and that eleven students in a class of seventeen made a comment. What is clear is that these students have learned *how* to engage in a classroom discussion.

[7]I often hear "my students aren't very good in an open-ended discussion." They can, though, learn how to engage in such discussions. Often teachers ask students to write some of their ideas first, so they have something to say when the discussion begins. They might also do some group work first, so that students can work out and rehearse their ideas.

[8]Some of the following might be useful texts to gain added insight and strategies for the use of cooperative learning: Cohen (1986), Johnson et al. (1986), Schniedeund and Davidson (1987), and Slavin (1986).

[9]Beginning a school year with skill development in relation to cooperative groups can help the remainder of the year be more productive. Teachers often believe they are sacrificing content if they take time on such things, but the quality of the content work reaches new heights when teachers take the time to provide occasions for practice of the complex tasks that are desired.

[10]To be intentional suggests putting students with different abilities, learning styles, and interests together. To be intentional is also to consider racial, linguistic, and gender differences.

[11]The Project Method was well developed by progressive educators in the 1920s and 1930s. See Kilpatrick (1926).

[12]I have observed settings in which students generated considerable enthusiasm for particular projects but didn't have the technical skills to carry them out. Because time wasn't made available to gain the skills, the work on the projects didn't go well, the products were not very interesting, and enthusiasm for the projects was greatly diminished.

[13]In the sports fields, coaches do a great deal of small-group and one-on-one teaching. They help students make small as well as large adjustments to enlarge and enhance their performance. They generally come to know their student-athletes extremely well. Academic coursework also benefits from teachers' "standing alongside" their students—giving individual assistance when it is needed; referring the student to a particular website, a particular book, or another student; suggesting an alternative way of thinking about something; and providing a focused explanation. Project work encourages a coaching stance on the part of the teacher inasmuch as the students are the workers (to use another Coalition of Essential Schools' conception).

[14]The Inquiry Demonstration Project represented an effort in the 1980s and early 1990s to share the instructional practices of the Urban Academy, a public alternative high school in New York City.

[15]Cook and Mack (1990).

[16]This is a natural response. Work that will go into print to be read by many others, usually elicits from students greater care and a larger commitment.

[17]I am currently involved in a research and evaluation project related to the Annenberg Rural Challenge. One of the principal ideas within Rural Challenge schools is "Curriculum of Place." Students are actively engaged in historical restoration and literary and entrepreneurial work related to their local communities. These are inquiry-oriented projects that end in the production of published booklets, museum exhibitions, restored buildings, community newspapers, and important environmental studies. What seems clear is that students have become major social and intellectual resources to their communities. Their work has become of great interest to community members. And student commitments to learning have enlarged greatly. Their work seems purposeful.

[18]It takes considerable time to respond carefully to student writing. When done, however, the quality of student writing is raised significantly. This is an important argument for reducing the numbers of students for whom teachers are responsible. At secondary schools such as the Urban Academy and Central Park East in New York City, teachers work with fewer than 50 students per day. One result is that students write far more and receive much more careful response than is the case in typical secondary schools, in which teachers work with 140–200 students per day. In the latter settings, there is very little student writing.

[19]Harold Stevenson's work comparing U.S., Japanese, and Chinese schools makes much of homework as a critical factor in the "success" of Japanese and Chinese students.

[20]He is suggesting the need to consider *generative topics*—something discussed more fully in Chapter 7.

# Curriculum Construction

In many respects, this discussion of curriculum construction represents an introduction to the chapter which follows on Teaching for Understanding. It provides a general overview of curriculum—the ways curriculum is generally thought about—and then moves directly to issues surrounding curriculum planning. The context of schools as we know them is always present.

Curriculum in the schools is most often defined as *courses* offered, the *content* within courses, or the totality of the learning experience a school provides its students. Sometimes it is defined as *everything* a student encounters in school, which brings forth in addition to the formal curriculum the conception of the hidden (or unofficial) curriculum. For the purposes of this discussion, however, I will define *curriculum* as the content—the ideas, questions, goals, performances, and means of assessment—around which teachers and students are engaged, whatever the course or teaching area is titled.

Among the many tasks a teacher is expected to perform in a school, the most important is determining *what to teach*. In general, teachers get a great deal of assistance with this decision making, much of it not wanted and a good deal not as helpful as they would like. For example, many school districts have developed curriculum guides for every grade level and subject matter, specifying in great detail the topics to be studied. Most states have also outlined frameworks to guide instruction or established regulations about the teaching of particular content.[1]

While there is a professed localism with regard to schools, there is also, for all intents and purposes, a national curriculum, at least at the macro level. In the primary-elementary grades, the guiding principle for curriculum development for much of the twentieth century has been to begin with what is most immediate and move toward the more remote. This "expanding horizons" approach has tended, for example, in the social studies, whether in Texas or Vermont, to focus on the home, school, and neighborhood in the earliest years, followed by the state in grade 4, the United States in grade 5 and a form of world history in grade 6. The middle and high schools have also had similar, fairly standard patterns—algebra 1 in grade 9; geometry in grade 10; algebra 2 in grade 11; trigonometry, math analysis, and pre-calculus in grade 12, although, with the interest in making calculus the standard twelfth grade course in math, algebra is becoming an eighth grade offering. This is not to say that there are not some modifications here and there or that some changes have not been suggested. However, they are not major shifts.[2]

The nationwide dependence on textbooks has contributed heavily to this "national curriculum." In virtually every curriculum area four or five textbooks dominate the market, and they differ little in regard to the topics they cover.

Codification of this "national curriculum" also gains support from the pronouncements of various subject matter associations, such as the National Council of Teachers of Social Studies and the National Council of Teachers of Mathematics, and from the curriculum regulations of the various states, which are, in turn, heavily influenced by textbooks and national curriculum organizations. The national curriculum has been solidified even further through the increased use of standardized tests developed to assess student knowledge, skills, and understandings at various levels of schooling. Given the tests' norm-referenced nature, it is only natural that the test publishers use the most frequently used textbooks and various state frameworks as a guide for developing the tests.

There have been times when the standard curriculum has been infused with new life—a greater use of local resources; more real text as opposed to textbooks; a broader range of multicultural literature; and increased use of manipulative materials, computers, and laboratory methods—but the main outlines haven't changed very much over the past century.[3]

Within the various courses and subject matters, however, most school districts have tried to incorporate some internal, locally developed coherence by establishing a particular focus at different levels or by defining common experiences at different levels. For example, they might determine that the sixth grade social studies curriculum will focus on the ancient world of Greece and Rome and one non-Western culture, with the tenth grade world history course beginning at a later point in Western history and adding one or two other non-Western areas of the world; that the eighth grade American history course will go through the Civil War, with the eleventh grade American history course beginning with Reconstruction; that all fifth graders will go to Plimouth Plantation and all eighth graders to Sturbridge Village; and that all ninth graders will learn how to write a formal research paper in the English course and all eleventh grade American history students will write a research paper. This kind of school systemwide ordering is usually a good idea to assure equity of experience and some reasonable sequencing of content, although it must always leave teachers room for their own inventions. The study of Greece and Rome, for example, can assume many forms.

School systems or schools within systems occasionally ask, "What do we want the students to learn in the course of their time in our system or school?" The responses become sets of aspirations against which to place all aspects of the curriculum. I was in a K–12 school that had the following aspirations (or, as they were called in the setting, "intentions") for the students:

- Learn very early that they have vast potential for being successful as learners; in large measure, this is a matter of enhancing personal identity

- Become fluent, confident users of language—persons who read, write, speak, and think
- Gain historical perspective, a sense of time, to understand the continuities that exist for them as well as surround them, to know what binds them culturally
- Understand the world of quantities—size and scale, estimation, certainties, and uncertainties
- Feel the excitement of learning, the fullness of a spirit of inquiry
- Learn the value of cooperation and come to know how much more they can know and understand, how much more personal satisfaction can be gained from collaborative thought and action
- Grow in their understandings of the importance of human relationships— over time and across cultures
- Understand and appreciate the natural, social, and political world in which they live, to see themselves as powerful and necessary participants in its well-being and ongoing construction and reconstruction
- Grow in their ability to take initiative, to set consequential personal directions and become responsible decision makers
- Engage their feelings and sensitivities through aesthetic experience—painting, dance, design, and the language of poetry and autobiography

Such intentions could easily find a place in all areas of the curriculum, regardless of the subject matter. The goals of developing such statements are to raise consciousness about large purposes and to give all teachers *and students* a sense of their unity, their active involvement in a community of learning.

However, even after all the collective understandings, the construction of general road maps, the teacher still has to do the finer work of planning what specifically to teach. The school system curriculum may call for the study of the growth of American industry at the close of the nineteenth century, but there are likely hundreds of different ways to proceed, many possible sources of material to examine, and many kinds of questions that could serve as starting points. Such a study could focus on technology or the conditions supporting industrialization, such as transportation, government policies, immigration, and natural resources, or it could flow from questions around human gains and losses, the labor movement, women, and child labor.

In most schools, teachers still have room for their personal interests, for genuine creativity with curriculum.[4] While some things work against the best curriculum work teachers might imagine, such as lack of planning time (in particular, with other teachers) and the shortness of class periods (especially at the middle and high school levels), some changes are beginning to occur. The length of the school day is being expanded, with more space built in for collaborative planning, and class periods in many settings are moving beyond the 42- to 45-minute periods that have been commonplace to 80- to 100-minute periods organized around fewer courses per day to accommodate different subject matters and more work that is interdisciplinary.[5]

How should teachers plan? I propose a process that builds on the Teaching for Understanding Framework, a pedagogical framework developed in great detail in Chapter 8. It represents a particularly good guide to curriculum planning, making the teaching-learning exchange more complete. My intent is to take you through a planning process that I find particularly helpful.

It is usually best when planning a curriculum to think about the course or year as a whole. *One question* might be "What do I most want the students going through the course/year with me to take away?" Here, the concern will revolve around "overarching purposes," habits of mind, attitudes toward the subject matter, skills, dispositions, and large understandings. In science, it might include modes of inquiry; in history, an understanding of multiple viewpoints; in math, patterns. The assumption is that everything studied will relate closely to those overarching purposes.

*A second question* might be "What *topics* ("generative topics" within the Teaching for Understanding formulation), defined to include ideas, questions, themes, and genres of literature, will I work around?" The assumption is that selections have to be made and that teaching a smaller number of topics deeply is better than teaching a larger number more thinly (the coverage route).[6] There will be a relationship between the topics and the overarching purposes. In fact, a teacher could ask with regard to the topics, "Will they further my more critical goals?" What teachers usually find is that some topics have more potential, are more generative than others. They are, in this regard, more likely to engage the interest of students; will enable the students to go on learning in important ways; will help students make more meaning out of what they see in the world, hear on TV or read in the newspapers; can be connected easily to other areas of curriculum, and central to the field of study itself.

In my work with a group of humanities teachers, some of the following topics came up as having been, in their experience, extremely generative. This meant for them that students were more engaged than usual, found some personal points of relationship, and were able to make more connections to other fields or areas of inquiry. The topics were immigration, equality, rights, power, democracy, identity, morality, religious belief, the nature of evil, survival, adolescence, growing up, friendship, revolution, conflict, change and continuity, love/hate, traditions, slavery, race relations, and the Holocaust. As the teachers described their work with these topics, there was an almost universal acknowledgment that they would be "naturally" engaging to teachers and students. They described them in the following terms:

- Are related to students' questions, interests, and intentions—there is an authenticity
- Are exciting to teachers
- Are visible in the world
- Can be applied easily to everyday life
- Are open to interpretation
- Lead to complex understandings
- Make connections to a network of other fields of inquiry
- Engender controversy
- Demand judgment
- Provide a basis for action in the world—a form of empowerment
- Have within them many diverse entry points over time and across cultures
- Have a powerful human narrative
- Lend themselves to different kinds of primary sources
- Provide inviting opportunities for detailed study
- Stimulate wonder
- Engage students in an act of construction (authentic in terms of the content and method related to the topic)
- Hold personal or intellectual challenges that can be recognized by students

When more of these characteristics are present in a topic, the more generative that topic is likely to be.

The National Committee on Science Education Standards and Assessment of the National Research Council (1993), National Academy of Science notes, "As the body of scientific knowledge has exploded, high school courses have become cluttered with so much new vocabulary, often exceeding that of foreign language courses, that terms can only be memorized rather than understood" (p. 1). The committee's solution was to think about science content broadly, in terms of large, *fundamental* conceptions—the nature of science (modes of inquiry, habits of mind, attitudes, and dispositions), the applications of science, and the contexts of science. While *generative topics* is not the language used by the committee to select content, the conception used—*fundamental understandings*—is closely allied. The committee notes that

> Subject matter is *fundamental* if it:
> - represents central scientific ideas and organizing principles;
> - has rich explanatory and predictive power;
> - motivates the formulation of significant questions;

- guides fruitful observation; and
- is applicable in many situations and contexts common to everyday experience. (p. 15)

With regard to the question of *generative* topics, I have been asked if this implies mostly something that has a catchy title that will get the attention of students. If the topic does have a catchy nomenclature, it might be helpful, but that is not what makes it generative. Its generative quality comes from its centrality, richness, and accessibility. For example, *immigration,* or *the peopling of America,* is a generative topic because it is so important in the history of the United States; it involves so many different people, cultures, and places; it has a recurring quality; it is so visible it is filled with controversy and human drama; and everyone in the class has a personal experience that relates to it (and these are only starters). I have been in classrooms, however, in which immigration was studied under such rubrics as

"Whose America Is It?"

"Where are All the People Coming From?"

"Where in the World Did We Come From?"

"The Builders of Our City"

"The Story of Human Migration"

"Ethnic Neighborhoods"

In this regard, I think also about the units constituting the Elementary Science Study. Their science content was related to electricity, compounds, energy, and bacteria, but the unit titles were "Batteries and Bulbs," "Mystery Powders," and "Pond Water." They are catchy titles but they worked and were generative for other, more important reasons.

A teacher in Springfield, Virginia, developed an interesting unit around public and private sculptures that he calls "Monumental Experiences" (James Percoco, *OAH Magazine of History,* 1992), a title with a naturally interesting quality. However, the unit's focus is on two monuments—Augustus Saint-Gauden's *The Robert Gould Shaw and 54th Massachusetts Volunteer Regiment Monument,* across from the Massachusetts State House, and Daniel Chester French's *Mourning Victory,* in the Sleepy Hollow Cemetery in Concord, Massachusetts. Beyond the artists themselves, who were part of the late-nineteenth-century American renaissance, the stories surrounding the monuments are enormously interesting. Who were the people being honored? Why were they honored in this form? Why at this time? What other monuments are there from the same time or earlier times? Are there ties to the Vietnam Memorial? How do these monuments interpret war, sacrifice, death, honor? How are these monuments similar to, different from, poems, music, and buildings that also commemorate important people and events? The questions are, again, literally boundless. The topic is a good starting point for interesting social history, helping students take so much more from their environments.

The *third question* to pose, after the selection of topics, is "What do I want the students to understand as a result of studying this topic?" It is important to work through a personal definition of *understanding*, recognizing that to assure importance it has to mean more than information, merely knowing about something. What we most want our students to understand—our understanding goals—might be posted in the classroom, alerting the students to what the unit is about and what they are working toward.

The *fourth question* to work through is "What will I ask students to do, read, and think about—essentially, the activities?" This will involve the most detailed planning—for a week as a whole and for individual days. What will you bring to the class? How will you introduce the materials? How will you organize the students for group work? What performances or exhibitions will exist to demonstrate understanding along the way? In the Teaching for Understanding Framework, these are called understanding performances.

This detailed planning is important to work through, not because everything will be followed precisely but as a way of assuring an ongoing thoughtfulness about our work. The careful planning also tends to bring forward greater confidence. I stress with my preservice students and with teachers who are just beginning to plan curriculum around the Teaching for Understanding Framework that the initial days are extremely important; that is the time when we bring the students into the topic. This is an occasion to help students *want* to pursue the work, see themselves in it, and come to consider possibilities. It is usually helpful if something active is planned to get the students involved.

Another thing I stress in the planning is that teachers ask, in relation to each day, how does the work planned relate to the understanding goals—the large purposes? Maintaining a conscious stance about these connections keeps the focus on understanding.

The *fifth question* has to do with assessment: "How will I stay in touch with students' understandings; what will cause me to say that they understand?" What should be clear is that assessment needs to be embedded and ongoing. The performance activities in question 4 need to be seen as central components of the assessment plan. There ought to be a minimum of one performance activity every other day.

Needless to say, the curriculum development task is immense, because it may be the teacher's most important work. However, it also opens up considerable room for creativity, for keeping large purposes up front, for keeping the teaching-learning exchange vital. It is what keeps teachers fully engaged, wanting to return each day, enthusiastic about the possibilities.

## FOR REFLECTION

What does it mean to understand something? If a person says, "I understand the civil rights movement of the 1950s and 1960s," what do you expect them to be able to do and to share?

Reflect on your life as a student in school. What units, themes, or topics of study are the most memorable—those that you enjoyed and did good work on, and that significantly expanded your understandings? How did those units proceed? What were the questions posed, the activities, and the materials?

During your life as a student, did you mostly cover material or uncover material, touch the surface of academic content or go deeply into academic content? What difference did it make?

Finally, as you think about yourself as a teacher, what are the topics you would most like to teach over the course of a year? What makes those topics important, worthy of spending many weeks on?

[1]While general outlines (to include scope and sequence delineations) have long been typical, the specificity of directions in this close-of-the-century "reform" period is particularly noticeable. From my point of view, it is much too heavy and limits the possibilities for teachers and students.

[2]The history of these curricular patterns is discussed in Chapter 3. See also Kliebard (1995).

[3]I make a point out of the national curriculum to make clear that education across the United States is not as haphazard as many critics suggest. Further, while I might hope for greater diversity than exists, I understand how our national curriculum has developed and why it will likely continue to exist.

[4]In many states, as I noted earlier, the curriculum frameworks being developed have grown in their specificity, and tests are being constructed to match the content being specified. These directions may place new limits on what is possible.

[5]I like the longer class periods and student schedules that focus on two to three courses/subject matters at any one period of time (trimester or semester), especially in the middle schools and high schools. I also understand that students aren't always prepared for the longer periods (having had a long socialization into shorter periods of time for the various subject matters), and teachers often wonder how they will keep students occupied for 80 to 100 minutes. Here again, teachers and students will have to work together to make the longer periods more productive. Teachers will clearly have to make use of a variety of approaches to teaching. Performance-oriented work should also become natural.

[6]In the work related to Why Math? discussed in Chapter 4, I ask beginning teachers to consider no more than four topics they might organize an entire semester or year around. If we could only teach four or five topics in a year in each of our subject matters, what would they be? I think we would profit greatly from thinking about our work through such a question.

# Toward a Pedagogy of Understanding

In many respects, this discussion complements the previous chapters on approaches to teaching and curriculum construction. It is mainly an explication of the Teaching for Understanding Framework that my colleagues and I have formulated to assist teachers in conceptualizing their work more powerfully.[1] Over the past decade, it has become the centerpiece of my teaching-learning work with teachers.

It may seem obvious that our teaching should be directed toward understanding, that being able to give back information on a Friday test, too often the typical fare, is not sufficient. In general, and in most settings, however, students tend to understand far less than we might desire. Systematic logic and algebraic formulas are often confusing, especially if any part of the context is altered.[2] Poetry is typically obscure as well as seemingly inaccessible, students often have trouble writing essays that bring forward the complexities in the topics they are writing about, and they generally see few connections between what they are learning in school and the world beyond school. Moreover, social studies is most often seen by students in schools as masses of names and dates, not content that is open to interpretation. And science is often defined in fixed and certain terms, not to be challenged.[3]

Do students understand the Civil War in the United States because, on an exam, they are able to provide the "five causes" listed in the textbook or enumerate the states making up the Union and the Confederacy? This would seem insufficient. If they can tell us the names of two Shakespeare plays, repeat the formula for determining the length of a hypotenuse in a right triangle, or provide the names of five of the planets in our solar system (including the largest and smallest), would we demand *more* before conferring on them our stamp of understanding?[4] I think so.

If students were able to describe the language of the American Declaration of Independence and connect it to ideas from two or three Enlightenment political philosophers (such as Locke and Rousseau), put into their own words critical elements of the petitions of complaint against King George, role-play what King George's response might have been, and describe the role the declaration has played in American life over time, would we, then, say they understand the declaration and some of the important issues surrounding it? If they could describe the Pythagorean theorem historically; show its uses in construction, surveying, and measuring; and argue for it in ways that go beyond prescriptive knowledge, would we say they understand that also? If they were able not only to name the planets but draw them in relation to one another, provide their sizes in reasonable scale, discuss their individual qualities, and relate their names to their mythic characters, would we say they are approaching understanding? Certainly, they are getting closer to what most of us would define as understanding, closer to what our schools should focus attention on.

As a way of helping preservice teachers get closer to their personal mean-ings of understanding, I ask them to think again about a deep interest, some-thing they are articulate about, feel in control of, have internalized, and are good with and at. It might be something they can make into a metaphor, pos-sibly draw pictures of, make personal connections to, and relate to the world more generally. It is likely something they can say they *understand*, not just know about. I suggest that it is toward *that kind of understanding* that teaching in the schools should be directed—something students can hold on to and use productively again and again in new settings as well as in familiar settings and beyond the Friday test, the end of the unit exam, and the school itself. Such a goal is, of course, large, greatly raising the stakes in the schools.

After students describe what they understand—the solar system, cooking, the periodic table, Russia, baseball, music, folktales, the poetry of Wallace Stevens, the life of Eleanor Roosevelt, density, the Federalist Papers—I ask for additional information, clarification, and more concrete examples, which in this activity is part of the process of making judgments about the person's under-standing or movement toward understanding.[5] For example, I asked last year, what would cause us to say that "Jeff understands folktales"? What should he be able to do to demonstrate his understanding? One person in class thought he should be able to tell us an interesting folktale. He did just that, vividly re-lating a folktale about turtles wanting to fly like birds, rooted in Caribbean cul-ture. In relation to another question, he also described the elements of folktales, what makes them a unique form of literature. It was agreed that he deserved "our stamp" of understanding.

Out of such discussions, we derive a set of "criteria for understanding," our ongoing process of seeking principles relating to teaching and learning that grow out of our ongoing, reflected-on experience.[6] Some of the following have become common: a person who understands something seems able to teach it to another person; can relate it to something else—another topic, another set of ideas, another environment; can draw a form of it; can manipulate it within a different context; has confidence about it and possesses a personal attach-ment to it; and can speak of things he or she is still not clear about and has questions about.

Virtually everyone involved in these kinds of discussions concludes that an education leading to such internalization seems within reach in the schools, especially if we set that task before us, putting all our efforts in that direction. That such understandings should be the end of what is taught in the schools seems fully logical. Why, the question is raised, would we want less? This be-comes even more clear as we engage in discussions about our own experiences, occasions in educational settings when we have been intellectually most fully engaged, when we have sensed that our learning was particularly profound and our understandings deeper than usual.[7] The common elements that have emerged over the past seven or eight years of such inquiries speak well to content and curriculum, whether the setting is an elementary or a secondary school. In the circumstances that mean something special

- The students have a role in defining the content (selecting the *particular* biography to read, the *particular* play to present).
- There is time to wonder, to work around the edges of the subject matter, and to find a *particular direction* and develop a personal commitment.
- Various forms of expression are permitted—even encouraged.
- Students' views are respected by their teachers, who learn something from them.
- There is an original product, something public—an idea, a point of view, an interpretation, a proposal, a paper, a presentation, or a performance. In the process, students gain "expertness."
- They do something—participate in a political action, write a letter to the editor of a newspaper or magazine, develop a newsletter, work with the homeless, talk about their work with others, and so on.
- They make personal connections to the content, are called on to place themselves in the setting. It is a "living experience."
- The content is connected to previous interests. Additionally, it is related to the interests of others in the class.
- Teachers are passionate about their work. The richest experiences are activities "invented" by the teachers.
- There is a sense that not everything is firm and predetermined, the results fully predictable.

If we were to act on such understandings, students' experiences in schools would be much different, far more productive. While we could certainly turn each of these characteristics into a pedagogical practice, this list is meant primarily to establish a firmer common base around the formulation of *understanding*.

The context for paying attention to understanding is clear enough. The students in our schools need an empowering education that goes beyond the classroom and into the world. They need to be able to *use* knowledge, not just know about something. Understanding is about making connections among and between things and not things in isolation, about deep and not surface knowledge, and about greater complexity, not simplicity.

To move this conception to a pedagogy, my colleagues and I have developed in our research what we call a Teaching for Understanding Framework, the elements of which are outlined in the following paragraphs. They are meant to serve as a guide for thinking more fully about teaching.

We begin with the question "what is to be taught?" Here the teacher should consider *generative topics*—ideas, topics, themes, issues, and questions that provide enough depth and variety of perspective to help students develop significant understandings. Implicit is a belief that some ideas have more possibilities of engaging students than others; some questions are richer in potential for helping students begin to see more complexity in the world or make connections to a wide array of issues and subject matters. The most generative topics are *central to a field of inquiry, accessible to students at many different levels, and rich in implications and connections.*

In this regard, I often ask what practicing scientists or historians would say are the *big* ideas in their fields—ideas that, if understood, could lead to ever more sophisticated work.[8] When pushed, students preparing for teaching as well as practicing teachers can imagine a small number of *central* ideas or topics around which their teaching *could* be organized—for example, at the secondary level, evolution in biology, the civil rights movement in American history, and relationships in mathematics. At the elementary level, the most generative topics relate to what children see around them—the natural habitat, physical structures, relationships, time, and size and scale. To speak of *accessibility* is to consider the richness of a topic, the fact that it can be entered at many different levels. A student with little previous background can enter it and have a powerful intellectual experience, and a student with considerable sophistication and knowledge also has a place to enter and can experience powerful learning. In this sense, generative topics are bottomless. There is likely never a point within them when there is nothing more to study or learn. And generative topics are *connected* to other topics and other fields, to life beyond school. In this regard, they don't stand fully alone. Moreover, they are topics teachers have a genuine interest in and are enthusiastic about.

One of the ways I suggest that students "test" their teaching topics, beyond the criteria previously listed, is through a mapping process. The larger the map, the more varied in its possibilities, the more possible entry points there are for students, the richer and more generative the topic is. In some respects, a map grows from discussing many possibilities, but it is also more than such brainstorming, calling on one's own understanding and enthusiasm for the topic. Figure 8.1 represents one example of the process.

I also make clear with this mapping process (and here I go somewhat beyond the Teaching for Understanding Framework) that it represents another means of planning—providing a sense of the materials that would be useful in support of the topic and a way to begin to match one's students to possible entry points, making sure there is a good entry point for each student. (This suggests, of course, that teachers know a good deal about their students and

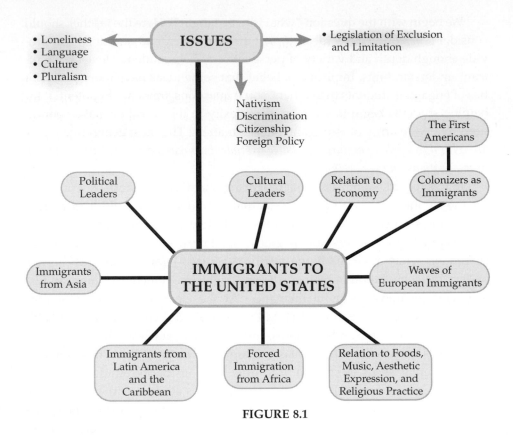

**FIGURE 8.1**

their interests.) As I note to my students, my best entry point for most subject matters is through biographical accounts.[9] It is interesting to hear from my students what makes for them the most productive entry points—through a fictional account, a hands-on exercise, or an opportunity to link the topic under study to something already understood.

I have been occasionally asked, "What isn't generative?" It is clear that imaginative teachers can make *any* topic generative but some topics represent better possibilities than others. Slavery has far more potential than the military events of the Civil War, because its effects are still present. Global warming in biology has more potential than the "anatomy of fish," because global warming is so heavily debated in the media and is understood to affect our immediate environment, now and in the future.

Evolution; states of matter; energy; the solar system; the life cycle; the environment and density in science; patterns, relationships, and size and scale in math;

and democracy, revolution, and immigration in history are certainly generative topics. Questions that have recurring qualities are generative. Why does it rain? What is the relation between what we eat and the quality of our physical health? How does disease spread? How is disease controlled? How do plants grow? What does it mean to be American? Technologies—machines, TV, computers, film, and robots—are also generative because their connections to so many aspects of a culture are rich. The point of all this is that we need to think deeply about *what to teach.* We can't do everything if understanding matters to us.[10]

The *second* key idea, *understanding goals,* represents what we want students to understand. Understanding goals answer the question "What do I want my students to understand about the generative topic?" Assume immigration as the topic—what would we most want students to understand—that there are large numbers of immigrants, that immigration has had a continuing quality, that leaving one's country and family roots is difficult, that great hardship accompanies immigration, that immigrants from some areas have faced extreme forms of discrimination, the contributions of immigrants to American life, the life stories of immigrants, immigrants' roles in building the infrastructure of the U.S. economy, ties between immigration from various foreign countries and migration within the United States, or what it is like to move? The list could go on. In the end, we have to decide on what we believe is *most* important.

For three week units, I suggest that teachers consider two or three understanding goals. And these understanding goals should be placed before the students so they know exactly where this unit is going and what they are expected to understand at its completion. They should be in a position of asking about everything being done and read, how it all relates to the goals. Teachers can also refer what is being done to the goals. Following are some examples of understanding goals:

*(geometry)* Students will understand the nature and purpose of proofs. Students will understand how to represent numerical information in clear graphs.

*(history)* Students will understand the importance of the First Amendment in relation to their lives.
Students will understand the relationship between rights and responsibilities in a democratic society.

*(science)* Students will understand why some things sink and others float. Students will understand how a biologist distinguishes between living and nonliving things.

*(literature)* Students will understand the different uses of language in *Their Eyes Were Watching God.*
Students will understand how authors create, develop, and sustain suspense in a plot.

*(language)* Students will understand the differences between Spanish and English, as well as the influence of other languages in Spanish and English. Students will understand how languages change over time.

What *aren't* understanding goals? There are many important goals that all teachers have that are not *understanding* goals,[11] such as the following:

- Wanting students to develop confidence in expressing their ideas
- Wanting students to enjoy learning
- Wanting students to know the facts of a particular passage or work (such as being able to retell the plot of *The Scarlet Letter*)
- Wanting students to be able to conjugate a verb form in a language

The *third* key idea of the Teaching for Understanding Framework, *understanding performances*, is classroom activities that encourage students to demonstrate their progress *toward* the understanding goals. In general, understanding performances ask students to go beyond the information given, to create something fresh and/or to share their current understandings in an observable way. In classrooms in which *understanding* is the ethic, students spend much of their time preparing for, demonstrating, and revising performances of understanding. This performance orientation, actually doing something, is central to understanding. It is the element missing in most classrooms. A good question to ask as we work through curriculum planning is "What might students *do* to develop and demonstrate their understanding?"

One of the ways I help students preparing to teach, as well as practicing teachers, understand this conception more fully is by asking of their *understanding goals* what would cause us to say that a student *understands* what we want them to understand? What would be the indicators? What would they be able to do? Once this has been described in detail, I ask, "What are some of the *steps* a student might take to get to that end (the steps along the way)?" The *steps* can be defined as understanding performances.

In general, in the course of a unit, students should have a number of opportunities to demonstrate their understanding—there should be a variety of understanding performances, such as the following:

*(literature)* To build their understanding of Hamlet's internal conflicts, students choose one of Hamlet's soliloquies and rewrite it as an entry in Hamlet's diary.

*(history)* Students compare two accounts of how the Revolutionary War began—one that claims the British fired first and another that claims the colonists did. They then discuss why the two reports are different and how they could find out what really happened.

*(mathematics)* To help them understand the concept of parallel lines, students experiment with two pieces of string, trying to arrange them so that they are always the same distance apart and never intersect. Students then describe to the class how they know that they've succeeded.

*(science)* To help them understand the physics of light and images as they relate to lenses, students experiment with a collection of concave and convex lenses and a light source. They try to find combinations that will serve as magnifying, telephoto, and wide-angle lenses and then draw diagrams to illustrate how light travels through the various lens series they have developed.

*(language)* To demonstrate their current level of understanding of poetic structures, students describe the poetic structures used by Pablo Neruda and Octavio Paz and present some of their poetry to exemplify these structures.

What are some examples of performances that do not necessarily show understanding? Just as there are many important goals that are not understanding goals, so there are many important performances that neither build nor demonstrate students' understanding:

- Writing memorized definitions on a vocabulary test
- Answering questions (either on a test or in discussion) about facts reported in a textbook
- Reporting the plot of a piece of literature
- Writing out the formula for solving quadratic equations

Even though these are not understanding performances, a teacher might view such activities as necessary for getting students to important understanding performances.

One thing to keep in mind with understanding performances is that they should occur at many points in the course of a unit. They place the teacher in a coaching role—helping students with constructions, getting them ready to present their findings, staying close to their data collections, seeing how they explain the solving of various problems, and helping them develop models of problems. It might be thought about as a continuous science, math, or technology fair.

*Fourth, ongoing assessment* allows both teachers and students to evaluate frequently the various performances of understanding as they develop over time. At its best, assessment has a cumulative quality. It never comes down to one final product. Through ongoing assessment, teachers always know how the students are progressing toward the understanding goals. In the best of circumstances, the students *also* know.

Ongoing assessment works best if teachers develop, possibly with students, sets of criteria around each understanding performance, a means of making an assessment about progress. Feedback, or ongoing assessment, can come from peers or from the teacher. Following are some examples of ongoing assessment:

*(history)* As students work on a research paper, they meet in small groups to describe their progress to others, to offer their own evaluation of their work up to that point, and to collect their classmates' reflections and suggestions for improvement.

*(literature)* As students work through a piece of literature, they write successive drafts of a paper on a topic, reflecting in journals about how their thoughts on the topic are changing. The teacher and a classmate read each draft, offering two or three suggestions for developing the ideas as well as for improving style.

*(science)* Students brainstorm a list of questions they have about a particular topic before they begin to study it. At the end of each week, they review the list and identify in their notebooks which questions they have answered, as well as any new ones that may have come up.

*(mathematics)* Working on a larger project, students periodically present their work to the class, both by sharing their written drafts and by making presentations. Students give feedback on the presentation, while the teacher offers comments on both the presentation and the written work.

*(language)* Students try out dialogues in several contexts and receive critiques about what worked well and what seemed to work less well, with the understanding that more work will be done.

If we were to stay with the process delineated, with many opportunities to determine progress, all students should reach the end of the unit with a valid measure of understanding. We will certainly not reach the end of a unit and be surprised that a student hasn't completed work along the way that was necessary for reaching the end product.

In addition to ongoing assessment, I ask students I work with to consider a culminating activity for each unit of study, which brings everything together. It could be a completed project, with a presentation; a portfolio of selections of work along the way, with an overview and concluding statement; or an exercise that calls on students to pull ideas together, to go beyond what has been studied. The pulling together of what has been learned over a few weeks typically creates constructive energy, a sense of genuine accomplishment.

Basic ideas surrounding the Framework are summarized in Figure 8.2.

I will now enlarge on some of the ideas as a means of providing additional directions. Since most teachers think about the year as a whole, I'll begin there. Whether at the university or school level, whether the work is exclusively in-

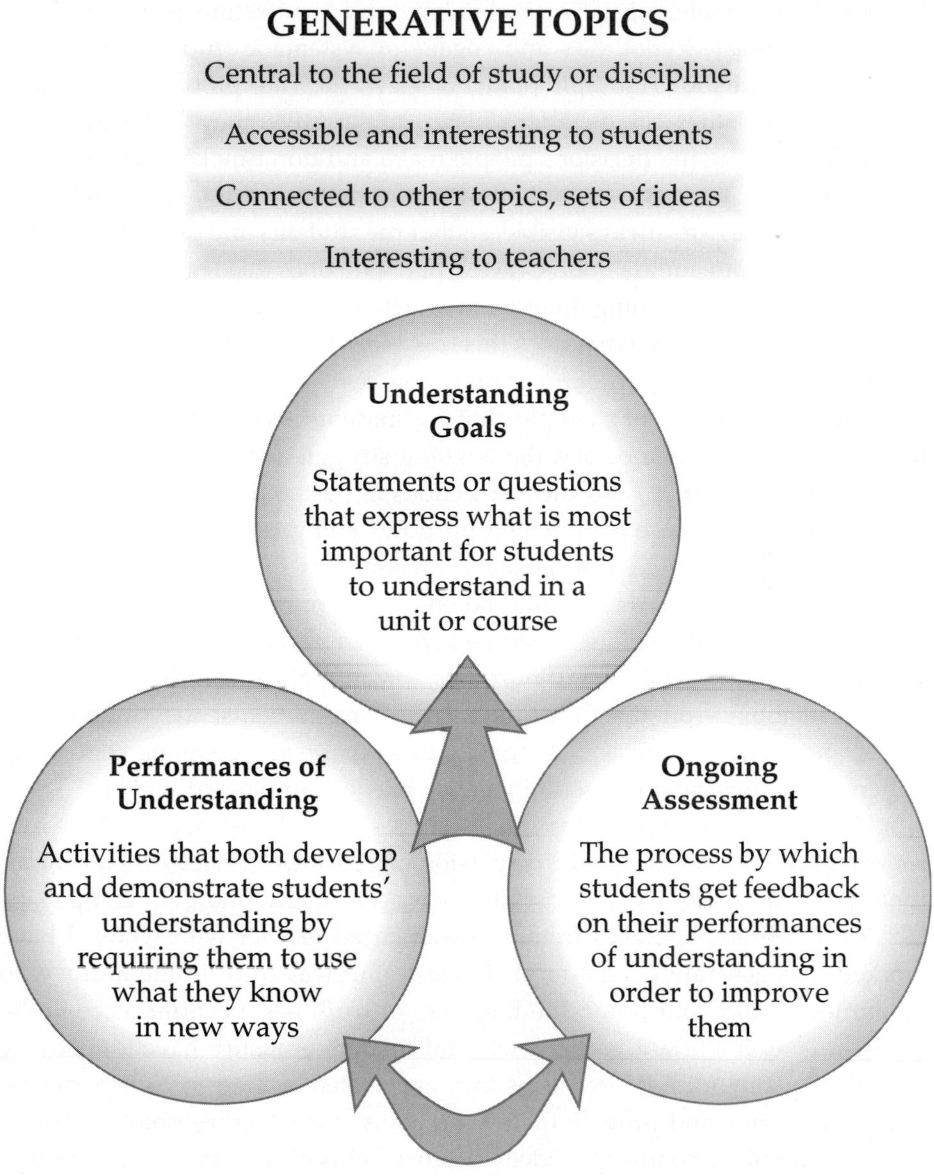

# GENERATIVE TOPICS

Central to the field of study or discipline

Accessible and interesting to students

Connected to other topics, sets of ideas

Interesting to teachers

**Understanding Goals**

Statements or questions that express what is most important for students to understand in a unit or course

**Performances of Understanding**

Activities that both develop and demonstrate students' understanding by requiring them to use what they know in new ways

**Ongoing Assessment**

The process by which students get feedback on their performances of understanding in order to improve them

**FIGURE 8.2**

terdisciplinary or based on a subject field, teachers typically ask (or should ask), "What do we most want our students to take away from the year?" Essentially this moves teachers to overarching goals, what they wish to be most intentional about, pay particular attention to, and come back to again and again. Among my goals for a secondary school history course, for example, are that students are able to use primary sources and know where to find them, recognizing that they can be in people, music, art, technology, and architecture as well as print; they can formulate hypotheses and engage in systematic study in relation to them; they can handle multiple points of view; they are problem posers and problem solvers; they can develop a historical narrative; they understand that history is made by the decisions people make and don't make; they are readers and writers. I might even put all of that on the board to assure that these overarching goals are always visible, so that the students and I can think about what we do day in and day out. One teacher, who does this regularly, asks students to measure everything done against such a list. Students are asked to say, for example, "Mr. Jones, what does this [the work being done] have to do with learning more about interpreting primary sources?" I might also define related understanding goals—for example, that the students *understand* the unfinished nature of American democracy, the ongoing struggle for equity, the idea that each of us is a historian, and the connections of past and present.

Given some of these overarching purposes and goals, I would make sure divergent primary sources were available for almost everything we studied. Getting materials together, then, would be one of my principal tasks as a teacher. There would have to be room for student choices, for inquiry, for interpretation, and for role-playing. Given my purposes, I would also likely have units—or generative topics—on the Constitution, the Amendments, the Courts, civil rights, and women's suffrage, along with units that revolve around continuing patterns of immigration, discrimination, violence, and peace making. These would help me reach my overarching purposes. I would ask against these topics what I outlined earlier in the discussion of generative topics—their centrality to the field of inquiry under study, their accessibility, and their complexity.

A fuller example comes from an experienced teacher with whom I have worked. His generative topic for a six-week unit was truth in literature: who determines justice and how? The literature of truth has a central place in the field—it is an important genre. Trials and matters of justice have a relatively engaging quality for adolescents as they are related to their prior experiences beyond literature and provide them with many diverse entry points. Further, students can likely connect the ideas to other fields of inquiry—social studies, film, and events in the news.

The *understanding goals* this particular teacher wanted students to achieve were to

1. Develop their own understandings of the balance between individual and social responsibility
2. Understand the central role of language—particularly, metaphor—in shaping thought and belief
3. Understand how guilt and innocence are defined and determined

4. Understand why particular definitions of justice prevail and others are crushed

5. Use evidence carefully to form and support their opinions on justice as presented in each of the literary works (the teacher used *Mutiny on the Bounty, To Kill a Mockingbird, Inherit the Wind,* and *A Jury of Her Peers)*

The teacher began the unit by asking students *to write about a time when they had been treated unjustly and about a time when they had treated someone else unjustly.* In class, they discussed how they had determined in each of these situations that an injustice had occurred. He then introduced the unit to students and asked them to think about why they would read literature (instead of history or sociology) as the starting point for thinking about justice.

Throughout the unit, students did nightly reading assignments. To track their developing understandings, the teacher asked students to *keep reading journals in which they recorded their responses to and questions about the works.* Students often began large-group discussions by sharing questions they had about the previous night's readings. In these large-group discussions, the teacher encouraged the students not only to wrestle with the answers to their questions but also to think about how they were answering them: which questions could be answered definitively? Which might have several answers? For the more complicated questions, they had to decide whether or not their answers were adequate and whether some answers were better than others. (This can be viewed as an understanding performance.)

At the end of each large-group discussion, students wrote a couple of sentences summarizing the most important things they had learned in the discussion. They also wrote down one new or lingering question in which they were interested. The teacher collected these and reviewed them to prepare for class the next day. (Embedded in this work is ongoing assessment.)

As they worked through each piece of literature, students *kept charts in their notebooks* to point out where they saw justice-related themes being introduced and how those themes were subsequently developed over the course of the work. In small groups, they shared these charts (which were performances) with one another. The charts also formed the foundation for more formal debates within small groups about questions of justice as they were played out in the literature. Students defended the points of view that seemed to them most valid (additional performances). Within groups, they critiqued one another's arguments after each of these debates (ongoing assessment).

Over the course of the unit, the teacher periodically shared with the students sample papers that defended particular points of view about justice in the works they were reading. (Some were papers he had written; others were the works of students from previous years.[12]) Some of the papers were well argued, while others were flawed. In large-group discussions, students analyzed these papers, weighing the arguments, evidence, and style of each. The teacher recorded their judgments on large pieces of newsprint, which he left taped up around the room. Eventually three lists emerged from these discussions—lists of the characteristics of a good argumentative essay, of an adequate one, and of an inadequate one. (These are essentially criteria against which students can judge their own work or the work of others.)

This exercise prepared students to write their own papers at the end of the unit. For these essays, they chose one aspect of justice and used two or three of the texts they had read to argue a particular point. Working in pairs, the students read and critiqued each other's work as it progressed. The final draft was assessed more formally by the author, a classmate, and the teacher.

I think the unit moved in a good direction. Justice became more than fiction for the students. What was learned could be transferred easily to discussions about such places and events as Waco, Bosnia, South Africa, Somalia, South Boston High School, the streets of Boston, and homelessness. It was not inert knowledge.

It is not easy to get from where we are to teaching for understanding. There are many barriers. Time is one critical barrier—time to reflect, time for collaboration, and the time pressures for coverage. Teachers ask, "Can I really afford four weeks on Reconstruction when I typically spend no more than two days?" Further, there are concerns about whether the students will have enough information to deal with the various college-entrance examinations (SAT and ACT). In this period in which "standards" are being emphasized, increasing numbers of tests are being introduced for the purposes of determining promotion and graduation. Teachers I know are asking, "Can I afford to teach for understanding?" It may, in fact, get harder to teach for understanding, yet the goal is *still* too important to be put aside.

What are some of the additional classroom-related questions my colleagues and I most often get in discussions of our work? "How can I manage this in the face of an unprecedented diversity of students—racially, linguistically, ethnically, and culturally?" (This is—particularly, in our urban culture—*the population*.[13]) A related question is "How do I really interest twenty-eight different students?" What this speaks to is that we need the many entry points that a pedagogy of understanding suggests—many performances of understanding that enable students at all levels to engage the content more fully, to be successful learners.[14]

I suggested earlier that a generative topic is accessible. To the degree that the topics fully invite questions that students can see *in* the world around them, that tap the issues that they confront, they have a naturally generative quality. So much of what we now do, with its singularity of tasks and commonality of requirements, assures that large numbers of students never deeply enter what we are teaching. Few have the intense learning experiences we desire. A pedagogy of understanding that aims at providing a more powerful education for all students has a better chance of generating greater intensity. It is also more interesting for teachers.

Another question relates to the fact that teachers most often work in schools with existing school districtwide curriculum guides and well-developed scope and sequence directions. Within a district's scope and sequence—which calls, for example, for a one-week unit on immigration—it is still possible to generate a topic related to it that can be pursued with reasonable depth (possibly the stories of five local immigrants, immigrant neighborhoods, the importance of immigration to a particular local industry, or the immigration from Laos).

I will close with a restatement of the primary premises undergirding the Teaching for Understanding Framework that I typically present to my students:

- All of our subject areas are so large that we couldn't possibly work through them with any serious depth.
- Given the foregoing circumstance, good selection of what we teach is critical—especially if student understanding of what we teach is at the center of our academic purposes.
- Our choices should be rooted in what we have called *generative topics* (defined as ideas, concepts, themes, genres, and movements).
- Generative topics are central to the field of inquiry, are accessible at many levels of complexity, and are easily and naturally connected to other topics, other fields of inquiry, and students' lives.
- In relation to our choices of topics, we need to select a small number of critical purposes—what we most want the students to take away, called *understanding goals*.
- The understanding goals we select help guide what we do day by day.
- As we plan activities day by day, we need to ask how they further and are related to our understanding goals.
- Within the day-by-day activities, we need to embed *understanding performances*, demonstrations of student understanding or demonstrations of critical growth along the path of understanding.
- Understanding performances imply that students *do* something—complete a construction, a play, a video, or an interview; engage in a role play; or argue several points of view—extending the ideas under study.
- *Ongoing assessment* occurs around the understanding performances, with feedback from teachers and student peers, and is related directly to the understanding goals.

- Self-assessment is embedded into the process of ongoing assessment.
- A unit culminates with a finished product, an exhibition, a major construction, a paper, or an "examination."
- The culminating activity or product brings together the understanding performances and is *related directly* to the understanding goals.
- Overall, the foregoing process relates to teaching for greater depth—it follows the Coalition's theme of "less is more."
- If carried out carefully, all students should be successful.

## FOR REFLECTION

Reflect on occasions in school when you were most fully engaged intellectually. What were the conditions?

Think about something you understand and have under control. What could you do, share, or discuss that you believe would demonstrate to others that you understand what you say you understand?

What do you believe schools would be like if *understanding* were the principal academic and intellectual aim? What would students be doing? What would teachers be doing?

Finally, consider a subject matter you are likely to teach. Within that subject matter, think about three or four topics you believe to be particularly generative—are central to the field of inquiry, are rich with possibilities, and can be connected to other topics, ideas, or fields. Regarding one of these generative topics, write one understanding goal. With regard to the understanding goal, consider at least two ways a student might demonstrate an aspect of that understanding goal.

[1]The Teaching for Understanding research project, out of which the Framework developed, was supported by a generous grant from the Spencer Foundation (Howard Gardner, David Perkins, and I were the principal investigators). I draw on many of the examples that arose during the research and were used by members of the research team. For a full description of the work, see Wiske (1997).

[2]I had the experience of discussing the meaning of *understanding* with a group of parents, students, and community members in a Boston area suburban community. A young woman responded as follows: "I have taken the full math curriculum at my high school, including calculus, in which I am now enrolled. I have an *A* average in math, yet I can't go beyond the text. If problems are not presented in the exact form of the text, if they demand something beyond the formulas I have memorized and use mechanically, I am lost. It is not really very different in my other subject matters, but math is on my mind just now. As you describe understanding, I have almost none. I don't plan to take any math in college because I don't understand it."

[3]Lewis Thomas writes persuasively in this regard that science is very uncertain. See *On the Usefulness of Biology* (1980), *The Lives of a Cell: Notes of a Biology Watcher* (1974), and *The Medusa and the Snail: More Notes of a Biology Watcher* (1979).

[4]I think here about a group of teachers in New York City who were contesting a citywide science test, believing firmly that it didn't get close to what children actually understood, that it didn't honor their slower, more intense, meaning-making, hands-on, observational, and experience-oriented approaches to science. Working with Ted Chittenden, a research psychologist from the Educational Testing Service, the teachers developed a science assessment that used the district's objectives and the questions asked on the citywide test but made them open-ended. They wanted to demonstrate the larger possibilities through a less restricted process. The citywide test, for example, asked, "Which of the following planets is the largest? a. Venus, b. Mars, c. Pluto, d. Jupiter." The teachers suggested that checking the right answer would not get them close to students' understandings. They asked students, in contrast, to *draw* a picture of the solar system. The drawings were, the teachers believed, far more revealing, getting closer to student understanding.

[5]Most of what students identify cannot be labeled in our subject matter terms. Most are activities they participate in—swimming, surfing, cooking, building. Interestingly, however, these activities are, in the end, connected to what are traditionally defined as subject matters. They tend to know something of the history, the related science, and the associated technologies.

[6]It is very important for me to draw out principles in virtually every activity we engage in as a means of keeping up-front the understanding that our collective thought has meaning, that our experience matters.

[7]As part of the Teaching for Understanding research project, I not only posed my question about "occasions when you were most fully engaged intellectually . . . " to my students but to students in middle and secondary schools as well as to practicing teachers. One of the discouraging aspects of these queries was that my respondents had had very few such experiences in school.

[8]At a meeting of Harvard scientists, the consensus was that a high school science course should focus on no more than four or five topics, and the associated textbooks should not be more than 100 pages in length. This was a clear view that our focus should be narrowed, that depth is better than breadth if understanding is the goal.

[9]As a senior in college, in a history course rather than a physics course, I read Galileo's *Dialogues*. They were fascinating. I am convinced that, had I read the *Dialogues* when I took my freshman course in physical science, I might have taken more courses in science and might have understood the science I was studying, rather than memorizing formulas for the exams and forgetting most of what I had learned.

[10]However, no topic will reach its generative potential if there isn't *time* to pursue work around it in-depth, to make the large connections, and to develop genuine understandings. Moreover, topics that should be extremely generative will be limited if the content is reduced to textbook accounts with predetermined right answers.

[11]Teachers with whom I work often ask about skills and wonder if the Teaching for Understanding Framework downplays them. Skills are, of course, learned best in a genuine context, not as separate learning activities. I think most of us know this intuitively, yet so much of the discourse surrounding schools and the commercial materials that find their way into schools make skills, learned apart, almost everything. There are many skills that need to be learned to move on to more complex tasks. And we need to teach them—if possible, within the content of our work—*but* they are not understanding goals, even though very important.

[12]While I say more about this in the previous chapter, which focuses even more on curriculum development, it is important to provide students with examples of the kind of work being aimed at. Often students don't complete good work because they don't know what good work looks like.

[13]The demographics of our schools have changed dramatically over the past three decades, but we need to stop making that the reason we can't do more powerful work in the schools. We need to see the circumstances as opening up new possibilities.

[14]I have found in my own work as a teacher, as well as in my observations of teachers working around the Teaching for Understanding Framework, that this performance orientation brings out greater levels of involvement among *many more* students. Those who are good observers, who take in considerable knowledge through those observations, and might not take as much from text, for example, can, in a performance-oriented classroom, publicly share their understandings and become active participants in classroom life.

# Developing and Maintaining Productive Classrooms

Young teachers tend to be particularly concerned about what is now most often called "classroom management" and what used to be called more simply "discipline." The literature they often receive tends to suggest that classroom management is the most critical aspect of teaching and that it is difficult to learn. They also learn early that administrators often judge teachers by how well they control student behavior—that "not smiling until Christmas" is one way of establishing that necessary control. I understand the concerns, but I devote my energy to altering the discourse, thinking about it differently.

I don't particularly like the terms *classroom management* and *discipline* or the literature surrounding them, as it seems to stand apart from concerns about critical instructional purposes and is filled with technical directions and steps to follow, rather than powerful ideas, generative content, and student learning. *Developing and maintaining productive classrooms* seems more appropriate, more useful as a formulation. It creates a more positive discourse.[1]

As we think about productive classrooms, we have considerable experience to guide us. I ask those with whom I work to reflect on such questions as the following: when did the classrooms you were in as students work well, were particularly productive? What did your teachers do and not do? What were the conditions? Such reflections can be enlarged and reconsidered by observing in a broad range of classrooms, a means of "testing" again the remembrances, whether we are just beginning our teaching careers or have been at it for some time.[2]

Preservice and inservice teachers with whom I have worked over the years have explicated the following principles relating to productive classrooms. They are essentially directed to teachers wishing to develop and maintain productive classrooms.

*Be well-prepared for each day.* There is a solid connection between good preparation and a productive classroom. To be well-prepared means having the purposes well in mind, making sure they are placed up-front. In this regard, teaching is intentional. Being well-prepared also means having materials available. The videotape is set and ready to start where we wish it to start. There is no fumbling about, while the students wait for us to find the right clip. The lab is set up. The original documents are ready to be passed out. The in-class library has been organized. The maps are present. The Internet addresses are posted. Being well-prepared also means having reviewed the materials and having rehearsed the flow, the questions to be posed, and the possible responses.

The conception of "being well-prepared" seems so obvious. In interviews with secondary school students, they cite this as extremely important, making clear they are aware of which teachers plan carefully and which teachers do not. Students in Harvard's teacher education program relate each year that their

internship classrooms are the *most* productive when they are teaching the three-
to four-week teaching for understanding curriculum they spent many weeks
developing. It is the segment of their internship in which they are the most prepared. And experienced teachers, when asked about the occasions when their
classrooms were most productive, when their students were the most interested
and the most engaged, cite units with which they were most familiar, for which
they had appropriate materials, and around which they *were the most prepared.*

*Use challenging ideas and materials.* This, again, seems natural as a principle.
The content in classrooms, the curriculum, matters greatly. It is difficult to maintain the interest of students if the ideas under examination—the questions being posed and the materials being used— don't cause students to wonder or
if they make little connection to student interests and the world. Real text—
something other than textbooks, workbooks, and summaries—demands interpretation, leaves room for invention, for multiple possibilities, and creates the
necessary potential for challenge.

Children and young people in the schools understand the nature of what
they are asked to do.[3] They know when the tasks are mostly "busywork," not
to be taken seriously. All of this becomes particularly evident in observations
of upper- and lower-track courses and classrooms, as well as in settings for
those judged "gifted and talented" and those deemed "regular" students, especially in relation to productivity, attentiveness, and cooperation. In upper-
track and "gifted" settings, disruptions are rare. Moreover, in these more advanced settings, the materials and assignments also tend to be more interesting,
more genuine. The projects more often call on the students to invent something, to construct their own experiments and research activities. There is more
often vigorous debate, and students are expected to exhibit some genuine understanding. Why should such experiences be reserved for these students and
not made the norm for all students? I have never witnessed an activity in an
upper-track or "gifted" program that wouldn't be just as good for *all* children
and young people.[4]

*Be reasonably consistent.* The qualification "reasonably" relates to situational
factors; consistency is not an absolute good. Classrooms are more productive
when students know what to expect in terms of teacher expectations and response. Students are often confused here. Sometimes homework matters and
sometimes it doesn't. Sometimes a paper can be rewritten, sometimes not. In some
respects, this formulation also relates to fairness and matters of respect, taking a
genuine interest in *all* of the students, being clear about how work will be assessed
and setting appropriate and agreed-on guides for behavior and being willing to
act on them. Much of the difficulty teachers have is related to not following
through on agreed-on understandings. Thoughtfulness here really matters.

*Be clear about what really matters.* In part, this principle is also closely tied to the need to keep large purposes in mind, guiding the day-to-day activities. It is being constantly aware that our work is about helping our students be successful with their learning. In this regard, it makes little sense to focus energy on all the things we believe our students should have learned before they ended up with us, a lament I hear often. Following the principle, it is always better to just get on with the work, providing the necessary base—that idea of scaffolding the work. If high-quality work matters, then we have to make sure the students know what high-quality work looks like and turn all of our efforts toward helping them reach that high-quality work.

*Show respect for the students.* Students know when they are being respected, when they are seen as persons capable of achieving and being responsible. When students are resistant to teachers and the content, the resistance typically has its base in feelings of disrespect, which leads, not unexpectedly, to student disrespect of teachers. In conversations with high school students who were suspended often and who had a history of difficulty in school, one of my doctoral students noted issues of respect and disrespect being dominant.[5] As it turned out, all of the students had at least one teacher they respected. They spoke of *that* teacher as being *patient,* providing ongoing encouragement: "You can do it," "Do what you can and we'll work from there," "I'll show you some ways to begin." The students described these teachers as persons who sat down next to them and got them started or helped them through something they didn't understand. These patient teachers "listened to the students" and "really cared—working with me was more than obligation." They "understood that we need time to talk—that many of us don't have other adults to talk things through with." For them, these were important signs of respect.

The *caring* theme was also dominant. Caring teachers, they noted, "maintained calm," "seemed to enjoy their work," "didn't embarrass the students," "weren't always looking for single right answers," "took time to help," "didn't just look out for the 'good' students," and "made sure students knew what was going on, why what they were studying was really important." They spoke of how little information students generally have about what is going on in the schools or why what they are studying matters.[6]

The students, however, had much more to say about teachers who didn't respect them or care about them. Such teachers, they noted, were contradictory about expectations and were quick to make judgments—"you are lazy," "you never listen," "you don't care about anything," "you don't want to learn anything." The worst thing, they suggest, is that such judgments were made publicly and were embarrassing. Moreover, such teachers, "spoke ugly to me," made it clear that they "didn't want me in their classes and would prefer it if

I didn't show up," "didn't really know anything about me—why I had difficulty getting to school some days," "didn't believe I really needed to be taught and wanted to learn," "didn't understand that I really did need to graduate from high school and the GED is not what I want." They spoke also about such teachers as being "negative," "indifferent," "not really very happy with their work," and "distrustful of everything I do." New teachers with whom I work understand all of this. They have many similar stories from their own histories as students. They have heard some of this language and this level of disrespect around them in their current schools.[7]

*Know the students.* It is very difficult to teach students well if you don't know them well. [8] What does it mean to know the students? It is obviously more than knowing their names. It means knowing their interests, what they care about, the ideas that motivate them, and how they will likely respond to different situations. It means being in a position as a teacher to anticipate, to plan more effectively, and to understand more fully when to push and when to step back, when to react and when to wait for one or two more lines. Knowing students in these ways comes from observing them, being involved with them in a variety of activities, finding ways to interact with them individually and in small groups on a regular basis, making use of exhibitions (a performance orientation to classroom work), and leaving room for students to chart some of what they do in terms of projects, biographies to read, and experiments to engage in. It means listening to the students and being close to their energy.[9]

A revealing exercise—good for us as teachers to do at least once a year—is to randomly select three or four students on a class roll and ask about each:

- How would I characterize the quality of her thinking?
- What kinds of questions does she raise in the classroom?
- Does she select projects and activities that challenge her to think? What are some examples?
- What does she value the most? What are her most strongly held values and beliefs? Is she aware of those values and beliefs?
- How does she interact with others?
- What is the literature that stirs her?

If our responses appear undifferentiated, it likely suggests that we do not know the students well enough. This kind of exercise is a good means of helping us reflect more on the issue of knowing the students.

*Be physically present—use the space to advantage.* Teachers need to be present when their students arrive, greeting them and acknowledging their presence. Teachers need also to maintain a physical presence, close by, able to speak in normal tones and be heard and serve in ongoing coaching roles, standing alongside the students. Teaching from a distance causes many students to feel distant. I think here of a recent experience shadowing a middle school student through his entire schedule for a day. Each class was different in a number of ways, but mostly in the ways teachers went about their work. The first three classes—French, English, and social studies— were fairly conventional but orderly. The teachers were *in control,* even though the activities were not overly powerful. They moved things along by being active and *very* present, making use of diverse activities and being well-organized. The fourth class was music. It was a more productive class than the three I had observed to this point but also the noisiest. The students were working in groups on lyrics to match the music they had developed earlier. Before the period was over, two groups had performed their pieces. They were humorous and inventive. The teacher moved around the room, coaching each of the groups as he went. Then came math. The students were the same (they traveled together) but *everything* was different. The students were inattentive, surprisingly (given what I had seen in the previous four classes) disruptive, and uninvolved. The teacher was in great distress, the student behavior getting worse with each scream. My student host told me, as the class was disintegrating, that it was usually worse. What was happening? The room was exceptionally large. The teacher didn't greet the students. She passed out to them recent test papers by calling names and the student called came to her for the paper. The process took a long time. The students were naturally unattentive and noisy. She announced that they had done poorly on the test and then proceeded to go over the test items one by one. She worked from an overhead projector that was at least twenty feet away from the nearest student. Others were as far away as thirty to thirty-five feet. Student desks were everywhere. There was no discernable pattern. I didn't think under the circumstances that the student behavior was surprising. I wondered, though, what the fallout would be during the next period— a science class.

The science class turned out to be the most productive class of the day. Students were seated at tables organized in a rectangular fashion. The teacher was seated with them, with no student more than ten feet away. He discussed their recent papers, narrative reports, reading from several of the reports to get from the students the differences they noted. He was trying to develop a set of criteria for good narrative reports of scientific phenomena. He suggested that they rework their papers with the criteria in mind. He then put four live lobsters on the tables. (They were studying crustaceans.) Interest was high as they physically examined and described the lobsters. The teacher posed interesting questions. As the productive class came to an end, he was asked if the lobsters would end up on his dining room table and he said, "Of course, why do you think I like this unit?" The playfulness was just right.

Other principles developed by my students have been *maintaining calmness* and *being culturally aware and sensitive*. The latter is related closely to knowing the students, having a genuine desire to learn from and with them, finding ways to construct an inclusive curriculum, and being conscious of language. It also represents a means of demonstrating respect.

There are always questions about rules. The most important rules relate to civility, respect, and safety. Students understand such rules, as they are easily justified. Many classrooms and schools have *too many rules*. We would all do well in school settings to ask ourselves regularly what the purpose is of each of the rules. Many of the rules create unnecessary problems. They are interpreted by students as arbitrary and disrespectful. Whatever the rules are, however, they should be clear, truly necessary, and up-front.

There are also questions among new teachers about power and authority. Teachers need to be authoritative in educational matters and fair and respectful in their dealings with students. Their greatest authority comes on moral, not status, grounds. In this regard, their seriousness of purpose matters, as do their expressed and acted-on commitments to the students. It is not about being physically imposing; having a loud, booming voice; or being able to threaten students.

Most schools *don't* have serious difficulties over orderliness. This is important to acknowledge, given the media discussions of schools that often focus on violence and disruption. In schools in which significant problems with students exist, the issues often go beyond individual classrooms. They are often settings in which the curriculum in too many of the classrooms is not particularly challenging, teachers are inconsistent about expectations, students are not highly respected, and materials are limited.[10] Even in these settings, there are teachers who do not have difficulties that can't be handled effectively. One lesson here is that schools need to have consistent practices in support of productive classrooms. Teachers need to be in conversation with one another about what matters.

Occasionally students come to believe that teachers who keep their students in rows, who permit no movement, and who don't make use of groups seem to have the most orderly classrooms and are most able to teach without interruption. I suggest to them that this may be the case in some settings, but it is hardly the universal case. Moreover, we need to ask what such structures imply for learning. Some seating arrangements support more passivity than active engagement. Active classroom-based research into what works most productively would be useful. [11]

All of us have some difficult days, when things don't go as well as we would like, when we feel discouraged, sometimes angry at the behavior of our students. On those occasions, it is easy to personalize everything. At such times, we need to bounce back, to become even more prepared, and to keep in mind that the students *do* want to learn (in spite of what they might say and often do), that they desire self-efficacy and respect, and that we must not ever quit on them.

Teaching is not easy. It is something that needs to be worked at all of the time. Seeing it in learning terms is important. This is one of the critical messages of this discussion on developing and maintaining productive classrooms.

---

## FOR REFLECTION

Reflect on classrooms that seem to work well, those you are observing or remember as a student, in which students and teachers interact productively. What are or were the conditions? What do teachers do and not do to get such productive classrooms?

What do you understand to be indicators of teacher-student respect in a classroom?

Think about a teacher who knew you well—your interests, your joys and struggles, and what you cared about. In what ways did this make a difference in how you approached your work with that teacher, the quality of what you did?

Why do you suppose challenging materials and ideas lead to greater student engagement than simple materials? What is your own experience?

Finally, as you think about yourself as a teacher, what kinds of relationships do you want to establish with your students? What will this cause you to be particularly conscious about doing and not doing?

---

[1] I do not want to suggest that there is nothing to learn or think about in the "classroom discipline" literature. In and of themselves, such ideas as follow, which come from a popular primer for new teachers, are not without some merit: "Establish classroom behavior rules at the outset in order to maximize instruction and minimize discipline problems." "Praise works wonders. Reinforce positive student behavior frequently. Students must be complimented when they do good work and behave properly." "Body language and verbal cues can thwart problems. A nod of the head, a glare, and movement closer to the offender often can solve minor problems. A reminder of the consequences for misbehavior is also effective." "Be assertive, but do not get angry when a student disrupts the class." My problem with such delineations is that they suggest teaching as a contest between teachers and students, and they are not tied closely to ongoing teaching and learning contexts. They are also the kinds of ideas that most of my students gather inductively from their focused observations in classrooms, within a genuine classroom they understand. More important,

however, working around such ideas is not where I want to focus my energy, because I want teaching and learning and its mutuality to be the center.

[2]While I ask my preservice students to make a large number of focused observations around which they write and engage in conversation and which are related to the way I think about productive classrooms, I pose many questions that might be more closely related to the ways classroom management/discipline are discussed in the literature. They are as follows: How do teachers get students' attention? What does a teacher do if he or she doesn't have students' attention? Does it work? How engaged and attentive are the students? How do teachers interact with their students? Do they demonstrate respect for the students? What are examples of this? How do teachers keep things moving and handle disruptions? The ongoing observations are helpful.

[3]Knowing this, we should bring our students into more evaluation of our work together. We should ask more often, "How is it going? Did this work? Was this assignment clear? How can we raise the level of intensity and make the work more engaging?

[4]There is more tracking in schools today than has ever been the case before. It grows from the belief that separating students by perceptions of gift, talent, or potential achievement will make the teaching and learning enterprise more productive. The negative effects are overwhelming, especially for those who are struggling to be effective and competent learners. It is a vehicle for maintaining social and academic inequities. This is, however, never easy to work through, as so many of us have completed much of our schooling in tracked courses. It is what we have known and what we may believe has contributed to whatever success we have had. In some respects, tracking is one of the byproducts of large schools and a view that resources limit possibilities. It is almost impossible to track in very small schools—which might be a reason for the greater success of small schools. Can schools that track heavily now go to untracking easily? Obviously not. They can, however, move toward less tracking as a step to untracking. Teachers will also have to develop more inclusive pedagogies. You might want to read Wheelock (1992).

[5]See Capella (1995).

[6]Occasionally I am in settings in which "caring" lacks any connection to genuine academic work and is all about "understanding why these children can't be expected to do high-quality academic work." That is *not* caring; it is *not* the point being made here.

[7]In relation to matters of respect and the need to actively engage the students, Paolo Freire was asked by my students during one of his visits to Harvard about students who were unwilling to take part in an instructional program. After suggesting that the typical response of teachers might be anger or a threat of punishment, Freire considered how it might be seen as another invitation to conversation. He thought we should ask, "Why do you not choose to participate? What do you believe would be more useful, that would help you more in your learning?" That idea of always keeping a dialogue open is important.

[8]This is one of the dominant principles of the Coalition of Essential Schools. It is the reason for its emphasis on the teacher-as-coach formulation and small schools.

[9]It is not surprising that students most remember with fondness and respect their athletics coaches, drama teachers/directors, journalism advisors, and band and choral coaches—those with whom they spent time beyond classes, during late afternoons and evenings, on weekends, in times of great joy and stress. These are teachers who came to know them and their families exceedingly well.

[10]Many of our schools are so deficient in resources, class sizes are so large, and facilities are so poorly maintained that many teachers and students have become demoralized. Schools with these conditions are disproportionately in settings of extreme levels of poverty and racial and linguistic isolation. This should be of great concern to us.

[11]New teachers should have beginning skills as classroom-based researchers, able to use their own classrooms as a critical venue for learning more about teaching and learning.

# CHAPTER 10

# Connecting Assessment, Teaching, and Learning

Chapter 12 presents a historical account of testing. In this chapter, however, I want to share another perspective about assessment that complements the discussion of ongoing assessment related to the Teaching for Understanding Framework yet also goes beyond it, in the process making connections to the intense external pressures currently faced by those who work in schools.

I begin with the premise that preservice and inservice teachers understand with little prompting the importance of assessment for classroom purposes. In focused conversations, they easily return to their own experiences with assessment as students, drawing on occasions when assessment practices were supportive of their learning and when they interfered. My discussions with teachers around this level of assessment have always been productive. Moreover, these teachers also tend to see much of the renewed interest in portfolios in relation to classroom assessment positively, primarily because portfolios make it easier to view work over time, offering that longer view of students' efforts that often gets lost, making student self-assessment more natural, and helping make parent conferences more productive.[1] Portfolios also place more responsibility in the hands of students, something that supports the more progressive teaching agenda that teachers wish to embrace. However, they also know that these directions are time-consuming. While encouraged in many school districts, portfolios haven't become potent enough to lessen the pervasiveness or the power of more external assessment efforts—the various standardized tests that are becoming decisive in regard to student promotion and graduation, as well as in judgments about the quality of schools. It is within this context that the following discussion proceeds. It represents part of the history and the possibilities that I want to make central to my work with teachers.

We need to begin, of course, with the understanding that student assessment is a critical aspect of the educational encounter. At its best, it provides us as teachers with important knowledge of students and their growth as learners, informs our ongoing curricular and pedagogical practice, is a basis for helping students reflect on their own learning, and serves as a window for parents into the power of the teaching-learning exchange involving their sons and daughters.[2] Without careful attention to assessment, the educational limitations for students and for our work as teachers are great.[3]

At the classroom level, there are some principles that might be useful to emphasize. They come from the collective experiences of teachers with whom I have worked over the years (in keeping with my ongoing commitment to collective thought/inquiry). They begin from the premise that assessment in our classrooms is about student growth and not just about *grading* students, a formulation teachers understand and almost universally support.[4] At their best, classroom assessment practices

- Are fair—students understand what the assessment practices are about, are provided the help they need to succeed, and are engaged in the development of clear criteria
- Are seen as opportunities for success—they are ongoing and include work that leads to understanding
- Are more than one thing—students have more than a single opportunity or single mode to demonstrate their learning
- Encourage self-evaluation
- Inform instruction—they help give direction to subsequent steps

You might want to add other principles that grow from your own biographies and from your observations in schools.

Moving to "assessment at its best," whether in classrooms or in relation to schools as a whole, however, has proven over the years to be far more difficult than expected. Assessment in many of our schools, at least the assessment that matters, has often been reduced to various norm-referenced and criterion-referenced tests, essentially, sampling processes aimed at determining what students have retained of relatively small elements of the various subject matters, mostly secondhand versions of students' modes of thinking and meaning making. Such efforts have fostered relatively low levels of teaching and learning while assuring, as Deborah Meier suggests, that "accountability is mostly a myth."[5] It is not encouraging that we are entering another period in which external testing is seen as a lever for making the quality of the teaching-learning exchange higher. There is no history to support such a belief.

Getting closer to students—having access to what they can actually do and seeing their learning over time, systematically and thoughtfully—is the challenge that many teachers have put before themselves in recent years, as they have explored portfolio assessment and the use of exhibitions of performance.[6] These efforts to move beyond the unsituated tests that have been so dominant in the past several decades have begun to take hold in increasing numbers of schools, even though they are not yet the norm.[7]

It is important to note, however, that some of the emerging discourse about portfolios, exhibitions, and situated learning is similar to that which surfaced alongside the progressive education reform period earlier in the century.[8] Teachers then, as now, were engaged in discussions about "documenting children's learning," making "real work" the focus of attention in assessment, getting closer to students' understandings, and helping students make learning their own.[9] However, such directions didn't come to dominate the educational landscape.

What seems clear is that these older progressive changes in the ways assessment was thought about and practiced demanded a major shift in the teaching-learning encounter. It was *not* merely a change in the form of the tests being used or the ways students were graded. It had more to do with (1) students assuming much more active roles and becoming the primary workers, engaged in content issues that mattered to them; (2) a curriculum that was flexibly organized and that called on students to demonstrate their understandings, with uncoverage as opposed to coverage of content assuming prominence; and (3) teachers learning to live with more uncertainty, being willing to alter (generally slow down) their pace, accepting the fact that students might pursue different directions or different topics and possibly learn different things. Those of us advocating for similar directions well understand that such practices are contrary to much of what is currently conventional practice in schools and classrooms.

What we should learn from the earlier experience is that a more productive system of assessment makes sense only if the teaching-learning exchange itself is equally powerful. For example, why develop portfolios of students' work if the work students are asked to complete is primarily sets of worksheets? Why record student presentations if the presentations are on topics about which the students had little choice and have little interest? Why ask students to select "best work" and share with their parents how they selected their work if they haven't had the time or resources to complete work they, in fact, honor and see as important?[10] Having a systemwide spelling list from which there will be a test each Friday, having a standard textbook with unit tests and year-end tests to prepare students for, and having a predetermined set of topics to study along with a list of things every child should clearly know leave teachers with greater certainty and with less to invent, stay in-touch with, observe, and respond to. Without question, it is an easier path. Given the organization of schools, it is not surprising that these less complex patterns of assessment, curriculum, and pedagogy remained dominant in the earlier period, even though there were teachers and schools in a variety of settings that pursued more progressive possibilities. Conditions may not now be so different.[11]

Many schools today are trying to make portfolio assessment and more performance-oriented exhibitions central features, and such directions have become prominent in the educational discourse,[12] yet the overall volume of tests developed beyond schools continues to grow.[13] Although teachers are encouraged through the various curriculum frameworks being developed by the states and the standards under construction by various disciplinary organizations to enlarge their thinking about curriculum and to make student understanding more central, there remain countervailing pressures to standardize what students learn. The path to "assessment at its best" remains as difficult today as at earlier periods of time.[14]

When assessment is discussed, whatever the definitions, the matter of *standards* is quickly brought forward. How standards are understood, however, makes a critical difference. One of the serious problems is that standards are being increasingly described and set by persons far away from classrooms. "Students *will* know X and be able to use X in three different ways by the time they complete grade three" may be thought of as a "high standard," but it may say very little about the power of a student's learning. Reaching such externally established standards may come at the expense of standards that are much more important to the students themselves and, ultimately, to the society as well.

In all the talk about standards, however, there is little acknowledgment that children and young people not only *hold* standards but also need to work toward the *next* level of standards. In the best of learning environments, standards have an active, dynamic quality. Anyone who has spent time closely observing children and young people, paying attention to their intentions, knows that there is this active side to standards. Patricia Carini (1994), an educator-philosopher associated with the Prospect Center in North Bennington, Vermont, notes in this regard:

> By working as I did for most of my professional life in [The Prospect School], I was mainly in the midst of children playing, talking, drawing and making things together. I was struck with how the give and take among children in a climate that offered plentiful time and materials influenced standards. It was a context in which standards could and did arise. It was a context in which standards could also be altered and reworked. That happened because the children were much in the company of each other and in the company of each other's work. In that physically and active workplace with many projects in the making, an idea or process sometimes gets carried further than that had happened before. What hadn't seemed doable proved through some child's efforts to be possible. (p. 4)

My experience is similar. When the first child writes a novel, novels become possible for others. When the first student uses visuals to buttress an argument, more visuals appear with student exhibitions. When the first student engages in an original scientific experiment, original work becomes common. When the first child makes a hook shot on the basketball court, others quickly follow. In active settings, in which students are encouraged to carry out their work in their own ways, to follow their interests and intentions, to take the time to do good work, the work gets better. In this manner, new and more complex standards are being developed all the time. Whenever I discuss this with preservice and inservice teachers, the examples proliferate rapidly. Virtually every participant has an example of such next steps, the higher standards that emerged. They remember when what they were able to do and enjoyed suddenly became for them "not good enough" anymore and they had to move to another level. For the majority, however, these remembrances related mostly to out-of-school activities. At the moment, most of our educational settings aren't organized to support these kinds of possibilities. Until they are, "assessment at its best" will continue to struggle for acceptance.

There is, then, little point in rethinking the assessment process without also rethinking the curriculum—what is taught and learned—and the pedagogy. (This is also the point of the previous chapters in this text.) As I noted earlier, I have seen too many portfolios that are mostly accumulations of simple responses to predetermined questions or writing prompts and lab reports of experiments developed exclusively by others with fairly predictable results. I have also been present for too many exhibitions in which the content has come directly from a textbook and clearly didn't relate to a serious student interest or commitment.[15] The teaching for understanding work, with its performance base, aims to create conditions for the more powerful intellectual work we should want in our schools.

In relation to changes in teaching-learning practices, it needs to be acknowledged that much that has existed in the assessment area has worked against teaching-learning practices that are geared toward intellectual challenge, serious writing, "teaching for understanding." That is why we need assessment practices that are *different* from those that currently dominate schooling. However, the commitment to these more powerful teaching-learning directions, a point I will keep stressing, demands far more than merely *beginning* a different path for assessment. That, too, needs acknowledgment. In settings in which the different assessment processes aren't tied to powerful curriculum content and pedagogy, portfolios (to include exhibitions and performances) will fade rapidly as another thing about which to remark, "It didn't work."[16]

As a means of making the foregoing more clear, I will offer some thoughts about writing and writing assessment—in part because writing has been in the vanguard of the change in pedagogical and assessment practices. Various teacher scholars (such as Don Graves, Peter Elbow, and Nancy Atwell) and programs (such as the National Writing Project and the Bread Loaf School of English) have been particularly active in promoting pedagogical and assessment practices in which student authorship is taken seriously, writing workshops are daily occurrences, students come to understand the power of collective thought through the encouragement of peer conferencing and engagement in evaluation of their own writing, and teachers understand more fully writing as a process and a meaning-making, interpretive activity. In this regard, Elbow (1991) notes that "portfolio assessment . . . is ideal for inviting students and teachers to be allies in the assessment process. Portfolio assessment takes the stance of invitation . . . " (p. xvi). Writing may be the best entry to such a stance.

Where writing activities match our best understandings of writing practice, portfolios have often come to mean something. They have been "measures" of students' growth, vehicles for student self-evaluation, ways for parents to see their children's work over time, a basis for teacher conversations about standards, and the meaning of good writing. In these circumstances, good practice and the presence of portfolios are fully complementary, naturally connected, and reciprocally powerful. While the portfolios in such settings have been useful in parent discussions, in most settings they have not yet become a basis for accountability—reporting to a community beyond the school, attending to the important political agenda that surrounds schools.[17]

For purposes of accountability, writing assessment, even in relation to good pedagogical directions, is still not too far removed from the current technology of standardized testing. Students *do* write for the various district and state tests that have emerged around writing, and this is an improvement, but their writing tends to be unsituated, disconnected from their ongoing work in a powerful classroom. It is usually about one single piece of writing. It is hardly a process that is likely to bring forth from children and young people their best and most committed efforts or to guarantee much teacher or public understanding of children's writing.

Those who are encouraging active writing programs make clear that serious writing for children (as well as adults) takes thought and time. It is almost never far removed from personal experience or interest and disconnected from an individual's way of interpreting the world. They recognize, further, that—in settings where children's ongoing school experience is rich; where teachers read a great deal to children, giving emphasis in writing to authorship and personal style; where active learning is promoted; where the world is permitted to intrude, to blow through the classroom—children have much more to talk and write about. In this sense, writing has a context, and that context is important to understanding the writing that is actually produced. Most current writing assessment efforts, even when they actually ask students to write, make little connection to such contextual matters.

The best person to judge students' writing, who can address constructively their progress as writers (their writing biographies, as it were) is in most cases the teacher closest to them. That shouldn't surprise anyone. It is the classroom teacher who is in the best position to know, for example, the questions a particular student has been raising about various aspects of classroom learning and make reference to, when reading a piece of writing, to previous pieces of writing, to the particular book he or she is currently reading, to the genres or authors the student is most inclined to read at the moment, to a painting just completed, to a new baby sister, to a trip recently taken, to the spring flooding across the community's many glacial lakebeds, to the special meadow colors, or to the classroom's human mosaic. Because this particular teacher's reading eye and thought are responsive to the surrounding context, never really separate from the text under development, he or she can bring about an interpretation. It is *that* teacher, deeply involved with the child as writer, who knows the next question to raise (when to push and when not to) and who can judge the meaning and quality of a piece of that child's writing. It is this outlook that should govern our perspectives about assessment issues as a whole.[18]

An example that has stayed with me for a long time relates to Judy Egan, a teacher with whom Don Graves, a teacher of writing at the University of New Hampshire, worked closely. It is drawn from her article "Thirty Two, Going on Eight" (1981). The subject of Judy's exposition is Heather, an 8-year-old, though Heather in this case is also the prism through which Judy sees her own writing. She writes,

> " . . . This tall eight year old (in my class now for two years) possesses strong will and determination. Heather is definitely in control of herself and, thus, her writing. . . .
>
> Heather's writing patterns had always intrigued me. I recalled thinking what an enigma she was because I was unable to predict her writing mood of the day. Just when I'd think that I'd hit upon a motivator—zap, it would no longer be successful and Heather would refuse to write. Yet other days there was no stopping her. . . . Heather was in control of her own writing. I've only begun to understand this. . . .
>
> Heather is now enjoying writing more. She has gained confidence in her abilities as a writer as she has become more aware of herself through her audience. Her topic choice has expanded to allow her to expose herself as a person. . . . (p. 2–3)

Judy then describes having seen Heather's doll collection, suggesting in the process that she might want to write about it. Heather responded, "But I have so many! It would just be too long!" Judy's fuller text proceeds as follows:

> The following day and for approximately the next fifty, Heather did not write about her doll collection. She continually told me she intended to. I remember pushing, probing, interviewing—all to no avail. She'd work on other pieces but it was obvious through their lack of content, detail and Heather's own lack of enthusiasm that her mind was elsewhere. The doll collection kept coming up (but nothing was started). . . . Weeks passed. More stories were started but never finished. I was finding it difficult to stay in the background but I tried to have confidence in Heather. On March 7th, two months after my initial interview with her, she skipped across the room to hand me a small booklet. Five blank pages lay beneath a cover where she had scribbled, *My Doll Collection,* by Heather.
>
> Now she had made a commitment, yet for the next few days there was always an excuse. "I just CAN'T go in writing today." "I have other plans." "Do I have to?" "It's not a good day for writing." I remember thinking at times that Heather was just being lazy, (hoping) to find an easy way out. . . . My encouragement and conferencing brought few results, perhaps a line or two but

seldom more. . . . Given the choice of another topic, I only received, "Nah, I WANT to do my doll collection."

The days continued to pass by and then, just as anticipated, Heather literally bounced into the classroom one early April morning at 8:15, forty-five minutes before the start of the school. She went directly to the workboard where the children are assigned the first activity of the morning. Finding her name tag elsewhere, she demanded, "But Mrs. Egan, I HAVE to go in writing first today. I have it all planned out!" Over time and through experience, I learned these days weren't to be taken lightly. No matter what my plans for Heather, I would allow her to take control of her morning. The school bell rang—she marched into the writing area—*My Doll Collection* out of her folder—pencil moving—add an illustration—conference—revise—rewrite. Three pages were completed when, to Heather's dismay, lunch stopped the morning's activities. The next two days followed a similar pattern until on Friday she uttered a desperate plea, "I HAVE to finish my book today—before the weekend. I just have to get it out of my head!" Once in the writing area, Heather elicited help, "I need a conference NOW. I have all these ideas to still put in. YOU know how many dolls I have. I feel like my brain is going to explode! " (pp. 3–4)

At this point, Judy describes her conferencing with Heather to help her bring focus to the writing project, as well as the assistance she receives from other classmates:

[An hour later], she was beaming beside me, "Guess what, Mrs. Egan? I finished it, I FINALLY finished it. What a relief!" Bending down to meet her outstretched arms, I took the small book from Heather. She read it to me and then, conferencing it together immediately, she made a few final revisions. Heather's book is now published in its final form between the covers chosen months earlier. . . . Completed on April 16th, three months after the topic found its place in her mind, it has been a little over one month since the piece had been actively started. (p. 4)

The story is full of detail and obvious commitment. Following are a couple of paragraphs—essentially one-fourth of the work:

My Doll Collection
By Heather Thomas

(Dedicated to my Mom)

My auntie and Grandad went to different countries. But my Grandad is dead. He was dead when my Mom was around 7 years old. What does that have to do with it? They brought back dolls from different countries. I have a lot of dolls. I have a favorite doll. She is from China. She had to have a hair transplant. I play dolls with my brother. Darryl was pulling her hair and it came out.

*Holland*

I have a Holland doll. She is pretty. She has a hat that looks weird. It comes up and it makes a point and it makes a curl. She has a blue apron and dress. Her hat is made out of lace. She is pretty. She has blonde hair and when she lays down her eyes close. She has wooden shoes. They are neat. (p. 5)

What would Heather have produced had she been forced to write on April 1st at 10:00 A.M.? What would the judgment have been of a reader sitting in a state capitol or national testing service office about Heather's blank page or to her one or two uninspired lines? How would Judy Egan have felt about it? Would her confidence have been undermined? In the context of Judy Egan's classroom, Heather grew as a writer, producing work honored because it was contextual and responded to by a person who knew Heather and her work over time. And it was this close understanding that gave to Judy Egan the confidence to support this child as she did. With each piece in Heather's portfolio, Judy could tell a story, provide a context.

Implicit in the foregoing example is the understanding that teachers who are deeply committed to being in a position to describe the growth of their children in writing—or in any other learning or subject area, for that matter—are persons who honor children's work as the products of thought, as well as being capable of evoking thought in others. They are authentic readers. While I may have overstressed the point, I have done so out of a belief that any talk of assessment that doesn't understand the importance of teachers being close to their student writers/learners and the surrounding context is doomed intellectually. It will certainly not lead to any lasting change.

This brings me to questions about assessment that go beyond where we are. Having already acknowledged the centrality of the classroom setting, the classroom teacher, and work over time, my principal direction is quite obvious. It is rooted in carefully organized and considered classroom documentation. Classroom teachers can, for example, systematically preserve copies of drafts of children's writing as well as finished pieces as a portfolio. Two or three pieces a month would provide a reasonable collection. Reviewing them periodically can inform a teacher's ongoing efforts to assist particular children. And, of course, this is an important purpose of the portfolio. At year's end, the accumulation—organized chronologically—can be subjected to careful review, with some of the following questions serving as a framework: Over time, what are the salient features and dominant motifs? How much invention exists? Is there complexity? What choices have been made about topics? What connections have been made to ongoing academic and social strengths? What kind of diversity exists in word use, voice, use of conventions? Such a review can be enormously revealing, often providing a perspective missed in the course of addressing work that stands alone. Such a portfolio is almost always revealing to parents, bringing the kind of comprehensive overview that parents often miss as they interact with their children about the school experience.[19] Having the work over time can also assist the children in bringing careful self-evaluation, more solid interpretation, to their own efforts as writers. That kind of opportunity ought not to be missed. This kind of classroom-based review can address concerns about the ongoing support of individual children and it can inform further ongoing instructional practice. It can also serve as a way for a teacher to describe children's growth over the course of a year, as well as inform more fully the children's subsequent teacher or teachers.

For purposes of a fuller schoolwide review, randomly selected children from each classroom in a school might be asked to select five or six pieces of their writing to be read by groups of teachers in the school as a whole—providing the readers with a statement of context for each work. At the level of the school, using such samples as a base, knowing that they were written within the instructional program itself and not apart from it should provide readers with more confidence about describing, for example, the writing of fourth graders in that particular school. And they should be able to do it with good authority. Moreover, such work can serve as the basis for a schoolwide report to parents and the community.

Further, and as important, by coming together themselves in the school as "a community of readers of writing," the teachers involved in this schoolwide review can greatly enhance their understandings of writing, very likely becoming better teachers and facilitators of writing. If assessment efforts don't produce these kinds of results, it is clearly a failed and faulty exercise.

While I focused in this account on writing, what I outlined could as easily have been about science, mathematics, or social studies. The use of portfolios in all the subject matters seems natural. Regarding the notion of teachers coming together as communities of readers of student writing, it should be obvious that teachers can also come together as communities of readers of children's and young people's understandings of history, as demonstrated in their completed projects and performances. Such communities are vital to change in school.

In closing this account, I wish to stress again the importance of tying assessment to powerful learning. Learning that matters is not inert —it has an intimate quality, it can be seen in the world, and it is useful in a way that can be understood. The period of Reconstruction in American history, for example, is not just a debate between conciliators and radicals; it has much to do with the way the United States developed socially, racially, and economically. What if Reconstruction had proceeded differently? Would race relations have taken a different direction? It is out of such questions that authentic content is constructed. Content needs to be at least this powerful to cause us to engage in an equally powerful mode of assessment.

In settings in which students are engaged in work they care about—in relation to questions that matter to them and that move them along in their mastery of a topic, an idea, a formulation, or a design—they also tend to know how they are doing, whether their work is at a beginning stage or quite far along. In such circumstances, they are capable of sophisticated self-evaluation. This is what we should want. Again, powerful content and self-assessment are reciprocal.

We have a chance to make a difference in the schools, to assure that children and young people receive an education of power and consequence. Movement toward assessment practices that "invite students and teachers to be allies," to draw on Peter Elbow, is an important beginning. Connecting that alliance to a powerful curriculum and to a more inquiry-oriented pedagogy of understanding will help us get closer to the schools we need.

---

### FOR REFLECTION

Think about occasions when assessment practices in schools—tests, grades, and responses to work—were particularly supportive of your learning and when they got in the way or were discouraging. What were the differences?

What causes you to say that work you have done is *as good* as you can do? What does this say about the kinds of standards you set for yourself?

Under what conditions do you do your best academic work? What might that say about how you might best organize instruction in your classroom?

Finally, think about a time when you wrote something, completed something, that you could truly honor—that you believed to be of particularly high quality. What were the conditions?

[1]Student portfolios are essentially collections of student work over time. They most often provide selections of what students and teachers consider typical work, challenging work, and representations of particular skills. They often include several stages of projects—from conception, to drafts, to a completed project. They generally include, as well, considerable student self-evaluation. Teachers might also maintain a classroom portfolio that accounts for the curriculum over the course of the year and might include segments of the teacher's planning and writing, along with photographs of students at work and some examples of, as well as reflection on, student work.

[2]I will discuss the connection to parents more fully in Chapter 11.

[3]My hope is that readers will understand how important assessment is and will learn to speak more articulately about its importance. I see this articulateness as a means of arguing for assessment that remains close to the students and the classrooms, rather than the external systems that have become so pervasive and so limiting.

[4]What is best practice regarding classroom assessment ought to be central, as well, to assessment for purposes of accountability, yet the worlds tend to be far different.

[5]See Meier (1995).

[6]Exhibitions are opportunities for students to present their work to other students and adults beyond their classrooms. They are public demonstrations of what they understand and are able to do.
[7]I note "dominance" here as a reminder that students are subjected to more tests today than ever before and they have a greater impact on students and their educational opportunities than was the case in earlier decades.
[8]It is important when engaged in discussions of educational change to acknowledge earlier efforts that are related. Too often, what is currently viewed as reform is spoken about as "new," not tried before.
[9]We should pay attention to this history—learning more about what prevented it from taking hold firmly and broadly. Such knowledge might help us as we try to strengthen current work along similar lines.
[10]A question being asked increasingly in this standards and testing time we are entering is "Why go through all this intensive work if what really counts is a score on an externally developed test?"
[11]I do not mean to be discouraging, but it is important to acknowledge that change in schools is difficult, yet teachers in many schools have created more supportive environments in which work with portfolios is natural and is tied to a powerful set of educational practices. This should provide encouragement that change is possible.
[12]It is hardly possible to read a professional educational journal today that isn't full of support for portfolios and inquiry-oriented teaching. There is, however, a long history of a gap between the rhetoric of educational practice and actual practice. See Cuban (1993).
[13]Haney and Madaus (1989).
[14]I understand that there is considerable optimism about portfolio assessment, but I also see the continuing power of tests and the belief that what students should know, year by year and course by course, needs to be made more explicit. There remains too much distrust in the capacity of teachers in local schools to construct a curriculum in relation to their own students and to engage in assessment that can be understood easily beyond a school community.
[15]Regarding the power of academic content, I have been asking college students regularly for the past eight years to think about a piece of work they completed in their K–12 schooling that they believed was "something wonderful," that they honored as being "the best work they could do," and that they thought was "worthy of saving" and "were eager to share with a parent, grandparent, and others." Most have been unable to bring forward any work that approximated such a description. Some have had one or two examples. In the settings we should strive to create, such work would be more common, the products of powerful pedagogy and assessment.
[16]I should note, however, that Linda Nathan's research in two schools involved with the Coalition of Essential Schools concludes that teachers' commitments to make use of portfolios affect the ways they think about and develop a curriculum, approach the teaching and learning exchange (pedagogy), and interact with students. She argues that portfolio assessment can help bring about pedagogical and curricular change. That assumption is certainly worth more examination. See Nathan (1995).
[17]Schools such as Central Park East and the Urban Academy, along with other Coalition schools, have parents, community people, members of the business community, and local academics act as judges for student exhibitions and portfolios, to assume important roles in the assessment of the academic quality of the schools. In Peacham, VT, children take their portfolios to the local library where they present their work to community people. Such efforts ought to be common. Later in this chapter, I discuss ways that portfolios can be used for schoolwide assessment.
[18]I realize that I have outlined in some respects an ideal context—a thoughtful teacher, who has a materials- and language-rich classroom, has come to know his or her students well, and takes writing seriously. I believe, however, that this ideal is more possible than not, that it could become more the norm if we were to make such an end a priority, providing to teachers the support they need to be the thoughtful practitioners most wish to be.
[19]I meet many parents who, because they see their children's work one piece at a time, lose perspective about their children's growth as writers. Seeing a year's worth of writing, organized chronologically, provides a far different view. Change is typically more evident, and a genuine, constructive parent-teacher conversation is more possible.

# CHAPTER 11

# Relationships with Families

It is essential for us as teachers to keep the families of our students in mind, to consider families as critical partners. After all, parents are their children's *first* teachers and likely over the years their most important partners in learning.[1] Keeping such a view in mind, though, is not always easy to do. New teachers, for example, are so busy considering ways of meeting their students successfully each day that families are hard to think about, but I remind the teachers I work with, as often as possible, that they can't afford to lose sight of the parents if they truly wish to serve their students well.

What do my students, as beginning teachers, see in the schools with regard to parents? Mostly, parents seem absent from ongoing conversations. There are occasional parent-teacher conferences and parent open houses, but enthusiasm for such activities is not typically high, especially beyond the elementary years. Some teachers call parents from time to time—in particular, when things have become extremely problematic with a student—but telephone calls are not the norm. Additionally, my students hear teachers and school administrators lament often, in regard to various aspects of parent participation, about how few parents are actively engaged in the life of the schools as classroom volunteers, tutors, and club sponsors and about *all* the parents who *don't* make it to various meetings at the schools.

Alongside the growing discourse about changing family circumstances—in particular, single parents, working parents, and parents and families under stress—the foregoing conditions and beliefs are quickly translated into "parents don't care about their children." Such views get stronger in settings in which the students and their families come from less advantaged circumstances, seem different culturally, or speak other languages. It is a particularly common refrain in many of the urban schools I visit, and it is discouraging.[2] We must keep such language from our vocabulary and our thought.

The most frequent and sustained contacts between the schools and parents, my students observe, tend mostly to be around special-needs placements (and the related Individualized Education Plans) or serious problems.[3] Announcements occasionally go out to parents but most are administrative—schedule changes, testing dates, special events. They tend to be impersonal, are not meant to enlist a partnership, and do not convey a sense that this school is *their* school. I meet too few parents who believe the schools their children are in belong to them. They are not often provided systematic information about what students are studying, the kinds of questions they are being asked to consider, the projects they are pursuing, or ways that parents might contribute to the project work. Reciprocity is lacking.

We need more constructive relationships between teachers and parents, a more uplifting and more encouraging discourse. It is not helpful for teachers to be so distant from the parents of the children and young people with whom they work, to think in terms of pathology, or to speak of parents as lacking interest in their children or their children's education. Parents *do* care for their children. They want for them the best education, the best life that is possible. That has to be our starting point. That is the place I push preservice and inservice teachers toward.

One of the activities I ask my beginning teachers to engage in is the preparation of a letter to parents or guardians that will be sent out during their first week of full-time intern teaching. (In our program, the full-time clinical experience begins near the end of January each year and continues to the end of May.) It is meant to raise consciousness about parents, to open the conversation about the need for a genuine partnership. I suggest to the students that, based on my experience in and around schools, parents are not particularly clear about what their children are learning in school and about whether their overall education is powerful or trivial, challenging or dull, and that parents should expect their children's teachers to explain fully what the school year will be like, what topics will be studied, what problems will be explored, what is to be read, what kinds of writing will be done, how the teachers will assess their children's progress, and how parents will be kept informed. This seems the least that should be expected. This letter is practically intended as an introduction (of the intern-teacher) to make clear to parents what the coursework will be about, what students will be expected to do, and how parents or guardians might be helpful and as a means for establishing a beginning teacher-parent communication. I view it as a beginning contract with the parents, an initial demonstration of respect.

The letters the students write are read in class, with the listeners assuming the roles of mothers/fathers/guardians. By and large, those serving in listening roles find the letters invitational, informative, and showing evidence of genuine caring for the students. Those acting as parents and guardians tend to be critical of any jargon and call attention to lines that appear to go beyond what parents need to know about (personal information such as the intern's age, sexual orientation, or number of children).[4] The most effective letters have some of the following qualities:

- The purpose and intent are clearly stated.
- The teacher's interest in the students and their learning comes through.
- What will be studied, along with a rationale, expectations, and a means of assessment, is outlined clearly.
- There is a promise of a follow-up letter, possibly a telephone call.
- There is an invitation to the parents to call and or visit the classroom.

What is interesting about the letters is that they provoke considerable conversation about their efficacy within the internship situation. Few of the students' mentors routinely write such a letter, although many consider it more seriously after seeing their interns' letters. Many also suggest that such a letter will place the teacher interns and the content they describe under unnecessary scrutiny, suggesting that parents may object publicly to aspects of the curriculum and may become critical of the choices. I continue to stress, however, the constructive possibilities, the fact that the care we bring to our students' families says a great deal about our care for the students themselves. Parents will notice that.

I encourage the students to consider such letters on a regular basis throughout a school year—prior to new segments of study, in relation to long, complex projects. Such an effort by the teacher is a recognition of the importance of parents. It is an important sign of respect and a way of helping parents engage their children more productively about their school lives. It helps parents move from "what did you do in school today?" and the proverbial "nothing" response to the possibility of asking, for example, about their interview of a recent immigrant, their research on cell division, or their solar-powered machine. Those with whom I work understand the importance of such conversations in the home. They also understand that the additional information makes parent-teacher conversations more productive.[5]

It is very rewarding to hear from graduates each year who describe in great detail their letters to parents at the beginning of the school year (in August or September). Many describe getting "thank you" letters from parents. They also discuss telephone calls from parents who have described aspects of their experience around some of the topics to be studied and have offered to share those experiences and related resources. They tell me after many such experiences, "It is one of the best, most productive things I have ever done."

I also introduce to my students some of my work with parents in response to their questions about what they should expect to go on in the schools. As one way of helping parents with this, I have prepared a document for discussion on *developmentally appropriate classrooms*.[6] My students find the document useful, something for them to think about, even an outline of ideas for them to address in a series of letters that they might send to parents or in conversations with parents. I indicate that I suggest to parents that they use the formulations as a basis for conversations with their children, asking, for example, "How much discussion occurs in your classes? Do you have enough time to do the best work you are capable of? Do your teachers respect your viewpoints? How well do your teachers know you, what you care about, and your interests? Do teachers read your work carefully? Do your teachers try to connect your work to other subject areas, to what you see beyond school?" Such conversations, I suggest, also enable parents to interact more productively with teachers. I ask new as well as experienced teachers to be prepared for such discussions.[7] *The developmentally appropriate classroom*[8] statement, which addresses the questions parents should expect, is as follows:

*Respect for the Students*
- Students' interests are important starting points for learning.
- Students' ideas and work are taken seriously.
- Students are understood to be actively in search of knowledge. Their questions, constructions, and observations are seen as part of the process of building knowledge.
- Students do as much talking as the teachers.
- Students have many opportunities to choose—the literature they read, the projects they do, the activities they participate in.
- Students have time to engage in work they can honor, work that means something for them.
- Students work cooperatively, helping each other.
- Individual, racial, linguistic, and cultural differences are celebrated. They are seen as ways of enriching the students' lives.

*Stimulation of Thought and Imagination*
- As students move beyond information to understanding, teachers respond to their ideas and questions in ways that extend their learning rather than encourage rote answers.
- Teachers (and students) ask more open-ended questions than yes-or-no questions. Teachers spark exchanges by saying, "What if you were to do it this way?" "How else could you do it?" "Is there another viewpoint?" "Why was it like that?" "How could it have been different?" "Why should we care?"
- Considerable attention is given to the processes of exploration and discovery, inquiry and investigation.
- Teachers encourage risk taking and provide a safe, supportive environment for it.

*An Abundance of Chances to Learn*
- Regardless of the subject area under study, all forms of communication are used: reading, writing, listening, and speaking. Classrooms are full of language.
- Classrooms are inviting and colorful, with a variety of interesting materials. The students know where these materials are kept and how to use them.
- Teachers help the students make connections among the various areas of study. As much as possible, knowledge is presented as an interconnected web, not as a handful of distinct categories that are unrelated to each other.
- Teachers keep learning, and they share what they learn with their students. They demonstrate that learning is a lifelong process and a source of delight.

- Notes, letters, poems, song lyrics, and all other forms of written information and expression are highly visible in classrooms.
- Students read real books by identified authors, not just committee-produced "readers" and textbooks.
- Teachers know that learning takes place over time and that students need numerous and related experiences before they are able to absorb critical concepts and to use these concepts effectively as the basis for new learning.

*Opportunities for Self-Expression and Connections to Life Outside School*
- Students have frequent opportunities to participate in the creative and expressive arts: music, drawing, storytelling, drama.
- Physical activities are seen as important for maintaining health as well as for building self-confidence.
- Parents are welcome in and around the school. They are encouraged to be active participants in their children's education.
- Teachers make an effort to connect students' lives in school to experiences outside of school, such as organized sports activities, films, work, and cultural activities.

In small schools, teachers can sit together and talk about the importance of such "developmentally appropriate classrooms" and the need to communicate effectively with parents. Efforts to make the connections, though, have to proceed regardless of school size. Letters are a beginning. Having family conferences can also be useful, especially if they are scheduled for the convenience of the families. Further, making use of parent interests, skills, vocations, and avocations can enrich schools and classrooms and can build greater levels of parent-teacher and parent-school relationships.

While acknowledging that school-parent connections have generally declined, I suggest that the connections can be rebuilt and revitalized. This will demand that those in schools assume much of the responsibility for the reconstruction of the partnership. The starting point is teachers and classrooms.

---

❧

## FOR REFLECTION

Reflect on the involvement of *your* parents or guardians in the schools you attended. Did they feel welcome or unwelcome? Why?

You might reread the practices outlined in the developmentally appropriate classroom statement, asking yourself what it would take to develop such a classroom.

Finally, consider drafting a letter to your students' parents (related to a classroom you are now working in or one that might come in the future). What would you want to say about yourself, the subject matter, the activities, your expectations, assessment, and the like? How would you expect parents to respond to your letter?

[1]Teachers at the elementary levels readily acknowledge this premise. It needs continuing acknowledgment. Adolescents need their parents every bit as much as younger children, even though the needs are different. Teachers in the middle and secondary schools often suggest that the content being taught, now more precise, is often beyond what parents are familiar with or can be helpful around. This speaks to a need for teachers to be even more in touch with parents, helping them be in a position to be more helpful to their children.

[2]There is no question that traditional forms of parent involvement in schools (particularly among mothers) have declined. This says something about changing social and economic conditions. But to extend this to parents "not caring about their children" seems self-defeating. Limited participation in schools by parents should not be seen as a sign that parents are not interested in their children or their education. If schools were to make participation a genuine priority, and if there were commitments to meet parents more on these terms, participation would be greater. Texas Interfaith, a community-organizing enterprise, has managed to help schools enlarge parent participation to extraordinary levels in settings of poverty and disenfranchisement. The key has been to get people in the schools out to community discussions in neighborhood churches, homes, and community centers. Once relationships have been developed in these "home" settings, parents begin coming to the schools. Some new thinking about how to re-establish a partnership is needed in many of our school settings.

[3]Teachers are often surprised when they do a careful log of all contacts with parents to note how much of it has a negative origin.

[4]Parents will come to know more about the teachers through face-to-face interaction.

[5]I share with these new teachers my own experience as a parent of seven children, which translated into 350 teachers—although some overlapped several children. The elementary grades were full of contacts. There were weekly letters describing activities, what was being studied/learned, and ways we could extend learning activities at home. But everything changed after that (which matches the research literature about parent contacts). From that point on, there was only one substantive letter from a teacher about a course/unit of study, homework, and overall purposes. That was a math teacher at the middle school level and involved one of our children. The letter told us about the teacher, that she had been teaching for fifteen years, that the course would involve particular algebraic concepts, that homework would be assigned each Tuesday and Thursday and would likely take about one hour, that she would call before the school open house (scheduled for a month later) to check in with us, and that we could call her at home if we needed to on certain days and at certain times. The letter provided a good entry into conversation with our son. We would have felt more like learning partners had we received this kind of letter and attention from all of our children's teachers.

[6]To speak of developmentally appropriate classrooms suggests the need to place students at the center, to ask, "Is this an 'appropriate time' to introduce a particular subject matter, to ask students to do particular kinds of projects?"

[7]Not all parents are this engaged or know how to be this engaged, but our task is to help them get to this point. One model of this is the weekly letter sent to all parents at the Mission School in Roxbury (Boston) by the principal, Deborah Meier. It actually takes up the kinds of issues outlined in this statement. It is educational and challenging. It addresses matters of controversy. It explores school practices and ways of extending students' work into the home. It stimulates good, ongoing conversation.

[8]Included here is the document related to secondary schools.

# Standardized Testing

*How Did We Get Here?*

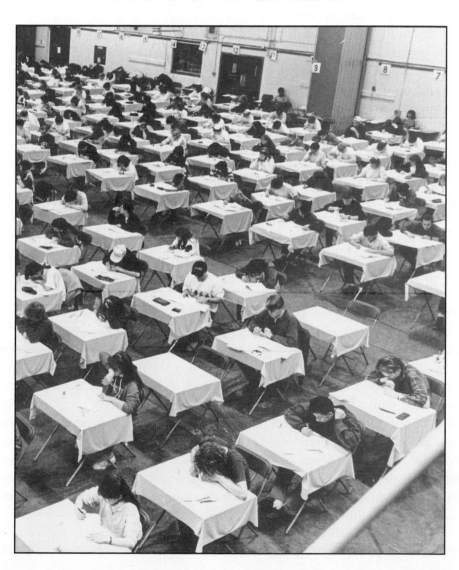

Those who go into teaching learn early on that various forms of standardized testing have come to assume a dominant place in their schools, often determining student placement, promotion, even graduation. Moreover, they often receive admonitions from school administrators about "getting the students ready" to take the various tests, coming to understand that their schools *need* to show improvement over the previously taken tests. They even learn in some settings that they are being evaluated on the basis of how well their students do on these tests. Not surprisingly, they ask, "Where did all this testing come from?" "How did it become so important?" "Why should these tests count more than my ongoing classroom assessment?" These are important questions that deserve some response.

Given the way testing has proceeded, over the years I have tried to provide preservice and inservice teachers some historical perspective about tests and testing as a means of helping them consider more fully what they face. Having an understanding of the history doesn't mean that the tests will not continue to matter too much, but teachers may be in a better position to help students and their parents understand what the testing is about and it might well help teachers engage more productively the fuller discourse about these tests and their uses. Teachers might even help lessen the power of these tests.

As we reach the end of this twentieth century, virtually every state is engaged with legislation and regulations to produce and administer tests at grades 3 or 4, 8, 10, or 11 for purposes of promotion and graduation. These tests are supposed to be aligned with the various curriculum frameworks and learning standards that the states, supported by the various subject matter associations, have produced. The expectation of policy makers is that these "high-stakes" tests will bring about a major improvement in the schools. And students are being told—although mostly warned—that their school lives will change dramatically, that how well they do on these tests will matter greatly.[1]

We certainly need more powerful schools. I meet few people in schools who disagree with the need. However, framing the need around "standards" and more tests doesn't necessarily move us in the direction of those powerful schools. I worry that standards will become little more than standardization and the tests will serve little real purpose, leading mostly to cynicism. Nonetheless, because tests for purposes of promotion and graduation are currently taking hold, popularized heavily through various media outlets as well as the educational press, it might be useful to offer first a historical account of these kinds of certifying (for purposes of promotion and graduation) tests before moving on to a fuller history of standardized testing.[2]

Historically, certifying examinations had their beginnings in this country in the 1840s as the Boston Schools instituted a common secondary school examination. In 1877, the New York legislature established a system of examinations "to furnish a suitable standard of secondary school graduation." By the turn of the century, most states had testing programs affecting promotion and graduation.[3]

These early examinations were not of the multiple-choice variety—that technology developed most notably in the post-1910 period—but their effects were similar. What were the consequences of this early testing? The tests had particularly negative effects for African Americans, immigrants, and the poor.[4] Their failure rates tended to be high and few went into the secondary schools. At the turn of the century, though, such a circumstance was not viewed adversely by educators, politicians, or societal leaders. A wide range of social, cultural, and racial inequalities was tolerated, and this testing was accepted as a legitimate means for selecting students into and out of educational opportunities. Equality of educational opportunity as a matter of public policy is, after all, a post–World War II development.

Was it disastrous at the turn of the century for an individual not to complete high school? While completion of the secondary school clearly opened up many opportunities inaccessible to those without a high school diploma, the lack of a high school diploma did not prevent most individuals from gaining an economic livelihood or place them in a radically different social position than most of those around them. After all, less than 10 percent of those who began school in 1900 completed high school. As school attainment expanded after World War I, not having a high school diploma became an ever increasing burden, but it wasn't until almost 1950 before it became a catastrophe.[5]

The overall increases in school attainment during the first half of the twentieth century took place as statewide examination systems that related to promotion and retention began to decline in number. By 1950, they had virtually disappeared. Accompanying the increased levels of attainment—and the growing commitment in America to expanding educational opportunities for all Americans—school programs also became more diverse. A natural consequence of this diversity was, as noted in Chapter 3, that high school diplomas lost whatever common meaning they had. Surprisingly, this consequence went unnoticed, to be interpreted in the 1970s as a sudden decline in standards.

What effect did the certifying tests have on curriculum? The evidence is that the tests influenced significantly what was taught. The diaries of early twentieth-century teachers were filled with accounts of the long periods in which they prepared students for the state examinations, in the process giving up what they considered to be more engaging for the students.[6] The *Regents Inquiry into the Character and Cost of Public Education in New York State* reported in 1936 that the Regents Examination had, in effect, become the curriculum.

What didn't appear on the examination was not taken seriously by teachers or students. The broad goals of locally established curricula were given little attention. George Madaus and Peter Airasian (1977), who have examined the history of certifying examinations in the United States as well as Australia and Europe, comment: "Faced with a choice between one set of objectives which are explicit in the course outline and a different set which are explicit in past certifying examinations, students and teachers generally choose to focus on the latter. This finding holds true over different countries and over many decades. . . . Most studies have found that the proportion of instructional time spent on various objectives was seldom higher than the predicted likelihood of their occurrence on the external examination." (p. 85)[7].

Currently the argument is that the problems in the past were technical, that we now know how to produce better tests, that the new standards are much more challenging than the older standards and are not as narrow. Teaching to the new standards, it is said, will not be as confining to teachers, that the newer tests go beyond information recall, asking students to use their acquired knowledge and understandings to do something—describe how they would set up an experiment, make sense of a historical document, interpret a stanza of poetry, or write with several different audiences in mind. There is, in fact, *some* of this; however, most items on these various standardized tests remain well within the longstanding technology of testing, primarily to support the mechanical scoring procedures. They still seem to be limited instruments with too much influence. I don't believe much will be different, that the negative effects will be as they have been, and school improvement will remain a serious challenge, much less amenable to these technical efforts to change them than to other possibilities that those in schools could more productively devise.[8]

It is important to gain some historical perspective of standardized testing in order to understand the intensity of debate that surrounds it, even though I do not wish to imply that the context today is necessarily the same as that which existed in the early years of this testing. There are some important differences.

Standardized testing, as we have come to know it, took form at the turn of the twentieth century. As I noted in Chapter 3, this was a time of rapid change in many aspects of American life. Immigration was reaching new heights, especially with a heavy influx of southern and eastern Europeans who were considered less assimilable than earlier immigrants; industrialization, aided by a growing faith in science and technology, was firmly rooted; what seemed an uncontrollable urban expansion paralleled the increased levels of immigration and industrialization; and schools were under intense pressures to enroll larger percentages of the school-age population, especially at the secondary school level.

In this period of change, psychology and education, as areas of academic inquiry, long stepchildren to more traditional academic fields, turned increasingly to science and technology as their base. It is not surprising that practitioners within these related fields adopted statistical procedures and scientific methods to support their work. The standardized tests they developed met many of the conditions of science as they were understood at that time. Moreover, and possibly more important in the early period, test construction and use appeared to support many of the cultural assumptions of the day. In a society clinging to egalitarian views, how could the great differences among people with regard to education, status, and power be explained? The Social Darwinists suggested that such differences existed because intellectual attributes among individuals and groups—racial, ethnic, cultural—varied significantly. The tests quickly "bore this out." Individuals and groups could, it seemed, be classified on the basis of "scientific measures," and selection processes could be established without any "blemish on democratic philosophy." While I would hesitate to suggest that Social Darwinism was the predominant philosophical orientation at the beginning of the century, it clearly had substantial support in the society—certainly among those who held privileged positions—and was actively called on to buttress the development of standardized tests.

Alfred Binet, an early champion of experimental psychology, is generally acknowledged as being responsible for legitimating standardized tests. In the years that followed the passage of compulsory education legislation in France (1881), Binet raised questions about the degree to which *all* children could benefit from regular school activities. At the turn of the century, Binet advocated special classes for those possessing "limited ability." Along with Theodore Simon, Binet was invited in 1904 by the Ministry of Education to develop an identification process that could be used to select children for special classes. Simon and Binet capitalized on the opportunity to develop a series of tests. The procedures they used for norming and validation were similar to those used today. (Another similarity exists in the results. Then, as now, scores reflected the social-economic structures.) While Binet was not immune from using such phrases as "mental ability" in relation to his test results, he had reservations about interpreting an individual's test results narrowly: he did not believe, for example, as many of his followers did, that the tests measured fixed *intellectual qualities* that were unamenable to further training.

After Binet's death, Lewis Terman of Stanford University began a revision of the Binet testing process. The Stanford-Binet test, published in 1916, was the result. In order to bring more specificity to the results, Terman attached a score, an "index of brightness," which helped popularize the term "Intelligence

Quotient." In *The Measurement of Intelligence* (1916), Terman described the "potential" for the test in a clear fashion:

> Intelligence tests will bring tens of thousands of these high grade defectives under the surveillance and protection of society. This will ultimately result in curtailing the reproduction of feeble mindedness and in the elimination of an enormous amount of crime, pauperism and industrial inefficiency. (pp. 6–7)

Those with IQ scores in the 70–80 range were of particular concern to Terman. He wrote further in *The Measurement of Intelligence*:

> [Such intellectual deficiencies are] very common among Spanish-Indian and Mexican families in the southwest and also among Negroes. Their dullness seems to be racial; or at least inherent in the family stocks from which they come. . . . Children of this group should be segregated in special classes. . . . They cannot master abstraction, but they can often be made into efficient workers. . . . From a eugenic point of view they constitute a grave problem because of their unusually prolific breeding. (pp. 91–93)

Does the foregoing sound familiar? It should. Such arguments, although less direct in tone, are not uncommon in the literature produced more recently by Arthur Jensen, William Shockley, Richard Herrnstein, and Charles Murray.[9]

Terman—along with others such as Henry Goddard (the Vineland Training School in New Jersey) and Robert Yerkes (Harvard), who had similar interests in "tests of intelligence" and later "tests of achievement"— eventually saw southern and eastern Europeans as also demonstrating mental deficiencies. It is not surprising that all three were active in the eugenics movement and were politically active in efforts to stem the flow of these "inferior" southern and eastern Europeans who were entering the United States as immigrants.

Goddard went to Ellis Island in 1912 to administer the Binet test, as well as others that he devised, to new immigrants. The results were hardly surprising, although to read Goddard's account it was shocking: he judged 83 percent of the Jews, 80 percent of the Hungarians, 79 percent of the Italians and 87 percent of the Russians as "feeble minded."[10] It was Goddard who also provided in 1912 the classic genetic tracing of the Martin Kallikak family, a set of pictures depicting ugliness getting more ugly (and more feeble-minded) over time. This reference could be found in psychology texts as late as 1955.[11]

When the United States entered World War I, Yerkes, then president of the American Psychological Association, proposed on behalf of several of his colleagues (including Terman and Goddard) that psychologists could perform a service by administering tests to draftees that might aid in their military placement. Tests were given to 1,700,000 men. While they were not used by the Army for purposes of placement, they did solidify the legitimacy of standardized testing and "improve" the technology of psychometrics.

The data from the testing were reported in 1921 by The National Academy of Sciences under the title of *Psychological Examining in the U.S. Army* (1921) and analyzed further in *A Study of American Intelligence* by C. C. Brigham (Princeton University Press, 1923). The results were predictable. Whites scored considerable higher than blacks; individuals from Scandinavian and English-speaking countries scored significantly higher than those from Latin and Slavic countries. Data showing correlations between the test scores and the length of time the tested individual had lived in the United States were essentially dismissed.[12]

The results of all of this testing were influential in the passage of the 1924 Immigration Act, which placed discriminatory restrictions on the immigration of non–Anglo-Saxon populations. It was a major victory for psychologists such as Terman, Goddard, Yerkes, and Brigham. In fairness, however, it should also be said that the victory was not theirs exclusively. There were many millions of Americans who were convinced about the need for restriction and did not need the psychological test scores for confirmation.[13]

W. E. B. DuBois, writing in *The Crisis* (1920), denounced the tests as one more effort to prove "scientifically" that northern Europeans were superior to all others. With regard to the Army tests and "Negroes," he noted:

> For these tests were chosen 4,730 Negroes from Louisiana and Mississippi and 25,052 white recruits from Illinois. The result? Do you need to ask? . . . The intelligence of the average southern Negro is equal to that of a 9 year old white boy and that we should arrange our educational program to make waiters, porters, scavengers and the like of most Negroes. (p. 1183)

Journalist Walter Lippman (1922, 1923) also raised a voice of protest about the tests and the meanings derived from the various scores, his outlet for criticism being the *New Republic* during the 1922–1923 years. In an early commentary (15 October 1922) he wrote, "The real promise and value of the investigation which Binet started is in danger of gross perversion by muddleheaded and prejudiced men" (p. 215). In the 15 November 1922 issue of the *New Republic*, Lippman wrote:

> Intelligence is not an abstraction like length and weight; it is an exceedingly complicated notion which nobody has yet succeeded in defining. . . . If the impression takes root that these tests really measure intelligence, that they contribute a sort of last judgment of the child's capacity, that they reveal "scientifically" his predetermined ability, then it would be a thousand times better if all the intelligence testers and their questionnaires were sunk without warning in the Sargasso Sea. (p. 297)

Lippman (29 November 1922) closed his original series of six articles on intelligence tests by suggesting that psychologists back away from their "pretentious" directions and "save themselves from the humiliation of having furnished doped evidence to the exponents of the new snobbery" (p. 10).

Terman's responses to Lippman also deserve reading. They are similar in content to what is produced by many contemporary apologists—namely, appeals to scientific authority, ridicule, and non-sequiturs. In one response (29 November 1922), Terman suggested, along with considerable ridicule, that Lippman had "some kind of emotional complex." Lippman's response is magnificent:

> Well, I have [an emotional complex] about this business. I admit it. I hate the impudence of a claim that in fifty minutes you can judge and classify a human being's predestined fitness in life. I hate the pretentiousness of that claim. I hate the abuse of scientific method which it involves. I hate the sense of superiority which it creates and the sense of inferiority it imposes.[14]

However, Lippman's charges, although powerful in tone, were not particularly influential. Tests, those producing IQ scores and those ever expanding achievement scores, proliferated rapidly in the 1920s and 1930s. They fit many school needs of the day by providing external procedures to justify promotions in the schools—now more committed to age-grade patterns than ever before. That they justified the continued preeminence of the privileged in American society seemed not to be a problem for most educators. And, as was noted earlier, they fit the scientific ethos of the period.[15] Progressives, who generally supported more democratic views of schooling, tended to give passive approval to the testing activities, especially in the 1920s. To attack "science" was not consistent with their basic approaches to education. In the 1930s, however, there were some shifts in progressive thought as efforts were begun to have standardized testing examined within the Progressive Education Association. But the Progressive Education Association, the principal outlet for progressive ideas, had begun its intellectual twilight by this time.

Were there other forces besides eugenics and the scientific ethos that helped make testing such a popular enterprise? There was a belief, expressed often in the early literature on testing, that the tests represented a democratic, objective process for selection into colleges and into particular professions, for passage to new grade levels, and for the awarding of academic honors. As some egalitarians argued, a test score removed the possibility of social status alone or faulty, prejudiced, teacher or school judgment determining one's entry, for example, into the elite schools. (Even though the elite schools received the same students after standardized testing as before standardized testing, the illusion of democratic practice survived the 1920s and persisted well into the 1950s and early 1960s.) How many times have we heard about the child who came from a lower socioeconomic and minority background who was singled out because of high test scores and given academic opportunities that might not otherwise have been available? There have been *many* such cases but, when we consider all of the individuals of lower socioeconomic and minority background who owe increased levels of academic opportunity and altered social or economic status to test scores, the numbers were surely small in the decades between 1920 and 1950 and there is little to suggest that conditions have changed.[16]

Ralph Tyler (1974), one of the dominant educators of the middle decades of this century, in his important critique on testing, commented that standardized testing began "as a means for selecting and sorting people and the principles and practices of testing that have been worked out since 1918 are largely the refining of means to serve these functions rather than other educational purposes (p. 4). "Sorting and selecting," as Tyler would suggest, were viewed in the early period as natural and necessary functions of the schools, resulting in a situation in which tests designed for such purposes would not be questioned seriously.

A stable force in the early testing movement was E. L. Thorndike (a prominent faculty member at Teachers College, Columbia), who, in the long run, may have had a greater longstanding influence on testing than the eugenicists. His *Introduction to The Theory of Mental and Social Measurement*, published in 1904, was an important contribution to the measurement field. The *Thorndike Handwriting Scale*, produced in 1909, was the first popularly used standardized test in the public schools.[17]

"Whatever exists at all exists in some amount" was a classic Thorndike phrase and one that says a great deal about Thorndike's basic approach to testing. In "Nature, Purposes and General Methods of Measurement of Education Products" (1918), Thorndike commented about some of the problems that were beginning to surface as early as 1917–1918: "[Those] directly in charge of educational affairs have been so appreciative of educational measurement and so sincere in their desire to have tests and scales devised . . . [that quality is being sacrificed]. . . . Opposition, neglect, and misunderstanding will be much less disastrous to the work of quantitative science in education than a vast output of mediocre tests for measuring this, that and the other school product, of which a large percent are fundamentally unsound . . . (p. 19). Thorndike continued to raise concerns throughout the 1920s (a veritable boom period for the development and marketing of tests) about the poor quality of tests, the uncritical acceptance of test scores, and what he perceived to be the unjustified judgments being made about individuals. His goal was the production of *better* tests and more knowledgeable test use. While it is possible to disagree with Thorndike's basic assumptions about education and learning, one must respect the way he carried out his commitments.

The technical quality of tests improved in the decades following the Depression, and these improvements are noted often in the educational literature. The eugenics advocates who were prominent in the formative years were gone, replaced by a growing corps of psychometric technicians. Norming and validation procedures became increasingly more sophisticated, and testing became a part of the "conventional wisdom" of schools.[18] Debates were few and criticism almost nonexistent.[19] In fact, the literature has very little criticism until the 1960s. At the same time, the standardized tests, while often basic to many of the positive and negative decisions made about students, were not viewed in the post–Depression years as overbearing. They did not appear to dominate curriculum or teaching. The *amount* of testing was not large in most districts, having what appeared to be a benign quality in many.[20]

Standardized testing received a boost with the ascent of *Sputnik,* as questions about the quality of schools accelerated. In 1965, with the passage of the Elementary and Secondary Education Act, however, testing, and the industry supporting it, exploded.[21] With the heavy influx of federal dollars came increasing demands for evaluation. And, unfortunately, in most instances evaluation became synonymous with outcome data produced by standardized tests. In part, this occurred because standardized tests and the technology supporting them were in place and evaluation paradigms that might have been more appropriate were not well developed or seemed to lack the "scientific construct" that was increasingly demanded as the evaluative process became submerged by a "single-score" mentality.

We are now in a period in which standardized tests *are* a major issue in schools. (It should be noted again that intelligence tests are not as much an issue now as they were. Their use has been diminishing rapidly over the past twenty-five years.) The level of criticism has grown significantly, related closely to the volume of testing that occurs. Test producers have been surprised at the harshness of the criticisms, feeling that the technical quality of their products is higher now than at any time in the past. They argue that the problems, and they now acknowledge that there are problems, are related to *use* or, more specifically, misuse.[22] While these are certainly considerations, the issues are deeper than use and misuse. Teachers and parents in many settings are going back to fundamental questions about the *purpose* of the schools, the ways in which children's development is being supported. They are asking the following questions: Do the tests support children's development? Do they bring greater quality to the teaching and learning exchange? Do they contribute to greater collaboration among teachers or among teachers and parents?

By the early 1970s, the formulation of "accountability" had taken root. Accountability was an engineering construct that state legislatures began to adopt as a basis for determining the success and failure of educational programs, as well as the degree to which money was being spent well or poorly in the schools. With standardized tests as the accountability anchor point, schools increasingly began to be involved in fall and spring testing and to get deeply enmeshed in numerical conceptions of "growth."[23]

The expectation was that children's scores on standardized tests would advance "one year" for each year they were in school. Dependent on a grade-level equivalency metric, a construct that test makers themselves argue against, teaching to tests—in particular, the spring tests—became for many teachers and administrators "a political necessity." Henry Dyer (1971), possibly America's most respected authority on testing in the post–1950 period, was especially critical of this development—in large measure, because he believed the grade-level equivalency scores that fueled it had no meaning. He wrote that they were "statistical monstrosities . . . which lure education practitioners to succumb to what Alfred North Whitehead called 'the fallacy of misplaced concreteness'" (p. 15).

The 1970s accountability movement, as it was being developed, led quite naturally and easily to the competency/basic skills testing movement of the 1980s. This testing, however, tended to make more use of criterion-referenced than norm-referenced tests. Virtually all state—and increasingly, local—district assessment programs are of the criterion-referenced variety. Similar in format to norm-referenced tests, they are generally written to test a set of specified learning objectives. Rather than being concerned with how a student's score (or the average score from a classroom or school) deviates from a norm, they focus on how far a student's score (or the average score from a classroom or school) deviates from a fixed standard. It might be determined in a state or local district, for example, that the standard is 70 percent. Those scoring *above* 70 can be said to have met the standard, while those below have not (although we need to recognize that the standard is arbitrary).

Because these tests tend to be state-specific, they offer no basis for state comparisons. The National Assessment of Educational Progress (NAEP)—essentially a criterion-referenced test—has long been engaged in national sampling, but not until the past few years, with a new mandate, did it ever test enough children to make any state comparisons. But, unlike other national-oriented tests such as the Metropolitan Achievement Test, the Stanford Achievement Test, the California Test of Basic Skills, the Iowa Test of Basic Skills, and the SRA Achievement Tests, which are the most used of the tests, the NAEP does not produce any individual student scores.[24]

We are in an era in which more children take more standardized tests than ever before in our history. Those who completed their schooling before 1960 likely took no more than three standardized tests in their entire school careers. Today it is commonplace for a student, especially in a large urban community, to take at least two each year, possibly twenty-four to thirty over a school career.

And it needs to be understood that this does not mean two 20- to 40-minute periods in the year. Typically a single standardized testing battery occupies several days, and in most schools it occupies several weeks of preparation time.
Further, while still not as universal as testing in the intermediate and secondary
school levels, testing now involves more children in the preschools and in the
primary grades.[25] In an increasing number of states and communities, it is "high-
stakes" testing in that children are, as a result of a single score on a test, often-
times kept out of a kindergarten or first grade, retained in one of the primary
grades, or labeled and placed in one or another special education program.[26]

The motivation behind the early testing is understandable, essentially the
belief that many of the problems of failure in later grades can be dealt with in
a "relatively painless manner" by identifying children who might profit from
"more time to mature" and "more practice with academic skills" or from placement in a specialized setting, where they can receive "remedial" help. The evidence to support such a belief is not, however, convincing. Lorrie Shepard's
(1987) research makes clear that children see the retention and special placement, even at these early ages, as "a failure" and that the achievement gains
that come with retention are most often not sufficient to justify the decisions
made. And it ought to give us pause that those who bear the brunt of the retention and "special" placement tend to be poor, minority, culturally different,
and limited English language users far beyond their actual number in the
school-age population.

Most states that have instituted "high-stakes" testing programs have made
grades 4, 8, and 11 the determining points for decisions regarding promotion
or retention. The presence of such tests in the upper grades, however, has an
effect on pedagogical and curricular practices in the lower grades. Shepard
(1987) notes: "Promotional gates at third grade or sixth grade are translated
downward into fixed requirements for the end of first grade. If a first grade
teacher is . . . reprimanded (by a principal) for having children below national
norms on standard tests, this teacher communicates to the kindergarten teacher
her unwillingness to accept children for first grade who are not ready to read"
(p. 7). Promotional gates at grades 8 and 11 have a similar effect.

Large numbers of teachers believe that the tests—whether norm-referenced
or the various criterion-referenced tests most often used by the states—often
negatively influence their instructional programs. They are right. I have found
myself in many classroom settings where children are reading mostly short
paragraphs and answering multiple-choice questions related to "the main idea
in the passage" or "the place where the accident happened" essentially preparing for the kinds of exercises common to the reading tests. Further, I have observed the Dolch list of basic words (200 words) being learned and relearned

because they appear often on early reading tests. I have also seen worksheets that were essentially facsimiles of the test used in particular schools. And preparation for the new state tests and the Scholastic Aptitude Test (SAT) is taking up increasing classroom time almost everywhere.

Eleanor Duckworth (1975) at Harvard, a collaborator of Jean Piaget, suggests that teaching answers has been the norm and, in fact, has been made a virtue, but she writes:

> The virtues involved in not knowing are the ones that really count in the long run. What you do about what you don't know is, in the final analysis, what determines what you will ultimately know. . . . It is, moreover, quite possible to help children develop these virtues. Providing occasions . . . accepting surprises, puzzlement, excitement, patience, caution, honest attempts, and wrong outcomes as legitimate and important events of learning easily leads to their further development. (p. 85)

The point is that we need to get beyond this history. During the late 1980s and early 1990s, the language and the practice appeared to be changing. The language of authentic assessment, performance assessment, documentation, exhibitions of learning, portfolios, process folios, all related practices, expanded greatly, as noted in Chapter 10. The changing language and practice grew from a belief that much that has stood for learning (mostly the rather indirect measures of these externally developed tests) does not get close enough to students—their growth, development, knowledge, and their understandings. They represented concerns about students who score high on reading tests and do not read or who are successful on computation exercises but cannot solve problems in the world. They relate also to the belief that assessment activities that do not inform teaching practice day in and day out are misdirected and wasteful, doubly wasteful if they do not inform students on a regular basis to make judgments about their own progress as learners. Student learning in regard to assessment is particularly important, although a fresher direction in the assessment arena.

This *different* direction, as it unfolded in the late 1980s, was typically set against *dependence* on assessment as standardized tests, information-based multiple-choice tests, spelling tests made up of words in isolation, and responses to end of chapter questions. While the different directions didn't necessarily call for the elimination of all the forms of assessment that have dominated our schools, they certainly called for their sharp reduction and for using them in far more limiting ways—for example, *never for major decisions or principal judgments* about students and schools.

Movement toward authentic assessment—mostly through performance assessment and portfolios—was understood as calling for serious reappraisal of the instructional program in the schools. If coverage were to remain the goal, for example, performance tasks would tend to be too limited. If worksheets, snippets of knowledge, were to dominate the day-to-day activities, rather than longer-term projects that produce real works, portfolios would not go any-where—they would just become folders of uninteresting and unmanageable paper. If students were not writing on a regular basis, across a wide variety of topics and in a variety of styles, for many diverse purposes, and *across* the cur-riculum, then staying in touch with growth and promoting self-evaluation would be of only limited importance. Further, if there were not opportunities and time for students to complete work they could *honor*, performance itself would be reduced in consequence. I cite all of this again to make clear that powerful ideas, powerful curriculum, and different assessment are linked ideas. Without a growing discourse about curriculum purposes, about students' understandings of history, math, literature, science and not their knowledge *about* those fields of inquiry, as well as about ways teachers can join together on behalf of student learning, portfolios and exhibitions will not have a very long or inspiring history. However, the climate is changing. What has begun around authentic assessment is being seriously challenged by the renewed em-phasis on testing.

Having provided a basic historical review, I will address several issues that relate generally to the technical aspects of testing and that tend to create mis-understandings and misuse. I make no attempt to be all encompassing; the problem areas are just too great.[27]

In discussions of standardized testing, one often confronts such terms and concepts as *objectivity, standardization, reliability,* and *validity.* These terms carry with them an aura of science; however, what do they mean in basic, nontech-nical language?

A test is considered *objective* if everyone takes it under the same basic con-ditions. The multiple-choice format, buttressed by a single "right" answer pat-tern, supports objectivity. However, objectivity has nothing to do with whether a test is fair, contains items of importance, or has ambiguous questions and an-swers. In other words, objectivity has *no relationship to quality.*

A test is *standardized* if norms have been established. Whether the norm populations are representative in more than a statistical sense is not the defin-ing characteristic. This concept, however, as in the case for objectivity, *has no relationship to quality.*[28]

*Reliability* relates to the consistency of the test—how close the results are for an individual or a group at two different testings or how close the scores are of individuals on two different forms of a particular test. Reliability is rather simple to establish; however, a test can have very high reliability (most popu-lar standardized achievement tests carry reliability coefficients of .87 to .93) and yet be a very poor test, measuring little considered important to large numbers of people who use or take the test, which relates to validity, which tends to receive much less attention.

At the most simple level, *validity* refers to the degree to which a test measures what it is supposed to measure or the degree to which the scores derived from a particular test can be related to what the test is supposed to be measuring—in other words, the inferences that can be drawn from the test scores. To say that a student's ability to label verbs in a test passage has little relationship to their ability to write is to raise a question about validity. Unlike reliability, validity is difficult to establish with any authority, especially for a single purpose or for a particular group. It is typically determined by having an expert examine a particular test and provide the equivalent of an imprimatur. This is content validation by opinion. Content validation is the focus of most standardized tests used in elementary and secondary schools.[29] Validity is also established by comparing (concurrent validity) the test results with other measures—that is, other tests, grades, or teacher judgments.[30]

So much for the terms. What can be said about test content? For many individuals with reservations about standardized tests, the content is the principal issue. This relates to the concept of validity but is, at the same time, broader. Most currently used standardized achievement tests, as was noted earlier, have been constructed to conform to instructional programs with predetermined objectives and materials that everyone is expected to work through. They have less relationship to programs that stress high levels of individualization and flexibility of objectives.[31]

How are the tests constructed? In preparing items for an achievement test, authors typically survey curricular patterns and basal materials; they attempt to learn about the sequence, if any, that tends to exist in various content/subject areas; and they make decisions about how to establish a balance between information items and concept items. Questions are prepared and generally tried out in a variety of school settings. (The particular items selected to try out represent, in effect, a statement about what the test authors consider important. This is not intended as a negative observation; it is, however, a condition that needs to be understood.) The items that most individuals get right or wrong are typically discarded. *Distribution* is desired inasmuch as, among a sample of students who take the test, the entire battery of items is designed to produce a *normal curve*, a construct in which half the students score below the average and half above. In such a process, items that many would suggest are important might be discarded and items of limited importance retained. Teachers, school administrators, and parents would do well to examine closely the questions that appear in the standardized tests used, or being considered for use, in their schools in order to make a judgment about the importance of the questions and their relationship to the local curriculum.[32]

Having developed the items, standardization procedures are entered into. This involves establishing a norm population and constructing norm scores. How long does all of this take? From start-up to publication, several years might pass, but what if curriculum changes are rapid or new goals emerge in schools? Might there then be a gap between the tests' curricular assumptions and the curricula that actually exist? This certainly has been the case for the past two decades in mathematics, in which math tests have been concerned with computation in a base ten system only. What if teachers really believed that a shift in educational direction was necessary? Is it possible that such a shift might not occur because of the risk of lowering results on an achievement test designed for different purposes? And, if the populations taking the tests change significantly from one standardization to another, do the scores derived then really have the same meaning?

It is important to comment briefly on test statistics—the derivations that bring scores relating to a norm population and that provide a basis for giving meaning to the *raw* scores (the number of "correct" responses on a test or subsection of a test). While it could be argued that everyone using tests should know a good deal about *derived scores* and their meaning, far too many do not.[33]

Test results are most often reported as percentile scores, stanine scores, or grade-level equivalency scores. A *percentile score* establishes where one stands on a distribution of scores. To say that one has a percentile score of 52 means that 52 percent of those who took the test as part of the norm population had a lower mean score (number of correct answers), and 48 percent had a higher score. Unlike percentile scores and grade-level equivalency scores, *stanine scores* are suggestive of a range. All raw and percentile scores are grouped to make up a 9-point, or *stanine,* scale. A stanine score of 5 is average; 40 percent of the scores will then fall above this average and 40 percent below. The percentile score of 52 will naturally fall within the 5th stanine, along with scores that go down to the 40th percentile and as high as the 59th percentile. (A stanine score has some stretch in it. It doesn't suggest so much precision.) A *grade-level equivalency score* is derived essentially by assigning to the median score of, let's say, a seventh grade norm population a grade equivalency of 7.0. Scores above and below the median are assigned grade equivalencies above and below 7.0. It is an *estimation*, nothing more. Based on extrapolation, a grade-level equivalent score in the 35th percentile might come out as 6.0, and a score at the 65th percentile might come out at 8.5. The imprecision, the distortion of meaning, with this metric is huge.

Of all of the derived scores, grade-level equivalency is still commonly used—and is certainly the metric that seems simplest to understand at the surface level—even though it is the *most misleading*. In their manuals, test publishers now regularly point out that grade-level equivalency scores are being questioned as an appropriate means of interpreting the test performance of individuals and groups. They suggest further that grade equivalents are not an equal-unit score scale and that statistical computations based on grade equivalency values, are not, strictly speaking, legitimate. However, grade-level equivalencies continue because school people have been lured, with all the accountability models, to measure *growth*. If children are in school for eight months, then the belief exists that they should make 8 months' gain. Only grade-level equivalency scores report in year-month terms.

What might it mean to learn that a third grade child (or class) is reading at a 7.9 grade level? Does it suggest, as I have often heard and read in the newspapers, that the particular child (or class) is reading as well as average-achieving youngsters completing the seventh grade? To begin with, what the tests measure as reading ability in grade 3 is not necessarily the same thing as reading ability measured in the seventh grade. A score of 7.9 is nothing more than an extrapolation above the mean. It has nothing to do with how well a youngster completing the seventh grade reads. Conversely, what interpretation is to be made for a seventh grade child with a grade equivalent score of 4.0 on a reading test designed for seventh graders? It implies that the youngster's reading score is much lower than average-achieving seventh graders who were part of the norm population. But does it establish that the youngster reads only as well as a fourth grader? The chances are that, if this seventh grader took the test designed for fourth graders, his or her grade-equivalency score might be 7.0. Remember, the tests were normed at particular grade levels. Third graders didn't take a test designed for seventh graders, and seventh graders didn't take a test designed for fourth graders. We are contending at best with a statistical construct, yet the use of grade-level equivalents goes on unabated.

Much of this discussion has dealt with test scores in a broad sense. The problems, however, grow as the context narrows and the tests are used to say something about *individual* students' achievement of particular skills or to determine specific instructional needs. Given the content sampling that is involved, the manner in which the tests have been constructed, the paper-and-pencil multiple-choice format, and the sources that exist for error, this clearly isn't an eminently valid use.

Let's examine some of the possible sources of error. A child's health on the day the test is given can affect the score. Noise in the classroom, teacher attitudes about the test, a child's experience with similar tests, a broken pencil, and any number of similar disturbances can influence a score. A child's mental state—depression, boredom, elation, or anxiety about the test—can also make a difference in how the student performs. Simple mechanical errors—such as marking the wrong box on the test sheet by accident, overlooking a question, or missing a word while reading—are relatively common test-taking problems.

Children experiencing difficulty with reading perform poorly on tests concerned with reading, but they also tend to perform poorly on social studies, science, and math sections of achievement tests inasmuch as they require reading skills. Thus, children's real knowledge may be considerably underestimated.

Many of these sources of difficulty, as well as many more, can affect an individual child's score, and they have little to do with how "good" the test is, how carefully it was prepared, or the validity of its content. In general, they are intrinsic to the nature of standardized testing.

How serious are these kinds of errors? It depends to a large degree on how the test results are used. In reports of test scores for large groups of children, it is possible to expect that many of the mechanical errors and related difficulties will balance out. The larger the group tested, the more likely such a balancing will occur. For an individual, however, the single score is often used for such purposes as curriculum placement and advancement.

Inasmuch as reading tests are common and are used for placement or for skill assignment, I will offer some general comment on them. The criticisms that I offer, however, are also relevant to the reading section of a general standardized achievement test, as well as to other subject areas. At the lower grade levels, reading tests are heavily dependent on a *particular* vocabulary. If a youngster's particular vocabulary does not include many of the words in the test, are we really to assume the problem is reading? In addition, many of the questions that appear depend on information that is not provided. A child can read the items and all of the responses and then select the "wrong" answer. The "problem" is a lack of information and not a lack of reading skill. It is also possible, of course, given the ambiguities in many items, for a child to select the "wrong" answer but read very well. Another issue is the obvious cultural bias that appears in reading tests, especially at the primary level. At this level, the tests use many pictures that reflect experiences that are not part of the experience of all American children.

These are possibly small issues. A more serious question, at least for those interested in reading as an area of inquiry, is related to the assumptions that underlie most standardized reading tests. In general, reading tests assume a hierarchy of skills. Exercises relating to words in isolation—decoding and syllabication, for example—are common, but there is no agreement among reading experts that any hierarchy of skills exists.[34] Many of the skill sheets that children are seen struggling with are related directly to a hierarchy of skills. In fact, several of the tests have correlative materials that can be assigned to students who score poorly in a particular skill area. There is some evidence that such activities will increase scores on reading tests, but there is little evidence that such activities enlarge a child's capacity to gain understanding from the printed page (the way in which many individuals define *reading*). The *time* taken doing skill sheets on syllabication, for example, might have been better spent *reading*, enlarging one's experience with words in new contexts.

Testing takes time. Does it add significantly to a child's learning, or does it take time away from other, more significant learning experiences? In many schools, actual testing time for most children takes four days in the fall and four days in the spring, but how much time goes into preparing children directly for the tests themselves? And, if a child is "targeted" under a special program, he or she is likely to be in for another dose of pre- and posttests in reading and math. The possibilities proliferate the more one thinks about testing in schools.

What is learned through all of the testing? The question that must always be asked in addition to all that has been said is *"Do the tests provide more information about a child's achievement in most subject areas than the child's teachers typically possess?"* In general, the answer is no. In most cases, teachers can provide more precise information to a parent about the quality of a child's reading or math skills than can any standardized test score. Do the test scores inform teachers about what they should do? There is nothing inherent in the tests or the scoring mechanisms that provides a capacity for informing teachers of what they should do. In this sense, tests' educational value is exceedingly small.

We do know how to use assessment to assist students in their learning, as well as to promote real accountability. There are many schools doing just that, but they have generally been freed from all the testing. We have much to learn from these schools.

In this chapter, I have conveyed an interest in helping teachers understand more of the history that surrounds standardized testing. There is nothing in the history that should cause us to believe that more testing will bring us to better schools or will promote higher levels of learning among all of our students.

---

## FOR REFLECTION

Think about your personal experience with standardized testing. What do you most remember? Do you see the scores you received as good measures of your knowledge, understandings, and academic skills?

What would serve as a good demonstration of your academic abilities?

In your opinion, why has testing for purposes of promotion, retention, entry into and out of various programs, and graduation become so pervasive, so popular? How might you respond to the kinds of arguments you are able to articulate?

Finally, what if there was a massive reduction in the use of standardized tests, with none given below grade 4 and none that had a high-stakes quality? Would schools decline in quality? Could they answer accountability questions? How might schools be similar or different?

[1]The Massachusetts State Board of Education has issued several press releases indicating that about 40 percent of high school students do not currently have the knowledge or skills necessary to pass the graduation tests being contemplated.

[2]It has been interesting to hear that this "high-stakes" testing we are venturing into on a substantial scale is new—another reason for all of us to gain greater historical perspective.

[3]The initial state tests came prior to the multiple-choice technology. They typically called on students to demonstrate their knowledge through essays, written answers to specific questions, and the solving of problems.

[4]It hasn't been different in the more recent testing of this kind—in the 1970s and 1980s. The evidence is that the testing had its most negative effect on students of color and lower socioeconomic populations. In a major publication at the time, *Testing . . . Grouping: The New Segregation in Southern Schools*, the Southern Regional Council presented its concerns about competency testing in the southern states contributing to a resegregation of the schools.

[5]In 1950, for the first time, most of the eighteen- and nineteen-year-old population completed high school. This attainment figure peaked nationally in 1967 at 76 percent and has remained stable since, but, throughout the twentieth century, the poor and various minority populations have carried most of the burden of limited school attainment.

[6]The following accounts of two North Dakota teachers are fairly common. Johanna Knudsen Miller described the North Dakota State tests in 1904 as "something I worried about for months. The first chance I had to work *only* with children in grades one through four, I took it because these children didn't have any State tests to take" (Perrone 1986). Grace Carlson, another early North Dakota teacher, remembers ending all the "interesting activities" for her sixth, seventh, and eighth graders in February in order "to concentrate on getting the children ready for the test." This meant going over answers to old tests and trying to determine what kinds of questions would be asked "this year." She was relieved when the state examinations ceased to be required at the end of the 1920s (Perrone 1974).

[7]Colleagues involved in a large-scale evaluation in one of our largest school districts note that virtually no challenging academic work goes on between January and April, when the high-stakes tests are given (and after that the students seem to quit doing anything). The curriculum during this period is the test curriculum. The school district recently celebrated an increase in test scores. This produced a political gain—but it is hardly an educational gain. This, I believe, will be repeated in most settings in which overall test scores have a history of being on average lower than the norm.

[8]Retention has a history of being used often as well as sparingly in the schools. Contrary to some of the recent discourse, "social promotion" hasn't been dominant through all periods of time. Many school districts have a history of retaining substantial numbers of students at various points. There is little evidence of salutary effects on the students or on test scores.

[9]Herrnstein and Murray's *The Bell Curve: Intelligence and Class Structure in American Life* (1994) has been heavily debated over the past few years. It makes its case for genetic differences among various populations on the basis of a variety of standardized tests.

[10]Kamin (1974, p. 16).

[11]Garrett (1955, p. 65).

[12]For a number of years, I have given my Harvard students the form of the Alpha test given under Yerkes's direction to those who were illiterate. They generally average, because some of the photographs have lost their context for this generation of students, about fourteen correct responses out of twenty—*not* a very good score. For the illiterates who took the test in 1917, mostly rela-

tively new immigrants and African Americans from rural areas of the South, the photographs had to have had even less context. It is not surprising that they also didn't score very well. The written tests had many of the same "lack of context" problems.

[13]The provisions of the 1924 act relating to national origin quotas were maintained in the McCarran Act of 1952. By the 1960s, however, pressures were building to bring an end to all this discriminatory legislation. In 1965, Congress passed the Immigration and Nationality Act, which eliminated the quota system based on national origins.

[14]Lippman (3 January 1923, p. 146). Such criticisms have continued and today IQ testing—that process which purports through a single score to measure intelligence, what Harvard psychologist Sheldon White calls a "mix of magic and pseudo-science"—is no longer a major factor in the schools. And increasingly those who write about intelligence as a construct do so in terms of multiple intelligences or talents—essentially, starting points for ongoing learning (Gardner [1983]). Related to Lippman's lament, teachers currently question how a score on a test, taken on a particular day, outside the norms of the ongoing instructional program, unsituated in this sense, can determine more than students' daily work over an entire year.

[15]Thorndike and Hagan (1962) write: "The testing movement seemed especially suited to the temper of this country and took hold here with a vigor and enthusiasm unequaled elsewhere" (p. 5). Readers should understand that standardized testing, with its multiple-choice response technology, has become in large measure an American phenomenon. It has never had very much consistent support in the rest of the world.

[16]Kendrick (1967) discusses the stark score differences between white and minority individuals who take the SAT. And Nairn (1980) has made clear that family income is the best predictor of how well students do on the SAT and other standardized achievement tests. Fair Test, a testing advocacy institution, notes that there are also large differences in scores between males and females, resulting in girls receiving fewer scholarship awards—even though they tend to get higher grades in high school and in the early years of college.

[17]By 1940, there were school tests available for every area imaginable—reading readiness, reading, writing, science, mathematics, spelling, creativity, self-concept, and uses of resources.

[18]David McClelland, a Harvard psychologist, suggests that standardized tests have become so thoroughly ingrained in American schools that "it is a sign of backwardness not to have test scores in the school records of children" (McClelland 1978, p. 1).

[19]As late as 1977, however, Oscar Buros, the long-time chronicler-reviewer of standardized tests and editor of the *Mental Measurement's Yearbook*, in a valedictory talk, could still write: "Most standardized tests are poorly constructed, of questionable or unknown validity, pretentious in their claims and likely to be misused more often than not" (p. 9). Surprisingly, he also noted: "So little progress has been made in the past fifty years—in fact, in some areas we are not doing as well. Except for the tremendous advances in electronic scoring . . . we don't have a great deal to show for fifty years of work. . . . Essentially, achievement tests are being constructed today in the same way they were fifty years ago . . . mistakes and all" (p. 10).

[20]Schools embraced the various achievement tests, in spite of their quality problems, generally as guides for thinking about schools and districts as a whole. Until the 1960s, scores on these tests were not the grist for the local newspapers or national reports. In most schools, there was reluctance to use the scores for important decision making about individual students. And the producers of these tests did not encourage their use for making large decisions about individual children. While teachers in schools where the tests were used referred at times to the test scores to support their judgments, their own assessment activities were primary, and they remained the critical evaluation decision makers. Further, at least into the 1950s, there was a fairly consistent view among educators that the standardized tests should not be given to children prior to grade 3.

[21]The volume of testing has grown at an annual rate of 10 to 20 percent over the past thirty years. (See Haney and Madaus 1989, pp. 383–389.)

[22]The test producers have attempted to reduce misuse by providing test users with very carefully prepared manuals relating to their tests. These manuals tend to point out painstakingly the particular test's limitations as well as constructive uses. They typically caution, in the case of achievement tests, that the test results ought not to be used to evaluate teachers, that Grade Level Equivalency scores are misleading, that growth is not unidimensional, that many external factors might

affect a child's score, and that the test measures a sampling of curriculum only. However, few teachers have ever seen the manuals and my experience is that few schools act on the cautions the manuals provide. This will be discussed more fully later in this chapter.

[23]I remember being in a school in the mid-1970s with a federal evaluator who wanted to know how well children in a classroom, all with books in their hands, were reading. I suggested that he sit with a sample of the children, selected randomly, and ask them to read to him. He quickly said, "That wouldn't tell me anything. . . . I want to know their grade level scores and whether they read better now than three months ago."

[24]The Clinton administration has been pushing hard for a national test at grades 4 and 8. While praising the NAEP, the administration wants to make individual student comparisons, as well as school district and state comparisons, possible.

[25]It is now the exceptional school district that *doesn't* test K–2 children (National Commission on Testing and Public Policy 1990).

[26]It is very disturbing to read about the numbers of kindergarten children who are retained because of test scores—in many districts, as much as 10 percent.

[27]Several of the references already cited in endnotes provide an extensive review of the problems inherent in standardized testing and its technical apparatus.

[28]Cronbach (1970), while acknowledging that this definition is often used, suggests that *standardization* is less related to the establishment of norms than to the establishment of precise procedures that "can be followed at different times and places" (p. 27). But, even with Cronbach's definition, one cannot infer quality because a test is standardized.

[29]Those who suggest that the tests often contain bias are, in essence, questioning content validity by claiming that the test content is not representative of the socioeducational experience of minority people.

[30]Several of the references in the Bibliography provide excellent technical discussions of validity— in particular, Cronbach (1970) and Nunnally (1967). I have obviously not made an attempt here to describe all of the expanding statistical/psychometric constructs relating to validity. When Deborah Meier (1974) asks in a monograph *What do the Reading Tests Test?* she is raising the question of validity. In essence, she argues that the reading tests are *not* measures of reading.

[31]This is supposed to be the strength of the new state tests that grow out of the various curriculum frameworks that have been established—namely, that they are directly related to what teachers are teaching.

[32]Parents are typically surprised when they see the tests their children are taking. Unfortunately, few see entire tests.

[33]Again, the test manuals accompanying most popularly used standardized tests are replete with information about derived scores, such as how to interpret them and what limitations need to be taken into account when using them. But, as noted earlier, the manuals are not particularly available in schools for teachers to read, and little information about derived scores goes out to the public to increase their understanding.

[34]Reading experts came together in Georgetown under the auspices of the International Reading Association in 1973 to discuss reading and reading tests. There was almost unanimous agreement that the existing norm-referenced reading tests were without a theoretical base. They agreed further that there is "no definitive knowledge regarding either the sequential learnings or component skills that children must acquire in order to read successfully" (Bussis 1973). There is little evidence that anything has changed.

# Maintaining Commitments

It seems appropriate to conclude in the same way I close out my year with pre-service and inservice teachers who have worked through with me the exercises and ideas that form much of what I have presented in the preceding chapters. I assume in this regard that readers have had a similar enough experience to make my usual closing remarks fully understandable.

We naturally close with many questions left to ponder—which tells us perhaps that our learning must inevitably continue; however, from a lot of experience, I know that teaching and learning situations are almost always like that. When I finished my first year of teaching, I thought about so many things I wish I had done, materials I should have shared, questions I should have asked. Out of this came a next year of teaching that was richer, but this next year, and every year thereafter, ended with just as many questions. This is likely one of the persistent qualities of teaching.

I wanted you to consider seriously your own histories as learners, to evoke in a number of different ways many of your memories of teaching and learning, your own understandings and expectations. We need to remember that we have important histories, we know something about constructive learning environments growing out of our many years in schools and classrooms and within families and communities. We also have many unique interests and understandings. And, by analog, we know, if we push ourselves, that our students also have important histories and more knowledge than they often reveal. They might not now understand what we wish them to understand about our various subject matters, but that doesn't mean they lack important insights into aspects of the world, about the importance of friendships and family relationships, about cultural symbols, and about ways of negotiating many aspects of their lives. One important point here is that we *and* our students have many places to begin with matters of teaching and learning.

I wanted you to reflect on questions of purpose in relation to your work with children and young people in the schools and to the content of your various academic fields. Our work is extremely important. It needs a powerful base, and it needs to be powerful in its hopes and in its vision of possibility. It is about means *and* ends: why this and not that? It is about why math and history. It is related to what we most want our students to take away, to make a part of them. I would like you to hold, keep cultivating, and value that inner voice that always asks *"Why?"* What is the purpose of this? What will it do for the students and their growth? How will it contribute to a healthier community life?

I wanted you to consider settings with one another that promoted conversation, some genuine showing about matters of teaching and learning, some of Freire's dialogue, a sense of colleagueship. There is much in the literature that defines teaching as isolating, *but* it doesn't have to be. In the best of situations, it isn't. The more we talk about teaching and learning, the more we are able to do so productively. Such ongoing conversation is a base for our ongoing growth as teachers and learners, our path to a powerful professionalism, to a voice of our own, to genuine empowerment.

I wanted you to become more observant about schools—what they are and what they could be. So much of schooling has become routine to the point that it is no longer questioned, hardly visible. Much of that routine, the ordinariness, keeps us from seeing alternative possibilities. Being ready to go beneath the surface, always asking how it could be different, is important.

I wanted you to understand that knowledge needs to be transformed, not simplified if understanding is our goal, and that ambiguities and uncertainties can be productive in classrooms. I think we know this, but breaking out of the patterns that keep learning so contained is difficult. Here again, our histories, especially around our passions, can be constructive. Those passions wouldn't have developed had there not been genuine challenges, puzzles to consider, and ongoing questions.

I wanted you to understand that idealism needs to be sustained, that the largest of possibilities need to be held, regardless of the setting and possibly because of the setting. My idealism was overwhelming when I began teaching. I was sure everything was possible, that all of my students could be engaged successfully, that our community could be more equitable, and that social justice could become a common ideal. My sense of possibility was even greater a decade later. My idealism has not waned with time—although I was told often over the years, as you will be as well, that "the real world just isn't what you want it to be." We need to know there is only one world, not an ideal world and a real world. Our idealism matters if we expect to help make that one world better.

I wanted you to understand that differences are to be celebrated, not bemoaned, that race and class need to be thought about, discussed, and made matters of personal and collective action, not matters of silence. We need to be persons who speak, who don't let all the talk about restricting immigration or inferiority and superiority of one racial or ethnic group in relation to others pass so easily. As teachers and citizens, our need is to be models of challenge—of persons who respect others and who care about matters of equity, of democracy writ large.

I wanted you to see teaching as a field demanding the best of our human resources and that teaching is always political because it is about change. We need to see teaching as a genuine profession of hope.

Of course, I also wanted you to become more thoughtful curriculum makers, persons able to meet students with growing levels of confidence, with an ever enlarging repertoire of constructive approaches in mind. Our seriousness of purpose will be evident to our students.

Did all of this come through? My hope is that together we made some good enough beginnings, something on which to build. If you are like others who have gone before you and have worked through the exercises and ideas outlined in this text, you will come to appreciate this base. It will help sustain you.

Will you or I cause the schools to be radically different this year or next year? Possibly not radically, but we can make the schools we work in better, providing more support to young people, their families, and their communities than would otherwise be the case. That may be good enough.

# *APPENDIX*

Included in this Appendix are a number of guides and outlines that have been useful to new teachers, helping them reach inside the teaching-learning exchange and bringing forward the dispositions so central to becoming students of teaching. They are as follows:

- Guide to Journal Writing
- Focused Observations/Journal Writing Directions
- A School Portrait
- Guide to Developing Curriculum
- Guide to More Precise Curriculum Planning
- Some Thoughts About Learning Style
- Scaffolds for Teaching and Learning
- Classroom-Based Research

# Guide to Journal Writing

(Journal writing is an effective means of keeping track of teaching. It has been a cornerstone of my work as a teacher since I first began some forty-three years ago. I asked my history students in secondary schools to keep "history journals," or "class journals," to record their observations, to keep them involved in the work. I also maintained journals to keep up with individual students, course themes, questions, and classroom issues. My teacher education students have found journal writing particularly productive. They have continued to keep journals as practicing teachers. As part of my instruction about journal writing, in recent years I have made use of the following guide, which I trust will be useful to those wishing to engage in journal writing.)

One important means of reflecting on our work as teachers, getting closer to our practice, is through journal writing. Such an effort often begins slowly, in the early stages yielding a lot of white space on the paper. The longer we stay with it, however, the more focus we bring to our observations, the more detailed the descriptions and questions become, and the more connections we are able to make.

The journal you are being asked to maintain is a teaching-learning journal. While it can serve as a vehicle for personal writing, the intent is to keep it focused on teaching and schools—a place to record useful ideas, interesting practices you have observed in the schools or read or heard about, responses to what you are reading or thinking about, questions, things you wonder about or worry about, and so on.

There are many journal styles. I suspect you are most familiar with a fairly free-flowing journal, in which ideas are recorded one after another. Such journals have a natural quality and may be easier for you to maintain. Nonetheless, I want to introduce you to another style, which makes use of a formulation that relies on connecting ideas and engaging in dialogue between ideas. Hence, I call it a *Dialectical Journal* (although I wish to credit Dixie Goswami, a wonderful teacher of writing at Clemson, and a regular member of the Bread Loaf Writing Faculty, for the basic term). In a dialectical journal, pages are divided, with the space on the right-hand side wider than the space on the left. Entries on the left will generally be quite specific—as concrete as possible—essentially, a referent. Those on the right are designed to be speculative—attempts to fill out understandings.

Some examples might be useful:

An entry on the left might relate to something that was read.

| | |
|---|---|
| 16 September 1999—I read the assigned selection from John Dewey's "The Child and the Curriculum." | Personal Commentary: What are my initial impressions? What questions did it raise? |
| | What did it cause me to think about in regard to my own experience? (You might return to this based on the class discussions or based on later personal thinking and reflection. The notations on the left make it easier to go back to particular discussions.) |

The referent might then be

26 September—The Child and the Curriculum
That is a general starting point. Ideally, you will move to greater specificity as your starting point. For example—the entire Dewey commentary may have engaged you, but was there a particular thought, expressed by a particular sentence or paragraph, that caused you to slow down a little? For example, note the following:

| | |
|---|---|
| The source of whatever is dead, mechanical, and formal in schools is found precisely in the subordination of the life and experience of the child to the curriculum." (p. 9) | How can the curriculum always be living—or always have a connection to the life and experience of children? Is there a role for the academic, the abstract, in school? at what level? What does it look like? Could it look different? (What I have started here is a subject that could engage me for a long time, something I might return to at many different times.) |
| "Interests in reality are but attitudes toward possible experiences; they are not achievements; their worth is in the leverage they afford, not in the accomplishment they represent." (p. 15) | I hear teachers speak often about their need to learn about the interests of their students. But what do they do with them? To say that a student's interest provides starting points for intense learning is, I believe, what Dewey implies. What does it mean in the classroom? Could a student's intense interest of outer space, for example, be turned into a full and balanced curriculum? |

The starting point might be something you read. For example, in Jerome Bruner's *Actual Minds: Actual Worlds,* another in a series of Bruner's reconsiderations, he writes:

"My model of the child in (earlier) days was very much in the tradition of the solo child mastering the world by representing himself in his own terms. In the intervening years I have come increasingly to recognize that in most settings it is a communal activity, a sharing of the culture. . . . It is this that leads me to emphasize not only discovery and invention but the importance of negotiating and sharing—in a word, of joint culture creating as an object of schooling." (p. 127)

My experience with cooperative learning has been positive. Why aren't Bruner's understandings more dominant in the schools I have observed? What causes the caution? I plan to examine cooperative learning more carefully, to see for myself how to make it work.

The starting point might also be something you heard—something that caused you uneasiness or caused you to wonder a bit. The starting point might also be an interaction. I'll provide one that I have returned to often over the years since I first heard it. An elementary principal shared it. He was in a kindergarten classroom, talking informally with a child. Their conversation, as the principal described it, was not unusual, but then the child said,

"You are talking to me because you want to, not because you have to." (That's an interesting starting point.)

That comment caused me to wonder about children's understandings of human relationships, and how we communicate with children, and what the possibilities are when children see our efforts as more than duty.

Another instance was a discussion with a group of history teachers about the use of primary sources. One teacher noted,

"My students could never read a primary source—so this discussion has no meaning for me."

I immediately thought about expectations. Such a belief immediately limits what students *can* do and learn. How could students be helped to read primary documents?

The starting point could also be a question that emerged as a result of an incident, something that caused you to *wonder*—to step back. One example comes from a school portrait I have read a number of times. Many of the teachers in this school speak of the diversity of the students—their many cultures and languages—as a kind of penance—"a killer."

"I wonder why the Hamilton teachers don't see the diversity as an opportunity filled with wonderful possibilities?"

(My dialectic response would likely be a statement of my understandings of possibilities. It might close with a plan to talk about this with a number of other teachers.)

Let me share two more pieces I wonder about. School tracking has reached unprecedented levels. Teachers tend to believe that greater homogeneity makes teaching easier and improves student learning. Why is that, when all of the evidence about learning and equity considerations are contrary?

School retention has enlarged greatly—20 percent of children in the primary grades were retained in this past year. I understand the pressures but don't we also know that the results are likely to be increased dropouts? Is that what we want?

The starting point can also be an incident you observed or read about. On the left-hand side, describe the incident as factually as you can, without embellishment or judgment. What you thought about it would be your entry on the right-hand side. You might return to the incident after a week. Do you think about it any differently?

I have obviously not exhausted the possibilities. Even if you choose not to try a dialectical format, possibly the foregoing discussion will assist you in thinking more about the process you will use.

In many respects, the journal can be a record of the year. At its best, it will also be a base for some of your ongoing thought. The important thing is to write as often as possible. Think of the journal as your means of ongoing reflection on teaching and learning, a basis for getting closer to your practice as a teacher, your entry into the scholarship of teaching.

# Focused Observations/
# Journal Writing Directions

(The intention of the following suggestions is to give focused direction to school observations and to provide a basis for some of the journal writing that I consider so critical for new teachers. As you will note, many of the tasks relate to mentor teachers, but they could be expanded to include other teachers. Overall, the writing seeks to help new teachers take in the landscape of schools and classrooms more fully, even as the particulars will stand out as the base.]

With regard to the focused entries, you should try to write as soon as possible, when the related observations or activities are freshest. Review particular entries prior to a discussion session and select what you believe to be the most critical issues, those most salient to you as you think about teaching.

## Focus #1

Take careful note of how two different classes *open* and *close* (if possible, observe two teachers). How do students enter, get seated, and get ready for the beginning of class? What is the teacher doing? How does he or she acknowledge students as they enter? How does the teacher begin? What does the teacher do if he or she doesn't have the students' attention? Does it work? How does the lesson proceed? How is it ordered? How engaged and attentive were the students? How did the class end? Did the teacher provide a summary, give an assignment for the next day, or pose a question? How would you judge the success of each of the two class periods? What causes you to make those judgments?

## Focus #2

Most schools have a variety of special-needs classrooms. Spend at least two periods in a special-needs setting. Take careful note of who the students are, the number of students in the class, the nature of the classroom instruction, the kinds of questions teachers ask, the materials being used, and the ways students respond. What did you observe that you believe you could take into your regular education classroom?

### Focus #3

Arrange a time to converse with a special-needs teacher. Inquire about the following:

- How an IEP (Individual Education Plan) is developed and evaluated
- Methods the teacher has found to be most successful in assisting students to be more effective learners
- The experience of special-needs students in mainstreamed classes
- How much interaction special-needs teachers have with regular education teachers
- How much help special-needs teachers are able to provide regular education teachers

### Focus #4

Engage in a conversation with your mentor teacher about how he or she plans— what to teach, what to focus on, what materials to use, what instructional activities to pursue, what homework assignments to make, how much writing to assign. Does he or she make out daily or weekly plans? What do you make of your mentor's process? Would it work for you? Why or why not? What questions are you left with after this conversation?

### Focus # 5

Carefully review the materials your mentor uses with the students—textbooks, lab manuals, original documents, trade books, anthologies. Do they seem clear? Are they thought-provoking? Do they seem challenging? Do they provide a broad, inclusive cultural perspective? Do they suggest that understanding is being sought? Are they readable? What kind of assistance do students receive to help them make sense of the text?

### Focus #6

A concern that most new teachers have is classroom management/discipline. Observe carefully how your mentor (or other teachers you are observing) handle classroom management/discipline. How do they interact with their students? Do they demonstrate respect for the students? Do the students appear to respect them? How do they get students' attention, keep things moving, and handle disruptions? In relation to the reading you have done, what do these teachers do and not do? What do you take from what you have observed?

## Focus #7

Prepare a brief case study of a discipline problem you have observed. Use the following format:

- A description of the setting (for context)
- A precise description of the incident, including the teacher's actions (without any judgment)
- Two questions that the incident raises for you that you would like to discuss with others

## Focus #8

By now, you have likely been present for a variety of assessment activities.

1. Write first about the various nonwritten performance activities you have observed — role plays, oral presentations, group activities that culminate in a report, drawings, and models. How did your teacher evaluate these kinds of activities?
2. Examine the assignments for writing. Were they clear? Did students have the required preparation? Were criteria established for how the writing would be evaluated?
3. Were there exams? What were they like? What kinds of questions were posed? How were they evaluated? How would you judge the assessment activities? What causes you to make that particular judgment?
4. Are portfolios maintained? How are they used? Do they lead to student self-assessment? Are they used in conferences with parents?
5. Is student work regularly presented in public forums—to audiences within and outside the school?

# A School Portrait

(As a means of understanding the complexities of schools, I have found it helpful to involve preservice and inservice teachers in developing portraits of schools. I usually suggest they focus on the schools they are working in. They can be done by individuals or collectives. This guide is meant to help focus the observations, to give the reflections as robust a field as possible.)

In this guide, I wish to take you through some of the questions that a school portrait might explore reflectively in order to weave together a rich tapestry.

## A School Has a Geographic Setting

Where is the school? What is the landscape like around it? How does it stand out, if it does? How long has it been there? What is the same and what is different about the geographic/ecological environment, about the racial, ethnic, and socioeconomic character of the community surrounding the school, and about the community served by the school? What does the school's presence mean?

## The School Is a Physical Structure

What is its shape and size, the distinguishing features? What thoughts does it inspire? What would stand out to a visitor walking into and around the building? What are its feeling tones—warm, soft, cold, inviting, isolating, bright, dull, vibrant, enervating, or energizing? Does it easily accommodate those who work and study in it?

## A School Has Purposes

What are this school's largest purposes? How are they talked about, shared, and made integral to what everyone does? How articulate are students and teachers about the purposes? What would cause a visitor to say, "I see those purposes in action—in what students, teachers, and administrators do; in the ways they interact; in classroom materials; and in various school programs?"

## A School Has Organizational Structures

What are the patterns? How are decisions made? What decisions are open to the school or not open to the school? Provide specific examples.

## A School Has a Climate

What is this school's distinguishing character? Is it competitive, cooperative, friendly, hard-edged, social, academic, intellectual, caring, vocational, community-spirited, safe, athletic, cliquish, loud, quiet, democratic, authoritarian, passive, or active? Are there stories that convey that character? How is this climate transmitted? Does it promote inclusiveness? What are the traditions, and do they continue to have meaning?

## A School Has Teachers

Who are they; where have they come from? How old are they? Are their backgrounds diverse or are they similar? What are their commitments in the school and beyond the school? How do they interact with each other? How much sharing do they do? Are they pleased to be in this school and interested in its growth, in its students, in the students' parents, in this community? Are they academically or vocationally oriented? Are they interested in new things, ideas, and ways of working? Are they independent thinkers? What are their largest hopes? What energizes them and enervates them? Are there stories that exemplify your description of the teachers?

## A School Has Students

Many of the questions posed about teachers can be asked in regard to the students.

## A School Is a Place for Teaching and Learning

What are the predominant pedagogical styles—the ways teachers approach the teaching-learning exchange? Is learning viewed as more active or passive? How much diversity exists? What are the dominant instructional materials? How is technology used for instruction? How much integration exists between areas of learning and across grade levels? Are there any common schoolwide themes? Where does the student stand in the teaching and learning exchange? Is the teaching-learning process characterized more by open-ended inquiry, a focus on uncertainty, or by fixed content and certainty—more by questions or answers? Do students work more together in groups or more as individuals, completing tasks alone? Is there grouping by perceived ability? To what degree are learning activities connected to the community? How deeply are topics pursued? Is service a requirement? What goes on that might cause you to say the teaching and learning exchange focuses on powerful ideas, concepts, and literature, or that students are growing as learners (able to extend their learning) and are becoming more independent as learners (able to establish more of their own directions and able to evaluate their own progress?)

## A School Is in a Community

How does the school relate to its community? What are the interactions? What are the reciprocities? How are the community's resources brought into the school, used by students for educational purposes, and made an extension of the school? Beyond the education of children and young people, how does the community use the school's resources?

The final question is "what does it all mean?" After pursuing all these issues, what do you wonder about?

# Guide to
# Developing Curriculum

(As a starting point for thinking about a course, a semester's work or a year's work, I suggest to teachers that they might want to engage in some writing and thinking about the following set of questions. In my curriculum development framework, it represents a precursor to more precise planning of units, themes, and day-by-day instruction. I ask that the teachers begin by considering a subject they might teach—composition, physics, algebra, history, American history, language arts, French, and so on.)

1. In relation to the foregoing subject, respond to the following: Why should students study such a subject matter? What is important about it? What would you say to students who ask, "Why are we doing this?"
2. Ask yourself what you most want students to leave this course or subject matter understanding, being able to do.
3. Given such a view, what four topics within the course or subject matter defined above are most likely to get the students to where you would like them to be? Why?
4. How will you know if the students have reached one of the understandings identified in item 2 above?

This paper is a precursor to more precise curriculum development. To help you think about an audience, you might consider writing a letter to your students (as well as to parents) around the foregoing questions.

# Guide to More Precise Curriculum Planning

(This guide relates to the specific topics and themes being developed within a course. It is related closely to the Teaching for Understanding Framework described fully in Chapter 8 of the text. For preservice students, it can be a good project to learn how to develop a curriculum. For those in schools, it is a productive process that can be engaged by individuals or collectives of teachers.)

The unit is to be organized around a *generative topic* to be addressed over a fifteen-twenty-day period.

1. Describe what you believe makes the topic generative.
2. Develop two or three understanding goals for the topic.
3. Organize fifteen to twenty days of instruction. What will you ask students to do and/or read each day? What questions will you pose? (Make a note of how this activity moves forward, is related to, your understanding goals.) At least every other day, define what you see as an understanding performance — an indication that students are moving toward understanding what you want them to understand. In relation to the fifteen-twenty days, try to vary your approach as much as possible.
4. Describe your overall assessment plan for the unit. How will you make use of the understanding performances within your plan for ongoing assessment? How will the unit culminate — a project, a paper, an exam?
5. Include a bibliography of resources and sampler of resources.

# Some Thoughts About Learning Style[*]

(There is increasing attention in schools to diverse learning styles, an understanding that children and young people learn in different ways. Being attentive to such diversity suggests the need to provide different instructional approaches—for example, a variety of materials, different kinds of assignments, and a range of questions and assessment strategies. As an entry into reflecting on learning styles, even before going to the literature, I have provided some of the following thoughts. The related discussions have been useful.)

When your computer freezes up, what do you do?
—Remove the computer cover and mess around inside
—Consult the manual
—Call an 800 number for service
—Call a friend

When you have to write a big paper, what do you do?
—Make an outline
—Start writing—anything
—Take a walk
—Talk it through with a friend

If you wanted to learn how to roller-blade, how would you approach it?
—Purchase an instruction book
—Strap on the blades and go
—Watch people blading for a while and then try it

When you read a book, how do you go about it?
—Read it through, cover to cover
—Read the first few pages and then skip around
—See if the movie is playing in town
—Check the reviews before finishing

Learning style is an important issue; systematic descriptions of it tend, though, to be artificial. Nevertheless, we and our students do exhibit preferences—and these preferences may vary according to the subject area or task.

- Some learners tend to be *sequential, ordered* thinkers; others are more typically *associative.*
- Some tend to take a very hands-on and *concrete* approach, while others take a more *abstract* view. (At Bruner's Woods Hole gathering to develop a physics curriculum, the educators wanted to establish learning objectives first, while the scientists wanted to mess around with things and figure out the objectives later.)
- Some like to watch and think things through on their own (*introversion*); others like to work or study in a group (*extroversion*).
- Some prefer to "see it in writing" (or diagram, charts, pictures); others would rather listen, getting instruction orally.

What do you think about this? How do you learn best? How do other friends or family members learn best? What do you observe in schools? What does this suggest for assuring that all students have opportunities to be successful learners? How might you plan for these many learning preferences?

*I wish to acknowledge the contributions of Rob Riordan, Cambridge Rindge and Latin School.

# Scaffolds for Teaching and Learning

(It is important to think about how we will scaffold our teaching to assure that our students are successful as learners. While not all teaching and learning is necessarily linear, nonetheless, it is helpful to be conscious about how we might get our students to the end points we desire, such as being able to swim, being able to make sense of primary documents, writing a research paper, and conducting scientific research. The exercise that follows is a means of thinking about this I have found particularly productive.)

You are to think about teaching *one* of the following—swimming, skiing, horseshoes, growing flowers, using a computer, playing a musical instrument, baking bread, or building a small structure.

What would you first do? Why?
What would you next do? Why?
Then what would you do?

The assumption is that you would do several things. Enumerate the steps. Remember, the person you are teaching should be able to perform the activity at the end. (We might want to plan many of our lessons around a similar scaffolding outline.)

# Classroom-Based Research

(Classroom-based research recognizes the importance of teachers being students of teaching. It starts from the premise that teachers can learn from thoughtful examinations of their own classrooms. While there is a large body of literature about classroom research, I offer the following guide as a starting point.)

One's own classroom is a source of knowledge about teaching and learning. When things don't work very well, when students don't seem able to complete the tasks assigned, when cooperative groups are not constructive enough, when parents seem unresponsive to our efforts, when there are disruptions that get in the way of what we understand to be good teaching-learning conditions, some of the difficulties can be understood better by examining our classroom practices carefully. In thinking about your own classroom, what do you wonder about? What is perplexing for you? What could you do to learn more about this? (Could you, for example, engage in focused observations, or ask someone else to come into the classroom and do focused observations? Could you engage in some focused conversations with small groups of students? Could you do some survey work? Could you alter some of what you do, carefully noting the response?) Develop a plan for your inquiry. Include a process for recording what you are learning. (You might want to discuss your plan with another teacher. There is always power in collective thought.) Carry out your plan. Write a reflection. Decide if you need to pursue the issue in some different ways.

One could argue that the reflective stance needed in teaching would suggest that inquiries into one's classroom practice must be ongoing. While this is certainly the case, more focused inquiries, using some of the foregoing ideas as a guide, can also be productive.

# BIBLIOGRAPHY

Addams, J. 1902. *Democracy and Social Ethics.* New York: Macmillan.

———. 1910. *Twenty Years at Hull House.* New York: Macmillan.

Aiken, W. 1942. *The Story of the Eight Year Study.* New York: McGraw-Hill.

American Association for the Advancement of Science. 1962. *Science: A Process Approach.* Washington, DC: American Association for the Advancement of Science.

Anderson, J. 1985. *The Education of Blacks in the South, 1860–1935.* Chapel Hill: University of North Carolina Press.

Annenberg Rural Challenge. 1997. *Learning from Rural Communities: Alaska to Alabama.* Cambridge: Harvard Graduate School of Education.

Apple, M. 1993. *Official Knowledge: Democratic Education in a Conservative Age.* New York: Routledge.

Ayers, W. and J. Miller, eds. 1998. *A Light in Dark Times: Maxine Greene and the Unfinished Conversation.* New York: Teachers College Press.

Bestor, A.E. 1953. *Educational Wastelands.* Urbana: University of Illinois Press.

Biddle, B. 1997. "Foolishness, Dangerous Nonsense and Real Correlations of State Differences in Achievement." *Phi Delta Kappan* (September): 9–13.

Binet, A., and T. Simon. [1916] 1973. *The Development of Intelligence in Children.* New York: Arno Press.

Bond, H.M. 1966. *The Education of the Negro in the American Social Order.* New York: Octagon Books.

Bridges, D., ed. 1997. *Education, Autonomy and Democratic Citizenship: Philosophy in a Changing World.* New York: Routledge.

Brigham, C. 1923. *A Study of American Intelligence.* Princeton: Princeton University Press.

Bruner, J. 1962. *The Progress of Education.* Cambridge: Harvard University Press.

———. 1965. *Man: A Course of Study.* Cambridge: Educational Services, Inc.

———. 1966. *Toward a Theory of Instruction.* Cambridge: Harvard University Press.

———. 1984. *Actual Minds: Actual Worlds.* Cambridge: Harvard University Press.

Bullock, H. 1970. *A History of Negro Education in the South: From 1619 to the Present.* New York: Praeger.

Buros, O. 1977. "Fifty Years in Testing: Some Reminiscences, Criticisms and Suggestions." *Educational Researcher* (July-August).

Bussis, A. 1973. "Memo for the Record," Princeton: Educational Testing Service.

Cahn, S., ed. 1997. *Classic and Contemporary Readings in the Philosophy of Education.* New York: McGraw-Hill.

Callahan, R. 1962. *Education and the Cult of Efficiency.* Chicago: University of Chicago Press.

Capella, G. 1995. *Young People's Perceptions of Teachers and Their School Experience: Two Dialogues.* Unpublished doctoral dissertation, Harvard Graduate School of Education.

Carini, P. 1979. *The Art of Seeing and the Visibility of the Person.* Grand Forks, North Dakota: North Dakota Study Group.

———. 1984. "Stories of Experience with Evaluation and Standards." North Dakota Study Group Meeting (February), Chicago, Illinois.

———. 1995. "Educational Values and the Child's Impulse to Value," Presentation to the North Dakota Study Group on Evaluation, Chicago, Illinois.

Chittenden, E. 1986. *The New York Science Test.* Princeton, NJ: Educational Testing Service.

Cohen, E. 1986. *Designing Groupwork: Strategies for the Heterogeneous Classroom.* New York: Teachers College Press.

Coles, R. 1986. *The Moral Life of Children*. Cambridge: Harvard University Press.

Cook, A., and H. Mack. 1990. *The Inquiry Demonstration Project*. New York: Urban Academy.

Cotton, K. 1996. "School Size, School Climate and Student Performance." *Close Up*, no. 20. Portland, OR: Northwest Education Laboratory.

Council of Great City Schools. 1991. *The Condition of Education in the Great City Schools*. Washington, DC: Council of Great City Schools.

Cremin, L. 1961. *The Transformation of the School*. New York: Knopf.

———. 1970. *American Education: The Colonial Experience, 1607–1783*. New York: Harper.

———. 1983. *American Education: The National Experience, 1783–1876*. New York: Harper.

———. 1990. *American Education: The Metropolitan Experience, 1876–1980*. New York: Harper.

Cronbach, L. 1970. *Essentials of Psychological Testing*. New York: Harper and Row.

Cuban, L. 1993. *How Teachers Taught: Constancy and Change, 1890–1990*. New York: Teachers College Press.

Delpit, L. 1995. *Other People's Children: Cultural Conflict*. New York: New Press.

Dewey, J. [1899] 1956. *School and Society*. Chicago: University of Chicago Press.

———. [1902] 1956. *The Child and the Curriculum*. Chicago: University of Chicago Press.

———. [1916] 1961. *Democracy and Education*. New York: Macmillan.

———. [1938] 1963. *Experience and Education*. New York: Macmillan.

———. [1938] 1976. "The Relation of Theory and Practice." In *The Middle Works of John Dewey*, J. Boydston, ed. Vol. 3. Carbondale, Illinois: pp. 249–272.

Dow, P. 1991. *Schoolhouse Politics: Lessons from the Sputnik Era*. Cambridge: Harvard University Press.

DuBois, W.E.B. [1903] 1969. *The Souls of Black Folk*. New York: American Library.

———. 1920. "Race Intelligence." *The Crisis* (July): 1181–1183.

Duckworth, E. 1975. "The Virtues of Not Knowing." *Principal* (March/April), National Association of Elementary School Principals.

———. 1987. *"The Having of Wonderful Ideas" and Other Essays*. New York: Teachers College Press.

Dyer, H. 1971. "Testing Little Children: Some Old Problems in New Settings." Paper presented at the National Leadership Institute in Early Childhood Education, Washington, DC, 1971.

Egan, J. 1981. "Thirty-Two Going on Eight." *Insights* 14 (November 1981).

Eisner, E. 1998. *The Kind of School We Need*. Portsmouth, NH: Heinemann.

Elbow, P. 1991. Foreword to Belanoff, P., and M. Dickson, eds. *Portfolios: Process and Product*. Portsmouth, NH: Boynton/Cook.

Fenton, E. 1966. *Teaching the New Social Studies in Secondary Schools*. New York: Holt, Rinehart & Winston.

Freire, P. 1971. *Pedagogy of the Oppressed*. New York: Herder and Herder.

———. 1997. *Teachers as Cultural Workers: Letters to Those Who Dare Teach*. Boulder, CO: Westview Press.

Froebel, F. 1912. *Education of Man*. New York: Appleton and Co.

Galileo, G. 1953. *Dialogue Concerning the Two Chief World Systems*. Berkeley: University of California Press.

Gardner, H. 1983. *Frames of Mind: A Theory of Multiple Intelligences*. New York: Basic Books.

Garrett, H. 1955. *General Psychology*. New York: American Book Co.

Gintis, H., and S. Bowles. 1976. *Schooling in Capitalist America: Educational Reform and the Contradictions of Economic Life*. New York: Basic Books.

Graves, D. 1983. *Writing: Teachers and Children at Work.* Exeter, NH: Heinemann.

Greene, M. 1978. *Landscapes of Learning.* New York: Teachers College Press.

*Guide to the Elementary Science Study.* 1967. Newton, MA: Elementary Science Study, Educational Development Center.

Haley, A. 1964. *The Autobiography of Malcolm X.* New York: Ballantine Books.

Hall, H. 1971. *Unfinished Business.* New York: Macmillan.

Handlin, O. 1959. *John Dewey's Challenge to Education.* Westport, CT: Greenwood Press.

Haney, W., and G. Madaus. 1989. "Searching for Alternatives to Standardized Tests: Whys, Whats, and Whithers." *Phi Delta Kappan* (May): 683–687.

Hawkins, D. 1965. "Messing About in Science." *Science and Children,* 2: 5–9.

Heller, E. 1959. *The Disinherited Mind.* New York: Meridian Books.

Herrnstein, R., and C. Murray. 1994. *The Bell Curve: Intelligence and Class Structure in American Life.* New York: Free Press.

Heslep, R. 1997. *Philosophical Thinking in Educational Practice.* Westport, CT: Praeger.

Hirst, P., and P. White. 1993. *The Philosophy of Education.* New York: Routledge.

Hoffman, N., ed. 1981. *Woman's "True" Profession: Voices from the History of Teaching.* Old Westbury, NY: Feminist Press (McGraw-Hill).

Hofstadter, R. 1964. *The Progressive Movement, 1900–1915.* Englewood Cliffs, NJ: Prentice-Hall.

Holt, T. 1991. *Historical Thinking.* New York: College Board.

Horne, H. 1917. *The Teacher as Artist.* Boston: Houghton-Mifflin.

Horton, M. (with Judith and Herb Kohl). 1990. *The Long Haul.* New York: Doubleday.

Horton, M., and F. Adams. 1975. *Unearthing Seeds of Fire: The Ideas of Highlander.* Salem, NC: John Blau.

Johnson, D., et al. 1986. *Circles of Learning.* Washington, DC: Association for Supervision and Curriculum Development.

Karier, C. 1975. *Shaping the American Educational State, 1990–Present.* New York: Free Press.

Katz, M. 1968. *The Irony of Early School Reform.* Cambridge: Harvard University Press.

———. 1971. *Class, Bureaucracy and Schools.* New York: Praeger.

———. 1992. *The Traditions of American Education.* Cambridge: Harvard University Press.

Kamin, L. 1974. *The Science and Politics of I.Q.* Potomac, MD: Erlbaum.

Kendrick, S. A. 1967. "The Coming Segregation of Our Selective Colleges." *College Board Review,* New York: The College Board.

Kilpatrick, W. 1926. *The Project Method: The Use of the Purposeful Act in the Educative Process.* New York: Teachers College Press.

Kliebard, H. 1995. *The Struggle for the American Curriculum.* New York: Routledge.

Kohl, H. 1994. *I Won't Learn from You.* New York: New Press.

Kohli, W., ed. 1995. *Critical Conversations in Philosophy of Education.* New York: Routledge.

Lazerson, M., et al. 1985. *An Education of Value.* New York: Cambridge University Press.

Lippman, W. 1922, 1923. Series of articles on testing, *New Republic* (15 October 1922, 29 November 1922, and 3 January 1923).

Lott, W. 1977. "Competency Testing." *Genessee Valley Personnel and Guidance Association Newsletter,* October.

McClelland, D. 1978. "Testing for Competence Rather Than Intelligence." *American Psychiatrist* (January).

McKenna, F. 1995. *Philosophical Theories of Education.* Lanham, MD: University Press of America.

Madaus, G. and P. Airasian. 1977. "Issues in Evaluating Student Outcomes in Competency-Based Graduation Programs." *Journal of Research and Development in Evaluation,* Vol. 10, no. 3.

Martin, J. R. 1994. *Changing the Educational Landscape: Philosophy, Women and Curriculum.* New York: Routledge.

Mayhew, L., and A. C. Edwards. [1936] 1966. *The Dewey School: The Laboratory School at the University of Chicago.* New York: Atherton.

Meier, D. 1973. *Reading Failure and the Tests.* New York: Workshop Center, City College of New York.

———. 1974. *What Do Reading Tests Test?* New York: City College of New York.

———. 1987. "Central Park East: An Alternative Story." *Phi Delta Kappan,* June.

———. 1995. "New Schools." North Dakota Study Group Meeting, 16 February.

———. 1996. *The Power of Their Ideas.* Boston: Beacon Press.

Messarli, J. 1971. *Horace Mann.* New York: Knopf.

Morison, S. 1965. *The Oxford History of the United States.* New York: Oxford University Press.

Nairn, A. 1980. *The Reign of ETS: The Corporation That Makes Up Minds.* Washington, DC: Aldan Nairn and Associates.

Nathan, L. 1995. *Portfolio Assessment and Teacher Practice.* Unpublished doctoral thesis, Harvard Graduate School of Education.

The National Academy of Sciences. 1921. *Psychological Examining in the U.S. Army.* Washington, DC: The National Academy of Sciences.

National Coalition of Advocates for Students. 1985. *Barriers to Excellence.* Boston: National Coalition of Advocates for Students.

National Commission on Excellence in Education. 1983. *A Nation at Risk.* Washington, DC: U.S. Government Printing Office.

National Commission on Testing and Public Policy. 1990. *From Gatekeeping to Gateway: Transforming Testing in America.* Chestnut Hill, MA: Boston College.

National Research Council. 1993. *National Science Education Standards.* Washington, DC: National Research Council.

National Society for the Study of Education. 1918. *The Measurement of Education Products.* Seventeenth Yearbook, Part II.

Noblit, G., and V. Dempsey. 1996. *The Social Construction of Virtue: The Moral Life of Schools.* Albany, NY: SUNY Press.

Noddings, N. 1995. *Philosophy of Education.* Boulder, CO: Westview Press.

Nunnally, J. 1967. *Psychometric Theory.* New York: McGraw-Hill.

Oakes, J. 1985. *Keeping Track: How Schools Structure Inequality.* New Haven, CT: Yale University Press.

Orfield, G., et al. 1996. *Dismantling Desegregation: The Quiet Reversal of Brown vs. Board of Education.* New York: New Press.

———. 1997. *Deepening Segregation in American Public Schools.* Cambridge, MA: Harvard Project on School Desegregation.

Parker, F. 1894. *Talks on Pedagogics.* New York: Kellogg.

Percoco, J. 1992. "Monumental Experiences: A Classroom Application of American Sculpture." *OAH Magazine of History,* Vol. 6, no. 4 (Spring).

Perrone, V. 1974. "An Interview with Grace Carlson." *Journal of Teaching and Learning,* Spring.

———, ed. 1975. *Testing and Evaluation: New Views.* Washington, DC: Association for Childhood Education International.

———. 1977. *The Abuses of Standardized Tests.* Bloomington, IN: Phi Delta Kappa Foundation.

———, et al. 1981. *Secondary School Students and Employment.* Grand Forks: Bureau of Educational Research and Services, University of North Dakota.

———. 1986. *Johanne Knudsen Miller: Pioneer Teacher.* Bismark: North Dakota Historical Association.

———. 1989. *Working Papers: Reflections on Teachers, Schools and Communities.* New York: Teachers College Press.

———, ed. 1991a. *Expanding School Assessment.* Alexandria, VA: Association for Supervision and Curriculum.

———. 1991b. *A Letter to Teachers.* San Francisco: Jossey-Bass.

Pestalozzi, J. 1885. *Leonard and Gertrude.* Translated by E. Channing. Boston: Allyn and Bacon.

Piaget, J. 1929. *The Child's Conception of the World.* London: Kegan-Paul.

Pierce, T. M., et al. 1955. *White and Negro Schools in the South.* Englewood Cliffs, NJ: Prentice-Hall.

Power, E. 1996. *Educational Philosophy: A History From the Ancient to Modern America.* New York: Garland.

Power, F. C., and D. Lapsley, eds. 1992. *The Challenge of Pluralism: Education, Politics and Values.* Notre Dame, IN: University of Notre Dame Press.

Pratt, R. 1992. *Philosophy of Education: Two Traditions.* Springfield, IL: Charles C Thomas.

Ratner, J. 1939. *Intelligence in the Modern World: John Dewey's Philosophy.* New York: Random House.

Rice, J. 1892–1893. "Our Public School System" [A series of articles]. *Forum.*

Rickover, H. 1958. *Education and Freedom.* New York: Dutton.

———. 1963. *American Education: A National Failure, the Problems of Our Schools.* New York: Dutton.

Rogers, A. 1899. *Modern Philosophy.* New York: Macmillan.

Rorty, A. 1998. *Philosophers of Education.* New York: Routledge.

Rose, M. 1988. *Lives on the Boundary.* Boston: Houghton Mifflin.

———. 1995. *Possible Lives: The Promise of Public Education in America.* Boston: Houghton Mifflin.

Sarason, S. 1982. *The Culture of the School and the Problem of Change.* Boston: Allyn and Bacon.

Sarton, M. 1959. *I Knew a Phoenix.* New York: Norton.

Schaffarzick, J., and G. Sykes. 1979. *Value Conflicts and Curriculum Issues: Lessons from Research and Experience.* Berkeley: McCutchan.

Scheffler, I. 1973. *Reason and Teaching.* Indianapolis: Bobbs-Merrill.

———. 1991. *In Praise of the Cognitive Emotions and Other Essays in Philosophy.* New York: Routledge.

Schneier, L. 1990. "Dancing in the Halls." Teachers Network, Harvard Graduate School of Education.

Schniedeund, M., and E. Davidson. 1987. *Cooperative Learning: Cooperative Lives.* Dubuque, IA: William C. Brown

Shepard, L. 1987. "What Doesn't Work: Explaining Policies of Retention in the Early Grades," *Phi Delta Kappan,* Vol. 69, no. 2, October.

Silber, K. 1973. *Pestalozzi: The Man and His Work.* London: Routledge and Kegan-Paul.

Sizer, T. 1984a. *Horace's Compromise: The Dilemma of the American High School.* Boston: Houghton Mifflin.

———. 1984b. *Principles of the Coalition of Essential Schools.* Providence, RI: Coalition of Essential Schools.

———. 1992. *Horace's School: Redesigning the American High School.* Boston: Houghton Mifflin.

———. 1996. *Horace's Hope: What Works in the American High School.* Boston: Houghton Mifflin.

Slavin, R. 1986. *Student Team Learning.* Washington, DC: National Education Association.

Southern Regional Council. 1983. *Testing, Grouping: The New Segregation in Southern Schools.*

Spring, J. 1972. *Education and the Rise of the Industrial State.* Boston: Beacon Press.

———. 1993. *The American School, 1642–1993.* New York: McGraw-Hill.

Stevenson, H., and J. Stigler. 1992. *The Learning Gap: Why Our Schools Are Failing and What We Can Learn from Japanese and Chinese Education.* New York: Summit Books.

Streib, L. 1984. *A Teacher's Journal.* Grand Forks: North Dakota Study Group.

Terman, L. 1916. *The Measurement of Intelligence.* Boston: Houghton Mifflin.

———. "Response to Walter Lippmann." *New Republic,* November 29, 1922.

Thomas, L. 1974. *The Lives of a Cell: Notes of a Biology Watcher.* New York: Viking Press.

———. 1979. *The Medusa and the Snail: More Notes of a Biology Watcher.* New York: Viking Press.

———. 1980. *On the Usefulness of Biology.* Enstone, England: Ditchley Foundation.

Thorndike, R. 1962. *Measurement and Evaluation in Psychology and Education.* New York: Wiley.

Tobier, A. 1988. *In Louis Armstrong's Neighborhood.* New York: Queens College School Community Collaborative Project.

Tolstoy, L. 1967. *Tolstoy on Education.* Translated by L. Weiner. Chicago: University of Chicago Press.

Traugh, C., et al., eds. 1986. *Speaking Out: Teachers and Teaching.* Grand Forks: North Dakota Study Group.

Tyack, D. 1974. *One Best System: A History of American Urban Education.* Cambridge: Harvard University Press.

Tyack, D., and L. Cuban. 1995. *Tinkering Toward Utopia: A Century of Public School Reform.* Cambridge: Harvard University Press.

Tyler, R. 1974. *Crucial Issues in Testing.* Berkeley, CA: McCutchon.

Weber, L. 1971. *The English Infant School and Informal Education.* Englewood Cliffs: Prentice-Hall.

———. 1997. *Looking Back and Thinking Forward: Re-examination of Teaching and Schooling.* New York: Teachers College Press.

Wheelock, A. 1992. *Crossing the Tracks.* New York: New Press.

Whitehead, A. N. 1929. *Aims of Education.* New York: Macmillan.

Wiske, M., ed. 1997. *Teaching for Understanding.* San Francisco: Jossey-Bass.

Yerkes, R., ed. 1921. *Psychological Examining in the United States Army.* Washington, DC: Government Printing Office.

# Index